Cultural Leadership

INSIDE AMERICA'S

COMMUNITY COLLEGES

BY

GEORGE A. BAKER III
AND ASSOCIATES

Published by the Community College Press, a division of the American
Association of Community and Junior Colleges
One Dupont Circle, N.W.
Suite 410
Washington, D.C. 20036
(202) 728-0200

ISBN 0-87117-241-0

This book is dedicated to former, current, and future students of the Community College Leadership Program at the University of Texas at Austin. Their experiences past, present, and future have and will provide the basis for team building and cultural leadership in America's great treasures—her community colleges. May they keep the spirit alive.

"When you ask people what it is like being part of a great team, what is most striking is the meaningfulness of the experience. People talk about being part of something larger than themselves, of being connected, of being generative. It becomes quite clear that, for many, their experiences as part of truly great teams stand out as singular periods of life lived to the fullest. Some spend the rest of their lives looking for ways to recapture that spirit."

Peter M. Senge
The Fifth Discipline: The Art and Practice of the Learning Organization

Table of Contents

Acknowledgments vii

Preface ix

Chapter 1
Creative Cultures: Toward a New Paradigm 1
By George A. Baker, III

Chapter 2
Community College Climate: The Signature of a Movement 17
By George A. Baker, III

Chapter 3
Creating, Managing, and Transforming Community College Culture: Presidential Perspectives 45
By Charlotte Biggerstaff

Chapter 4
Culture and Communication 61
By Tessa Martinez Tagle

Chapter 5
Empowering the Leadership Team 79
By Mary Ann Roe

Chapter 6
Instructional Leadership: Building a Culture of Excellence in the Teaching-Learning Community 97
By Rosemary Gillett-Karam and Eli Peña

Chapter 7
An Organizational Culture Consciously Shaped to Foster Creativity and Innovation 113
By Michele Nelson

Chapter 8
Cultural Leadership: The Founder 133
By *Phyllis Barber*

Chapter 9
Cultural Leadership: The Successor 163
By *Phyllis Barber*

Chapter 10
Culture, Leadership, and Organizational Systems 187
By *G. Allan Clark*

Chapter 11
**The Future of the Community College in Evolution:
Approaches to Analysis of Organizational Culture
and Functioning** 207
By *George A. Baker, III*

References 235

Index 253

About the Authors 259

■

Acknowledgments

The authors acknowledge the participation of the presidents and their institutions who were identified in the Shared Vision study. Data and interviews provided for that study were re-analyzed, and additional data were gathered for various chapters of this book.

The president, faculty, and staff of Santa Barbara City College, California, provided exceptional support for Chapter Seven. The founding and succeeding presidents, the administration past and present, the staff, board members, and faculty of Central Piedmont Community College, North Carolina, played a major role in the development of Chapters Eight and Nine.

The chancellor, president, administration, staff, and faculty of De Anza College and the Foothill-De Anza Community College District, California, played major roles in the development of Chapter Ten.

Susan Moore, director, learning resources at Monroe County Community College, Michigan, played an important role in editing and revising sections of the book.

Sophia Arditzoglin, lecturer, science education, Department of Curriculum and Instruction, the University of Texas at Austin, took responsibility to edit each chapter and develop a common format. She also researched and developed material for various chapters.

David McKay, director of research in the Human Resources Department for the city of Austin, Texas, took responsibility for the final editing of the manuscript.

Without the quality efforts of these individuals and groups, this literary effort would not have succeeded.

Preface

This book is the result of the collective efforts of several professionals, all of whom are in pursuit of a common goal: access and excellence in leadership toward student learning and student success in community, junior, and technical colleges.

From 1988 through 1990, we worked together to explore the various aspects of organizational culture as they applied to leadership challenges in the community, technical, and junior college movement.

We believe that we have crafted a work that will help colleges survive and succeed in an environment that has been shaped by the powerful socioeconomic and political forces of the 1980s. Not only was there a revolution in the Soviet Union, the results of which are rapidly reshaping the hegemony of the world powers, but there also was a "quality revolution" occurring in organizations in the United States. This "quality revolution" is destined to reshape the hegemony among the various components of public and private organizations, thereby increasing the competitiveness of American corporations and businesses in the world economy and enabling educational institutions to produce a quality work force.

The cultural leadership description and prescription that we offer calls for a new paradigm in a period of rapid change. For community colleges, the old status quo paradigm existed in an era of growth and expansion characterized by increasing enrollments, adequate retention rates, legislative delegation of authority, stable literacy rates, a traditional student population, and program development based on demand. However, the new paradigm will be played out in a period of turbulence, scarce resources, declining enrollments, soaring attrition rates, increasing illiteracy, student diversity, and shrinking program offerings. Moreover, the challenge for colleges will be to meet the needs of underprepared students while fulfilling the demands for a quality work force in an era of scarce resources. Colleges will be doing more with less. Furthermore, political forces will demand more accountability while seeking to increase control of the bureaucracy.

We believe that the study of leadership and organizational theory and behavior provides presidents and colleges with a theoretical framework for transitioning from the old to the new paradigm. In short, we believe that leaders, by empowering their leadership teams, will be able to embed a culture of values, attitudes, and beliefs and develop competencies for the organization and its members in such a way as to meet political and educational demands for effectiveness and quality. We believe that leaders hold the power to facilitate the paradigm transition through the empowerment of the teams they build. Their behavior reinforces culture as they pay attention to quality indicators, measure and control organizational energy, and respond positively to turbulence caused by external and internal pressures. Leaders shape behavior in others by deliberate coaching, teaching, and role modeling. Leaders increase motivation, satisfaction, and performance through the allocation of status and rewards just as they enhance organizational quality and mission accomplishment by establishing and monitoring programs for staff recruitment, selection, promotion, retirement, and separation from the organization.

The research reported herein has led us to conclude that the new quality-focused paradigm will require leaders who are self-confident, group-oriented, facilitative of change, catalytic toward quality, and persuasive with all external and internal constituencies. Leaders will find themselves: 1) moving from growth to crisis, 2) being tested through total quality approaches, 3) attempting to move those who want to maintain the status quo, 4) working with boards who expect repeated success in crisis management, 5) refurbishing the existing structures in their organizations, and 6) dealing with the consequences of the cultural change that external and internal demands have placed on them.

While the founders of community colleges created an environment that attracted followers and encouraged them to unite in following a new course, their successors must not only maintain the existing culture, but must also reconcile the diversity that multiculturalism has delivered. While founding presidents used their personal skills to lead the rites of integration, their successors will deal with rites of renewal and resolution. While effective founding presidents were often charismatic and autocratic, the new leaders will need to be inspirational and participative.

Cultural leadership is based upon the assumption that leadership influence depends on follower expectations. Thus, if a follower generally expects the status quo to be maintained, a leader will not only need to innovate, but also to behave in a way that truly empowers the follower to become the leader of his or her domain.

The thesis of this book is that we can destroy the illusion that organizations are created of separate, unrelated, and often competing forces. When we learn to give up this illusion (the old paradigm), we can begin to build the learning organization (the new paradigm). In the new organizational setting, followers continually expand their capacity to create the results they desire. It is an environment where individual and group patterns of thinking are nurtured, where the collective spirit of excellence and quality can grow and develop, and where the college learns how to promote and participate in lifelong learning. Therefore, we believe that the ferment in leadership will continue to grow until we are able to build a quality culture that is more consistent with our higher aspirations and higher levels of self-actualization.

Perhaps the most important reason for studying leadership from a cultural perspective is the fact that we are only beginning to understand the new capabilities that community colleges must possess in order to survive in a dynamic and demanding environment. Insufficient research has been conducted on leadership in general and leadership in community colleges in particular. Researchers such as those who have helped develop this book will provide us with the tools to distinguish quality-oriented learning organizations that have been transformed out of traditional, authoritative, controlling organizations. We can then master certain basic organizational disciplines. The basic discipline and learning presented in this work will be vital as we move steadily toward an increasingly more difficult and unpredictable future.

Chapter One is an overview of leadership and culture in community, technical, and junior colleges. In this chapter, we present the concept of organizational culture and link it to leadership. A new paradigm is presented, along with leadership requirements within this paradigm.

Chapter Two provides a framework for dealing with a major aspect of organizational culture. Organizational climate, as it relates to leadership, motivation, communication, decision making, rewards, and job satisfaction, is developed in this chapter. The chapter concludes with the climate profile of three typical community colleges.

Charlotte Biggerstaff, dean of continuing education, Northeast Texas Community College, developed Chapter Three from her doctoral dissertation. Biggerstaff studied the population described in *Shared Vision: Transformational Leadership in American Community Colleges* (Roueche, Baker, and Rose, 1989) and determined how fifty of the most effective presidents attempt to influence culture in their colleges. The study also dealt with the presidents' responses to critical incidents. The behavior of leaders in modeling and teaching others is described in Chapter Three, and the author reports how presidents reward, recruit, select, promote, and retire or terminate followers. The chapter concludes with a discussion of systems employed by presidents to control and manage their organizations.

Chapter Four is a study of culture and communication in the community college. Tessa Martinez Tagle, campus president at the Medical

Center Campus of Miami-Dade Community College, Florida, authored this chapter. Tagle outlines organizational proficiency in community colleges and explains how communication linkages are formed. Several cultural communication issues are discussed, including the communication of shared values and symbolic behavior, staffing processes, information systems, and an emphasis on quality in communication.

Mary Ann Roe, dean of institutional advancement at Texas State Technical College, developed Chapter Five. Roe discusses cultural leadership from a team-building perspective. She describes readiness for leadership in a transformational environment and discusses leadership development and leading and following in a college setting. She reports on transformational themes in her research and completes the chapter with a discussion of implications for leadership in community, technical, and junior colleges.

Chapter Six was jointly developed by Rosemary Gillett-Karam of Austin Community College and the University of Texas at Austin and Eli Peña, chairman of the biology department at Texas Southmost College. This chapter focuses on instructional leadership and the aspects of building an excellent culture in the teaching-learning community. Gillett-Karam and Peña use path-goal theory to analyze the results of two studies they conducted on presidential influence. The authors draw a connection between teaching and leading and show how community college presidents can improve teaching on their campuses by modeling excellent leadership behaviors. When CEOs work to satisfy student needs, clarify the path to success, raise expectations, maintain standards of excellence in teaching and learning, and promote an intellectually stimulating college culture, teachers follow in kind.

Chapter Seven is a discussion of cultural leadership in an environment where influence is used to foster creativity and innovation. Michele Nelson, acting dean of communication/fine arts at Grossmont College, California, presents her findings from a study of the leadership of Peter MacDougall and the culture in transition at Santa Barbara City College. The author deals with the cultural indicators of freedom and control, leadership, challenge, resources, encouragement, recognition, and sufficient time. Nelson concludes her chapter with recommendations for the development of a creative and innovative culture.

Phyllis Barber, assistant to the president at Central Piedmont Community College, North Carolina, developed the two case studies that constitute Chapters Eight and Nine. Chapter Eight focuses on the founding president of Central Piedmont, Richard Hagemeyer. Chapter Nine analyzes the culture developed by his successor, Ruth Shaw. Barber discusses the embedding mechanisms of systems and procedures, communication, decision making, planning, staff development, and budgeting. Perspectives on relationships with the Board of Trustees and state officials are also developed in Chapter Eight. Chapter Nine is similarly structured and includes a discussion of Shaw's strategy to reshape the college's culture.

Chapter Ten was developed by Allan Clark of Camosun College of Victoria, British Columbia, Canada. Clark presents a case study of De Anza College, part of California's Foothill-De Anza Community College District. Clark describes the relationship of the leadership structure provided by Tom Fryer, district chancellor, and A. Robert De Hart, president of De Anza, to the culture and climate of the college. In this chapter, the values of innovation, quality faculty and staff, mutual trust, shared leadership, learning, change, community, organizational integrity, planning, and communication are discussed.

Chapter Eleven views the community college as a organism in evolution. The concepts of organizational life cycle and situational leadership are employed to project the community college movement into the twenty-first century. The Community College Effectiveness Model is presented to link the movement to the two driving forces of institutional effectiveness and total quality improvement.

To understand the research that forms the basis for this book, the reader needs some historical information pertaining to research methods for dealing with organizational culture and leadership. Methods for determining organizational behavior have vacillated between empirical measurements and case studies. Today, ethnographic research and qualitative methods command a great deal of attention, as they do in this book. Ouchi and Wilkins (1985), quoted elsewhere in this work, assert that studies of organizational culture constitute a major tool for the study of educational institutions and that the qualitative methods and case study techniques can replace quantitative numbers with "thick descriptions" of organizational phenomena.

We believe that this book will strengthen the focus on organizational culture as a major means for studying the American community college. We also believe that this volume will help ensure that organizational culture is not seen as a passing fad. Moreover, this volume helps define the concept of organizational culture through studies that have been conducted on community college presidents, their leadership teams, staff, faculty, and students.

The lack of precision and agreement regarding the definition of organizational culture has been well documented in the literature. For the purposes of this book, we will rely on Schein's definition, which states that culture is the pattern of basic assumptions that a group (in our case, the college, through its leadership) has invented, discovered, or developed in learning to cope with its problems of external adaptation and internal integration. If we add to that definition Martin's (1985) view that culture is a set of commonly held attitudes, values, and beliefs that guide the behavior of an organization's members, we have both a collective and an individual view of culture.

Finally, we agree with Peter Senge, who writes in *The Fifth Discipline* (1990) that there are five new component technologies that are converging to guide change in innovative organizations. The first technology is systems thinking, which Senge believes is a means of dealing with all organizational events though they may be distant in time and space. Each event has an influence on the rest. In addition, all human endeavors are systems and are bound by invisible fabrics. To view organizations from a cultural perspective allows us to see all parts of the complicated lacework.

The second technology is personal mastery. Mastery is the discipline of continually clarifying and deepening our personal vision, of focusing our energies, developing our patience, and seeing reality objectively. Personal mastery is attained through the empowering aspect of cultural leadership and is explored in several chapters.

Mental models constitute Senge's third component of the fifth discipline. The mental models are presented in Chapter Two and are related to organizational climate as a major component of organizational culture. The mental model turns the mirror inward and allows us to unearth our internal pictures. This mirror allows organizational members to think effectively and to make that thinking open to others. The various studies presented in this book facilitate this process.

Building shared vision is Senge's fourth aspect of the fifth discipline. When leaders share a genuine vision, people excel and learn not because they are told to, but because they want to. *Cultural Leadership* focuses a great deal on this fourth concept.

Team learning is the final aspect of the fifth discipline. Senge asks how a team of committed managers with individual I.Q.s above 120 can have a collective I.Q. of 63 (1990). The discipline of team learning confronts this paradox. *Cultural Leadership* emphasizes team building, decision making, and problem solving. This aspect of cultural learning is vital because teams, not individuals, are the fundamental learning units in community colleges.

Cultural Leadership is really Peter Senge's model in a particular organizational culture, the community college. The book's framework allows the five disciplines to develop as an ensemble, with systems thinking as the chief integrator. Our chapters allow the reader to fuse these concepts into a coherent body of theory and practice. This book, like *The Fifth Discipline*, lets the reader see something "out there" and learn to create a lever long enough to shift the paradigm from the old to the new. As Archimedes said, "Give me a lever long enough and I can move the world."

George A. Baker
Austin, Texas

■

Chapter 1

Creative Cultures:
Toward a New Paradigm

By George A. Baker, III

"There is a twilight when everything remains seemingly unchanged. And it is a twilight when we all must be most aware of change in the air—however slight—lest we become unwitting victims of darkness"
(William O. Douglas in Guy, 1989, p. 3).

The dawn of a new epoch in the history of the American community college is at hand. Decisions about a number of critical issues have the potential for profoundly impacting the character and functions of the community college as the twenty-first century approaches. Some community colleges may consciously and systematically develop a process for organizational renewal by creating an agenda for action; yet others will placidly experience organizational decline if they confront the future by using only the anachronistic methods of the past.

Today, as never before, American community colleges, as well as the American corporate world, are being challenged by an increasingly chaotic environment. The organizational structures, dynamics, and leadership that have worked comfortably in the past are being dramatically challenged by a milieu charged with countervailing forces that became particularly problematic in the late 1970s and continues today.

The former world of the American community college and its founding presidents—one of growth and environmental stability—is vastly different from that faced today by the successors of those presidents. The complex environment of today's American community college is characterized by: declining initial student enrollments, alarming attrition rates, shrinking economic resources, encroaching controls by state governments, astounding levels of adult illiteracy, rising average student ages, rising pressure

1

being placed on curricula by rapidly expanding and changing technologies, new challenges related to increased diversity in the work force and among students, and the challenge of increasingly underprepared students at a time when business and industry are requiring higher skills in both old and new jobs.

This environment is forcing a re-examination of mission and purpose within the community college. Calls for access and excellence, innovative teamwork and collaboration, and leadership capable of turning education around echo across America. For example, the AACJC Commission on the Future of Community Colleges in 1988 decided to turn community colleges toward excellence through a more inclusive and purposeful theme of "building communities." Several sources in recent years have declared that a leadership crisis exists in higher education. The Carnegie Foundation for the Advancement of Teaching concluded that the central issue facing higher education is presidential leadership, and the Association of Governing Boards of Universities and Colleges commission, led by University of California President Emeritus Clark Kerr, determined that the need for effective leadership in today's colleges and universities has become critical for institutions to continue to respond effectively to the needs of society (Fisher, Tack, and Wheeler, 1988).

The American corporate world has fared a little better. Giants like IBM were considered leaders in the corporate world in 1982; four years later they discovered they had much to learn about serving customers and speeding products to market. Increasing foreign competition, the revolution in labor-management relations, deregulation, rampant buyouts and takeovers, changing consumer tastes, and rapid technological change have escalated the pace at which corporations must evolve and adapt in order to survive. The key to successful adaptation, according to Peters (1988), lies in the ability of the corporate world to embrace impermanence, to thrive on chaos while providing excellent quality and service, to create new markets and niche markets for products and services, and to increase environmental responsiveness through improved flexibility. Concomitant with the need for corporations to evolve and adapt is the requirement for a corporate leadership capable of flourishing amidst chaos and ambiguity while meeting environmental challenges and shaping a corporate culture of quality and excellence. Bennis and Nanus (1985) acknowledge that a clarion call has been issued for effective leadership and that everyone agrees this commodity is at a premium.

The crises and the paucity of leadership exist in both the educational and business worlds. Finding a set of solutions must be the nation's highest priority. The appearance in 1982 of In Search of Excellence by Tom Peters and Robert Waterman, relaying stories of successful leadership behaviors of effective chief executive officers, indicated that the corporate world had begun to move forward from its period of crisis. A new model replaced the old view of the CEO as manager. The traditional manager was more interested in how things got done than in the meaning of decisions and actions for employees (Zaleznick, 1988). In the companies of *In Search of Excellence*, management is balanced with the skills of leadership; Peters and Waterman (1982) found CEOs not only doing things right, but doing the right things. Since 1982, a large volume of literature has been produced that identifies leadership behaviors that have led to organizational change and success for companies in turbulent environments. Through their sheer volume, these studies have provided a sense of continued revolution for leadership behaviors and skills development in the corporate world. In general, those organizations that have adjusted to current turbulence have prospered, while those such as the automobile industry of Detroit are facing cutbacks and decline.

In Search of Excellence also prompted the community college world to write about its success. Roueche and Baker (1987) examined the leadership behaviors that led to organizational change and excellence at Miami-Dade Community College, Florida; the eight basic principles of excellence reported in *In Search of Excellence* were found to be applicable to the American community college setting. However, unlike the plethora of studies on exemplary leadership and leadership behaviors spawned in the corporate world by *In Search of Excellence*, only two major studies of community college leadership have emerged. A study by Vaughan (1986) and a study by Roueche, Baker, and Rose (1989) examine the community college presidency. The former devotes one chapter of ten to the topic of leadership and isolates the traits that prior leadership research evidence suggests are related to leadership behaviors. The latter is a more comprehensive, detailed study of selected successful and exemplary leaders in American community colleges—presidents who demonstrate the transformational behavioral attributes identified by Bass (1985a), Burns (1978), and Tichy and Devanna (1986). A third major publication specifically discusses transformational community college leadership behaviors. As a case study, *Access and Excellence* provides a model, but generalizations are difficult (Roueche and Baker, 1987). While these three studies identify traits and characteristics associated with effective leadership and explore their transforming effects on the community college, none of them focus on specific situational leadership behaviors that can be effective in the turbulent times colleges and corporations alike currently experience.

Leadership in Turbulent Times

The report of the AACJC Commission on the Future of Community Colleges, *Building Communities* (1988), recognizing the more complicated and risky nature of today's community college presidency, concludes that as leaders approach the twenty-first century they must have strong management skills, be coalition builders, possess vision, create new decision-making strategies, build trust, strengthen the campus community, and be capable of inspiring others. According to the findings of a Carnegie Foundation survey (1984), these leadership behaviors, required for the dynamic and rapidly changing environment of the present and future, differ significantly from those that have traditionally been used.

In Vaughan's 1986 study of traits of community college leaders, the 591 presidents responding to the Career and Lifestyle Survey represented 48 percent of the 1,220 public two-year college presidents nationwide, of whom approximately 12 percent had occupied their current positions for longer than fifteen years. Over half of the respondents were over 51; 11 percent were over 60 years old. A large number of this group has retired or will be retiring in the near future as founding presidents of their institutions. Their successors must be prepared to evince leadership behaviors to effect organizational change that will enable their colleges to deal effectively with changing constituencies and the turbulent environment.

To expand the knowledge base available to emerging community college leaders faced with replacing founding presidents at this critical time, it is essential to identify specific leadership behaviors that can be used effectively in specific types of situations to institute organizational change. This can be accomplished by identifying leadership behaviors used by college presidents who have been recognized as performing effectively in their environments. Once such behaviors are identified, they can be examined for their consistency with the leadership behaviors used successfully in turbulent times by corporate CEOs. The existence of a relationship may permit the transfer of more corporate strategies to the community college setting, empowering community college leaders to more effectively face the challenges posed by the dynamic and changing American community college educational environment.

The community college has been viewed as an institution with a unique set of purposes and functions that have evolved in response to societal demands. However, the expectation that such an institution will continue to provide comprehensive and creative learning and accessible education to a diverse constituency has been broadened. Increasingly, community colleges of the future will be called upon to demonstrate evidence of quality teaching and learning and student success; leaders will be required to take major steps to reform and reshape their institutions in order to satisfy the increasing expectations of clients and resource providers. Unfortunately, many community college presidents have been inadequately prepared to initiate such expected reforms, largely because they have become conditioned to manage rather than lead. Although the phenomena of rapid change is not unfamiliar to these presidents, their personal internal need to control tends to interfere with efforts to transform the organization for the future, thus complicating, and sometimes confounding, the leadership process.

Emerging external pressures have caused many presidents to turn their attention away from the needs, expectations, and power of their internal environments. A recurring theme that emerged from the research studies cited earlier in the chapter is the observation that as community college presidents have directed more and more of their effort toward problems of external adaptation, many of them have alienated themselves from the energy potential within their institutions. Threat, rather than opportunity, has increasingly become the focus of administrative energy. Inattention to the ever-evolving institutional culture has isolated these presidents from their constituents, and the goals of individuals have often superseded those of the institution. As conflict among subcultures has proliferated, the college may have never achieved a system of shared values and beliefs, or the system may have disintegrated over time.

New Paradigms for Cultural Leadership

The leadership strategies, organizational cultures, and processes by which organizations achieve their goals that were appropriate and effective in an era of growth and relative prosperity have become anachronistic in today's environment of rapid change, declining resources, and seemingly diminished options (AACJC Commission on the Future of Community Colleges, 1988; Bennis and Nanus, 1985; Chafee and Tierney, 1988). New ways of seeing our organizational processes—new paradigms and mental models—are critical to successful adaptation to the future.

Just as a new paradigm emerges in science when old theories stop working, the new paradigm in organizational leadership began to take form when the old school of management thought started to crumble during the '70s and '80s. A conscious reworking of organizational culture would allow community colleges to assume an essential, integral, and contributory position in an interactive national economic recovery structure like the one suggested by Smilor, Kozmetsky, and Gibson in 1988.

A reasonable question would be, "Why would community college CEOs want to embrace a new model?" "Because the old paradigm is not working" would answer reasonable critics of the community college approach to building community. One example of evolving a new paradigm that is responsive to changes in the environment relates to the role of the community college in working at a high level toward *building communities*. The AACJC Commission on the Future of Community Colleges succeeded in 1988 in evolving a new, inclusive paradigm by suggesting that community colleges orient toward excellence. This model emphasizes developing highly interdependent collaborations with employers—industries, businesses, public organizations, and organized labor groups—for the training of the work force, for the economic development of the community, and for excellence in transfer education. For many colleges such an undertaking represents a fundamental shift in the way they see the institution's role in the community: organizational boundaries become less well-defined, and interdependence of groups of organizations working toward common goals becomes intensified, requiring high levels of flexibility and a high level of trust among organizations. This kind of shift, or organizationwide change, in the way the college sees itself and its work constitutes the development of a new paradigm for organizational functioning.

It is essential that effective community college cultures, those characterized by creative and innovative responses and adaptations to their environments, be examined in detail to identify and describe operative organizational characteristics and cultural paradigms. The insights obtained can provide other community colleges with tools to enhance their ability to respond and adapt to their changing external environments. In short, we expect to offer a new paradigm—a light toward the twenty-first century. It is a paradigm based on expanding our awareness of and responsiveness to the cultural process at work in American community colleges. However, before our account of the paradigm can be developed, a better understanding of the nature of community college culture is necessary. A number of approaches to analyzing the college culture are demonstrated in this book.

Organizational Culture

Although the concept of organizational culture is difficult to define, measure, or study, it has been demonstrated to be a crucial dimension of effective organizational functioning by researchers who have confirmed its presence and its influence on the behavior of the people who make up organizations. Theorists and practitioners who are interested in organizational culture generally reflect an interest in studying the creation, growth, development, and survival of organizations (Ouchi and Wilkins, 1985). Although many research studies have been conducted employing an organizational culture approach in the business world, only now has an interest in organizational culture begun to surface in higher education. Studies of organizational culture in community colleges can enable us to better understand why some colleges continue to thrive in times of uncertainty while others lose ground (Biggerstaff, 1990).

Corporate and public awareness of the powerful culture phenomenon gained impetus during the early 1980s with the publication of three best-selling, non-fiction books that chronicled aspects of organizational life: Ouchi's *Theory Z* (1981), Peters and Waterman's *In Search of Excellence: Lessons from America's Best-Run Companies* (1982), and Deal and Kennedy's *Corporate Cultures: The Rites and Rituals of Corporate Life* (1982). Collectively, these popular works extolled the virtues of humanizing the work environment; valuing creativity and innovation; and recognizing the importance of symbolic cultural activity to sense-making and unity within the organization. These seminal studies illuminated the concept of organizational culture as a system of shared values and beliefs that contribute to and interact with organizational structures, processes, and people.

Following paradigms presented in these important studies, much of the corporate world immediately began examining itself for evidence of functional and dysfunctional culture. Education, however, was slower to respond. The thinking in educational circles has long centered on the belief that the teaching/learning enterprise is of a higher moral order and, as such, must vigorously resist the intrusion of forces that suggest a profit motive. Past attempts to systematically apply behavioral objectives to the teaching process, or measure learning according to predetermined competencies, ran counter to the prevailing pedagogical belief that real learning could not be quantified. In time, however, the value of these principles became recognized among community college educators, with the result that many curricula were profoundly transformed. The fact that the organizational culture phenomenon was first identified and popularized in business-related literature may have contributed to the initial recalcitrance of educators to accept its relevance for their field.

However, closer examination of the cultural approach to organizational studies has revealed that its origins are deeply rooted in the traditions of anthropology, sociology, and psychology (Kuh and Whitt, 1988; Ouchi and Wilkins, 1985). That these disciplines are considered "legitimate" by educators may well explain why higher education institutions are at last beginning to address cultural issues. In other words, the multidimensionality of the culture concept may have broadened its appeal and opened up a new way of perceiving and understanding how educational institutions work.

This "cultural perspective" appears to hold considerable promise for higher education leaders who value not only outcomes, but also people, processes, and contexts. It further proposes new approaches to solving what Schein (1985a) referred to as "problems of external adaptation and internal integration" (p. 9). Today, a college's external public is demanding that leaders more effectively manage declining resources; specify, measure, and defend learning outcomes; and respond to conflicting expectations of diverse constituencies (AACJC Commission on the Future of Community Colleges, 1988). At the same time, the internal public of the institution expects leaders to demonstrate a strong value for teaching and learning, to recognize and reward excellence, and to involve vested interests in setting new directions and making decisions.

While such environmental imperatives have focused increasing attention on effective leadership in higher education, scant energy has been directed toward helping leaders find artful as well as technical solutions to these growing pressures. Toward this end, the cultural perspective suggests a new way of looking at the higher education organization: as a holistic entity that cannot be altogether intervened upon, as the rational model would suggest, but can be nurtured and directed toward a common purpose. This perspective suggests a new way of conceptualizing, studying, and developing organizations.

Organizational cultures have been studied from a wide range of perspectives in an effort to understand their essentially non-rational properties. Abundant and diverse definitions in the literature (Clark, 1972; Mitroff and Kilmann, 1984; Pettigrew, 1979; Sathe, 1983; Schein, 1985b; Tierney, 1988) and frequent use of colorful metaphor to elucidate the concept (Jelinek, Smircich, and Hirsch, 1983; Pascale and Athos, 1981) further verify its highly interpretive and subjective nature. Culture has also been described in terms of the degree to which it exhibits certain properties: adaptability or fluidity (Albrecht and Albrecht, 1987; Smircich, 1983); strength (Deal and Kennedy, 1982; Peters and Waterman, 1982; Pfeffer, 1981; Sathe, 1983); and health (Albrecht and Albrecht, 1987; Gregory, 1983).

One of the fundamental reasons why culture is so difficult to define is that much of it is subtle and implicit. To better explain the phenomenon, Schein (1985a) developed a conceptual hierarchy, which ordered culture into three levels: artifacts, values, and assumptions.

At the first level, culture is made visible and tangible through symbolic form, that is, artifactual manifestation. Rites, ceremonies, rituals, myths, sagas, stories, language systems, and norms are all manifestations of culture at the artifactual level.

The second level of the cultural hierarchy—values—reveals how people explain and rationalize what they say and do as a group. Values link artifacts to assumptions by explaining the obvious and providing a foundation for the development of deeper beliefs. As standards for guiding action (Rokeach, 1968), values are testable, debatable, and ordinal (Goodstein, 1983). The degree of congruity or conflict among seminal values often determines how strongly members are socialized in a common direction.

Assumptions comprise the third and deepest level of the hierarchy and are the essence of culture. They represent learned responses to environmental expectations and exert a powerful influence over what people believe, how they think, and what they do. At this level, values and beliefs are taken for granted and seldom articulated.

Although culture is revealed through its artifacts, symbolic meaning is authenticated through an understanding of the values and assumptions that undergird the manifestations. The challenge for an organization, and its leaders in particular, is to look beyond the obvious and manage culture at all three levels.

The development of a body of cultural artifacts, values, and assumptions over time is encouraged by a number of important factors, including (1) external issues, which define the environment and its boundaries and specify what is necessary to survive within it; and (2) internal issues, which clarify member behavior group cohesiveness around common purpose (Nadler and Tushman, 1988; Schein, 1985b). Culture is inclined to develop when a group solves problems together over time, membership remains relatively stable, alternatives are absent, and interaction is common (Wilkins and Ouchi, 1983).

One of the most important issues organizations face when they attempt to bring people together to solve common problems is the reconciliation of conflict between individual needs and those of the organization in which they have chosen to work (Pascale, 1985; Schein, 1985a). In the case of higher education and other professional organizations, this conflict is further complicated by loyalty to the profession or subculture (Gregory, 1983; Hoy and Miskel, 1987). Thus the socialization of members to the larger or overall culture is critical to the continued survival, healthy development, and ultimate success of the parent organization (Pascale, 1985; Pettigrew, 1979; Schein, 1968).

Culture and Leadership

From the cultural perspective, the relationship between leadership and the creation, development, and transformation of an institution's culture is of particular interest to the researchers who developed this book. The interdependence of organizational culture and leadership makes studying one apart from the other difficult, yet there is growing pressure to determine both the origin and effect of this relationship. The discovery of the ways in which each exerts influence can have considerable impact on all aspects of organizational development. For example, the knowledge that leadership can mobilize significant cultural change might influence the selection of a new president. Or, a better understanding of the pervasiveness and power of institutional culture may help explain why certain management principles operate better than others in a specific situation. Thus, the study of organizational culture in relation to leadership in colleges and universities has the potential to explain both success and failure and to illuminate both efficiency and effectiveness. As higher education is called upon to become increasingly accountable for its actions, such information can be invaluable to key decision makers.

A keener comprehension of how culture affects organizations can also help to surface significant issues that tend to elude the members of an organization, particularly those requiring heightened attention by leadership. If, as Schein (1985a) has suggested, "organizational cultures are created by leaders" (p. 2), then one of the most critical functions performed by leaders may well be the creation and management of this culture through whatever influence can be brought to bear.

According to Pfeffer (1981), the construction and maintenance of systems of shared meanings, paradigms, languages, and cultures comprise the essence of all important administrative activity. Similarly, Pondy (1978) argued that leaders' effectiveness can be measured by their ability to make activity meaningful for organization members. Thus, leaders in higher education have a primary responsibility to immerse themselves in their institutional cultures in order to achieve a higher level of understanding and better confront the challenges ahead. In this way, the leader's vision for a particular institution is grounded in both the present and past, which heightens its credibility as a valid image for the future.

Culture and Community Colleges

The relationship between leadership and the creation and management of institutional culture is critical to the success of community colleges. Having come of age in the past decade or so, these colleges are now generally recognized for their unique contributions to the education of a growing and highly multicultural population. As the "people's colleges," they have specialized in adapting to their changing environment, recognizing emergent needs, developing academic and technical programs to strengthen their communities, and meeting head-on the challenge of illiteracy (Cohen and Brawer, 1984; Eaton, 1988; Gleazer, 1980; Roueche and Baker, 1987). But they have done so with varying degrees of success; the successes of one institution have often not been replicated in other settings.

Understanding how effective presidents create and manage their various cultures may well clarify the reasons why some community colleges have been more successful than others at solving the problems of external adaptation and internal integration. More importantly, viewing the community college as a culturally generative and culturally interactive organization suggests alternatives for leader behavior that foster the development of a shared belief system and encourage commitment to it.

The research reported in this book focuses on the efforts of exceptional community college chief executive officers to create and manage their institutional cultures. (Hereafter in this research, these executives are collectively referred to as "presidents.") Specifically, the researchers identify and describe what it is that such presidents do to transmit and influence culture in their institutions and how they go about doing so. This presentation of research findings was precipitated by a four-fold belief that (1) a number of presidents are unaware of the importance of monitoring their cultures for functional and dysfunctional qualities; (2) others, who may be aware of the need, are unsure of what to do about it; (3) still others primarily attend to pressing external problems, believing the internal environment can survive through delegation; and (4) many community college presidents experience difficulty in building integrated, well-functioning leadership teams that are in effect extensions of the presidential power and influence. Furthermore, since the literature implies that too little attention has been paid to understanding critical interaction processes in organizations, this book attempts to highlight the value of cultural perspectives for leaders who are working toward fulfilling the promise of open-door colleges.

Scant research has been performed in higher education that would help leaders understand the value of the cultural perspective or the means by which it can become useful. This is a particularly acute problem for community college presidents, whose institutions generally have been quick to respond to the demands of the external environment, often at the expense of internal culture. As these colleges have matured, they have become increasingly differentiated, and original values around shared purpose have been compromised. The time has come for serious introspection and revitalization. The time has come for a significant paradigm shift in American community colleges.

Nowadays, the responsibility of community college leaders lies in mobilizing a shared commitment toward a common vision, a feat that can be accomplished by focusing more attention on symbolic and cultural processes. Viewing the institution from a cultural perspective will eventually generate significant insights and the development of effective strategies that would be of value to leaders, members, and constituents alike.

In their definitive report on expectations for community colleges in the twenty-first century, the AACJC Commission on the Future of Community Colleges (1988) defined the term community "not only as a region to be served, but also as a climate to be created" (p. 7). In keeping with this emphasis on the climate of organizations, the present studies are directed toward the potential of the "climate to be created," which derives its essence from the evolving culture inside and surrounding the institution. By identifying exceptional, transformational community college presidents and describing their orientations around the five themes of vision, influence, people, motivation, and values, Roueche, Baker, and Rose (1989) examined how exceptional presidents have attempted to create and manage cultural meaning within their colleges. Their study was precipitated by a belief that such insights could help other leaders rethink and reorder their priorities in a direction that respects the potency of the culture phenomenon in unifying an organization around common purpose.

Specific references to culture in community college literature are rare. Applying a cultural perspective appears warranted, however, given the changing and highly complex nature of these institutions. Throughout its relatively brief history, the community college has advocated accessibility, diversity, and comprehensive educational programming. This is no longer enough, however. Increasingly, community colleges are being called upon to address the key issues of quality, leadership, and the future (AACJC Commission on the Future of Community Colleges, 1988; Eaton, 1988). Leaders are advised that as they focus more on these external expectations, their responsibility to the internal environment cannot be ignored.

The challenge for community college leaders, then, is not only envisioning the future, but also mobilizing the shared commitment of an increasingly differentiated membership (Roueche, Baker, and Rose, 1989). Community colleges are advised to analyze and address cultural issues if they are to effectively meet this challenge. It is incumbent upon leadership to see that such internal analysis takes place. As community college presidents come to understand the symbolic and cultural aspects of their environment, they become better able to create, alter, and subsequently manage meaning for others.

The Structure of the New Paradigm

The point made earlier in the chapter is that researchers have only recently begun to consider the importance of studying the relationship of leadership and organizational culture in higher education institutions. Noting that conventional models generally have failed to explain the complexity of educational institutions, Masland (1985) and Kuh (1989) suggested that less orthodox approaches that consider the educational institution as a holistic entity hold more promise for theory-building in these highly complex organizations. Other contemporary research has proposed that employing a cultural perspective in educational institutions can clarify the role of leader as an effective change agent in the service of a shared vision for the future (Eaton, 1988; Firestone and Corbett, 1988; Miskel and Ogawa, 1988; Roueche, Baker, and Rose; 1989; Tierney, 1988).

Although higher education researchers have generally ignored the culture phenomenon, recently it has been the subject of numerous anthropological and sociological studies that do not specifically focus on higher education. The reasons underlying these studies are numerous; two, however, are particularly relevant to the thesis of this book. First, as the rate of change continues to escalate and environments become increasingly uncertain, the need for internal unity around common values and beliefs becomes more critical to organizational survival (Deal and Kennedy, 1982). Second, understanding organizational culture provides leaders with insights into purposive patterning, performance motivation, and subculture conflicts and resolution, all of which must be considered when implementing change (Schein, 1985a).

With respect to higher education, Kuh and Whitt (1988) and Tierney (1988) suggested that analysis of symbolic and cultural activity can explain why actions work in some institutions and not in others. The cultural perspective has also been found to be useful for understanding colleges and universities as organizations where the internal parts do not function well together (Masland, 1985). These studies suggest that a better understanding of the interaction between diverse and changing internal and external environments is essential to effective functioning of organizations noted for poor internal collaboration.

Leadership and the New Paradigm

Whether culture can be managed is a subject of considerable debate in the literature (Graves, 1986; Jelinek, Smircich, and Hirsch, 1983; and Martin, 1985), but evidence indicates that, at least to some degree, leaders can influence culture formation and transformation (Deal and Kennedy, 1982; Peters and Waterman, 1982; Baker, Roueche, and Gillett-Karam, 1990; Schein, 1985b; Siehl, 1985). Several chapters in this book demonstrate how insight into organizational culture can be helpful in determining which leader behavior is most appropriate for given situations. Most importantly, several of the research studies reported in this book indicate that leaders must engage followers in a shared commitment toward cultural reform, if change efforts are to be successful (Biggerstaff, 1990; Barber, 1990; Roe, 1989; Nelson, 1990; Peña, 1990; Tagle, 1988; and Clark, 1990).

Literature on organizational culture tends to refer to leaders as either founders or transitioners. Founders are important in the initial stages of cultural development, and their effectiveness can be measured by the degree to which they successfully envision and communicate a future for the organization and motivate others to commit to it (Schein, 1983; Pettigrew, 1979). They are viewed as prime movers in major historical events (Clark, 1972; Deal and Kennedy, 1982; Peters and Waterman, 1982) and are credited with directing the process which results in shared beliefs (Martin, Sitkin, and Boehm, 1985). On the other hand, transitional leaders are seen as change agents with significant opportunity to redirect the culture of an organization (Lundberg, 1985; Siehl, 1985). Research suggests that it is not enough for these leaders to envision and communicate a future; rather, they must establish trust (Bennis and Nanus, 1985), create readiness for change (Cameron and Ulrich, 1986), and identify the guardians of the current culture (Tichy and Devanna, 1986), if they are to engage their followers in a common effort.

Cultural leadership also embodies an important symbolic character. In their efforts to transmit and embed culture, leaders manipulate a variety of symbolic forms, including language, stories, gestures, and procedures, all of which help members make sense of their environment (Dandridge, 1983; Tierney, 1989).

A Conceptual Framework for Cultural Analysis

As leaders become conscious of the meaning of their own behavior, they are more likely to clarify it for others—a critical step in achieving consensus around shared values (Schein, 1985b; Tierney, 1989). Believing that conceptual frameworks can be useful for stimulating awareness of behavioral meaning, Schein (1985a) developed a model for categorizing the cultural and symbolic activity leaders employ in their daily activity. Hereafter, this model will be referred to as the Cultural Embedding Mechanisms Framework (CEMF) and will be discussed in detail later in this book. Schein's model provides a format for analyzing how leaders influence the cultural and symbolic fields of their organizations. As a conceptual device, the CEMF was designed to classify seemingly random activity in order to make it more comprehensible and meaningful.

The CEMF suggests that leaders transmit and embed culture throughout the organization, using primary and secondary mechanisms. It implies that leaders affect the cultural development of their organizations both consciously and unconsciously. It highlights the importance of making leaders aware of the nature of their behavior, in order to more appropriately select and target cultural and symbolic activity in the future. The CEMF model enables identification, classification, and description of leader behaviors, with reference to how they create and/or transform the culture of an organization. The three case studies presented in this book are well-developed examples of cultural analysis and outcomes.

Conclusion

An organization's culture and its leadership are integrally entwined, and organizational effectiveness is linked to the role of leadership in creating and managing culture. Culture must be the focus of well-developed research if we are to learn how to better build upon our colleges to support the communities we serve. Conversely, leaders who understand and value the cultural aspects of their organization can effectively intervene in the culture evolution process by consciously working to create a common value and belief system that motivates commitment around a shared vision for the future.

The first section of this chapter has been designed to orient the reader to the turbulent environment for today's American community colleges. It describes the context where community college leaders call for an orientation toward building communities as the macro-mission for community colleges into the twenty-first century. As a result of these clarion calls, a new paradigm for cultural development in community colleges is proposed.

In the second section, the cultural concepts based on current research were articulated. While the concept of organizational culture remains elusive, difficult to define, perplexing, and challenging to measure, community college researchers are converting abstract concepts to concrete and indurate visions that they believe can be understood and put into practice. The researchers in this book have employed the best principles of research in anthropology, sociology, and psychology to bring to the reader what really happens inside America's premiere community colleges.

These principles establish a foundation to link culture and leadership in ways that the following chapters will illuminate. This overview and the subsequent chapters describe the link between the leadership and development of organizations and the building of community in community colleges.

In the final section of this chapter, the structure of the new paradigm and specific tools for studying the exceptional community colleges and their leaders are identified.

Chapter Two focuses on community college climate as a means of examining the relationships or subcultures among separate entities within an existing organizational culture. Using a weather metaphor, climate may be generally defined as the atmosphere of the college itself. More formally, climate can be used to describe the relatively enduring properties of the college's internal environment. Thus culture is the social architecture that translates the "blooming, buzzing, and confusion of organizational life" (Bennis and Nanus, 1985, p. 110). Climate is a set of properties of culture that can be measured and described. This study of climate allows us to examine the complex and multifaceted transactions occurring between individuals and a college. From a cultural perspective, climate provides a baseline for cultural analyses. Understanding the properties of climate allows us to translate a mixture of feelings, values, and responses of leadership onto a canvas on which the deeper aspects of culture can be illuminated and integrated.

■

Chapter 2

Community College Climate:
The Signature of a Movement

By George A. Baker, III

I nformal day-to-day behavior, with its underlying attitudes and values, makes up that aspect of organizational life that is referred to as the *climate* of the organization. Climate is not the overt behavior or visible artifacts that one might observe on a visit to an organization. It is not even the philosophy or value system as articulated by the founder, or written down in charters or policies. Climate emerges from the assumptions that underlie the values (Schein, 1985a). It is a complex mesh of social forces and unwritten rules that influence the behavior of each member of the organization and thus shape behavioral norms (Allen and Pilnick, 1973). Once fully developed, every organization has its own distinct organizational climate (Brown, 1979). This normative system of the organization, its feel, its tone, its atmosphere, its set of internal characteristics distinguishes one organization from another (Hoy and Miskel, 1987).

In recent years, both academic and business executives have become increasingly interested in the subject of organizational climate. One of the nation's largest management consulting firms, McKinsey and Company, has studied how individual and group motivation could increase productivity. McKinsey personnel working in association with university consultants have published five books, three of which made the nation's best-seller lists (Peters and Waterman, 1982; Ouchi, 1981; Peters and Austin, 1985). The other two have been widely read by corporate executives (Pascale and Athos, 1981; Deal and Kennedy, 1982).

Although some experts speculate that organizational climate has become a fad, with large amounts of questionable material published, most researchers believe that important organizational dynamics are behind

17

the rising interest in climate. The authors of this book are among them. Between 1960 and 1975, both academic and business executives criticized large, complex organizations as being "too bureaucratic." Such a reaction was partly due to organizations' unresponsiveness to human needs and their ineffectiveness in reaching even their own goals in society. During this period, the American research community became interested in studying individual human motivation, small-group dynamics, face-to-face relations, and work design. By studying such micromanagerial subjects, we learned about the evils of too much bureaucracy and how to manage small work units more effectively.

Beginning in the early 1980s, however, there was a strong need to determine how to constructively coordinate and manage those large, complex, and relatively impersonal organizations by understanding the role of climate in achieving their objectives. Extensive reviews by Hellreigel and Slocum (1974) and James and Jones (1974) reveal three major perspectives that have been used to define the variable concept of organizational behavior. The first treats climate as a set of attributes from which an organization can be studied. The second treats climate as an interaction between the organization's attributes and the individual members' perceptions of these attributes. The third approach identifies organizational climate as a psychological approach where individuals' perceptions are studied in order to get a measurable understanding of the organizational climate. This third explanation forms the foundation for the research conducted by the senior author of this book from 1987 to 1992.

Organizational Climate

Organizational climate has been regarded as an important construct in organizational research for more than 20 years (Field and Abelson, 1982; Joyce and Slocum, 1979, 1982; Litwin and Stringer, 1966). Major theoretical and methodological questions still remain (Field and Abelson, 1982; James and Jones, 1974). There is broad agreement, however, that organizational climate identifies relatively enduring characteristics of an organization and can be used to distinguish among organizations (Campbell, Dunnette, Lawler, and Weick, 1970; Tagiuri, 1968). Organizational climate should, therefore, display organization-specific variance and can be expected to be relatively homogeneous within organizations and relatively heterogeneous among them (Drexier, 1977; Ansari, 1980).

Researchers have taken a variety of approaches to exploring organizational climate. Allen and Pilnick (1973) refer to it as the "shadow organization." Davis and Newstrom (1985) define it simply as "the human environment within which an organization's employees do their work" (p. 23). Tagiuri and Litwin (1968) describe organizational climate as one of the relatively enduring qualities of the internal environment of an organization that is experienced by its members, influences their behavior, and can be described in terms of the values of a particular set of characteristics (or attributes) of the organization.

Organizational climate, then, is the pattern of basic assumptions that a given group has developed in learning to cope with its problems—a pattern that has worked well enough to be considered valid and, therefore, is to be taught to new members as the correct way to think and feel in relation to those problems (Schein, 1985a). According to Lawless (1979), such unwritten psychological contracts exist between employees and managers, and these psychological contracts reflect the organizational climate.

Climate has been described by Schein (1985a) and Tagiuri and Litwin (1968) as a relatively enduring quality of the internal environment of an organization. This climate is experienced directly by the organization's members and influences their motivation and performance. Climate can be measured and described in terms of the values of a particular set of characteristics.

Various procedures of arrangement or systems have been used to judge the quality and excellence of an institution of higher education. Roueche and Baker (1987) defined organizational climate as the atmosphere within which an organization functions. It includes "the overall environment, values, shared beliefs, and personality of any given educational institution" (p. 24). Using, as a metaphor, the idea of visiting a home in which the physical characteristics of the home and the living that is going on within the home are observed, Roueche and Baker contend that one obtains a "feel" for the house and the people within the house. The same is true of organizations. By making observations, one can get that same "feel" for the organization. Theorists use the term "climate" to describe that feeling. Organizational climate is defined as the "atmosphere of the workplace," or the answer to the questions, "What is it like to work here? What is in the air? And what is the prevailing mood in this workplace?"

While some of the research findings on organizational climate are contradictory, for the most part the results point toward a correlation between organizational climate and organizational effectiveness. Deal and Kennedy (1982) found "evidence that the impact of values and beliefs on company performance was indeed real" (p. 7). Allen and Pilnick (1973) reveal similar findings: "Our research has shown that there is a direct relationship between the profitability of an organization and its climate" (p. 11). On a more conservative note, Hellreigel and Slocum (1974) cite eleven studies that demonstrate "a significant relationship between job performance and organizational climate" (p. 263).

This connection between climate and effectiveness gives managers a number of reasons to study organizational climates and cultures. First, climate can be used to predict organizational phenomena (Field and Abelson, 1982). Several research studies have demonstrated a strong relationship between organizational climate and concepts such as job satisfaction, job performance, group communication, organizational structure, organizational commitment, and organizational performance (Bowers, 1973; Joyce and Slocum, 1982; LaFollette and Sims, 1975; Lawler, Hall, and Oldham, 1974; Likert, 1967; Muchinsky, 1977; Schneider and Snyder, 1975; Weish and La Van, 1981).

Second, the concept of climate is useful for organizational development (Kets de Vries and Miller, 1984; Offenberg and Cernius, 1978; Likert, 1967). Third, organizational climate has been found to influence motivation and behavior of individuals (Friedlander and Greenberg, 1971; Litwin and Stringer, 1966). Fourth, the construct incorporates a perspective that moves analysis away from the more static and structural qualities of "organization" and toward the more dynamic view of processes of "organizing" (Weick, 1979; Pettigrew, 1979).

By thoroughly understanding the positive and negative impacts of their practices, managers can take specific actions to improve the climate and thereby improve performance within the organization or institution. Allen and Pilnick (1973) put it thus: "Once we have determined the organization's norms, the obvious question is: If we have norms that are detrimental to our organization's effectiveness, what can we do about them?" (p. 12). The research demonstrates that while changing organizational culture is slow and difficult, organizational climate and, hence, organizational effectiveness can be improved (Lawless, 1979; Allen and Pilnick, 1973; Deal and Kennedy, 1982; Becker, 1975).

Understanding Organizational Climate in the Community College

American community colleges are organizations in their own right, containing all the characteristic problems and potential possessed by other organizations. Community college administrators are faced with many challenges in assuring that their schools run as effectively as possible. Although some special considerations need to be taken into account when translating the extensive research of business and industry (community colleges' extremely diverse clientele and employees, and their unique mission, for example), much can be learned from this type of research. After all, people and groups operate in a similar manner in many different situations.

The cultural network, or pattern of measurable organizational norms, is the primary means of communication within any organization (Deal and Kennedy, 1982). The climate determines the norms of the cultural network. "We have no choice as to whether norms will exist in our organizations, but we do have a choice as to what norms will exist" (Allen and Pilnick, 1973, p. 17).

Since norms within an organization develop with little conscious influence by the people whose lives they shape, an organization or work group may embrace the norm of mediocrity without the people in that organization or group ever considering whether they prefer mediocrity or excellence. New employees joining the work group are rapidly caught up in this web of existing structures (Allen and Pilnick, 1973).

In the book *Three Thousand Futures*, the Carnegie Council on Policy Studies in Higher Education (1982) examined what is happening to the "private" or internal life of individual campuses of higher learning throughout the country, in relation to quality and excellence in education. The conclusion was startling: "This life is threatened by the cessation of growth" (p. 113). The council asserted that growth is a requirement for any healthy entity, even academic enterprises. When enrollment ceases to grow and the flow of financial resources accompanying it diminishes, a self-confirming sense of failure sets in, causing further decline by stultifying energy and promotional activity.

With such concerns accelerating throughout the country, now would seem to be the time for institutions of higher education to examine their strengths and weaknesses. The people who administer colleges and universities in the United States should look at the elements of organizational climate at their campuses and determine whether the level of their leadership meets the institution's standards of excellence. Educators and leaders bear the responsibility to ensure that their colleges achieve both access and excellence.

Approaches to Measuring Organizational Climate

Intensive efforts to conceptualize and measure organizational climate first began in the early 1960s, for the most part consisting of structured perception questionnaires. Hellreigel and Slocum (1974) identified thirty-one studies using organizational climate constructs as a key variable. With some exceptions, the instruments used in these studies can be used to examine any business organization.

A major means of measuring organizational climate is the model developed by Likert (1967) and adapted by Roueche and Baker (1987) (See Figure 2.1). Likert identified four management systems ranging from "exploitive authoritative" to "participative group." Likert's research found that the participative group system, System Four, generally produced better results in terms of productivity, cost-reduction, absenteeism, and turnover.

Figure 2.1
Likert's Management Systems

System One: Exploitive Authoritative

Motivation is derived from fear, threats, punishments, and occasional rewards; very little upward communication exists; there is little interaction, and when it exists, it is with fear and distrust; decisions are made at the top without adequate and accurate information; lack of teamwork exists; there is mediocre productivity.

System Two: Benevolent Authoritative

Motivation is derived from rewards and some actual or potential punishment; attitudes are sometimes hostile and sometimes supportive; management feels responsible; very little upward communication exists; there is competition among peers; policy decisions are made at the top while others are made at the lower levels but within the framework; information is moderately adequate and accurate; teamwork is discouraged; goals are overtly accepted but covertly rejected; there is fair to good productivity.

System Three: Consultative

Motivation is derived from rewards, occasional punishment, and some involvement; attitudes may be hostile but more often they are favorable and supportive; substantial portions of personnel feel responsibility and generally behave in ways to achieve the organization's goals; cooperative and favorable attitudes toward others generally exist; some job dissatisfaction and job satisfaction exists; there is considerable upward and downward communication; broad policy and general decisions are made at the top with more specific decisions at the lower levels; goals are set after discussions with subordinates; some pressures exist to protect self and colleagues, hence, there is a tendency to distort information; there is good productivity.

System Four: Participative Group

Motivation is derived from economic rewards based on compensation systems developed through participation; there is group participation in goal setting; all personnel feel responsibility; favorable and cooperative attitudes exist; there is high job satisfaction; good upward, downward, and lateral communications exist; there is substantial adequate and accurate information; decisions are made widely throughout the organization; there are strong pressures to obtain complete information to guide one's own behavior; there is excellent productivity.

Adapted from Likert, 1967.

System Four also produced a more effective organization characterized by better communication, higher peer-group loyalty, higher confidence and trust, favorable attitudes toward supervisors, high job satisfaction, and overall organizational climate.

System Four is characterized by three overriding principles: (1) leadership's use of supportive relationships; (2) use of group decision making and group methods of supervision; and (3) establishment of high performance goals. Likert states that the more these principles are applied throughout the organization, the greater the extent to which motivational forces arising from the needs of members will be compatible and will result in cooperative behavior focused on achieving organizational goals.

Roueche and Baker (1987) attempted to measure the climate of community college cultures through a questionnaire that asked community college employees to rate their leaders on a five-point Likert-style scale. The assumption was that attitudes, values, and perceptions of organizational members could be measured and correlated with the System Four model. If the scores fell between one and two, we could assume that a System One climate (Exploitive Authoritative) was perceived as existing at the college. Scores falling between four and five on the scale would be representative of a System Four (Participative Group) environment. In some cases, where a seven-point scale was used, scores could be standardized to correlate with the System Four concept.

Baker and Roueche, from 1986 through 1987, and Baker, from 1988 through 1991, conducted climate studies in more than forty community colleges. These studies were generally conducted at the request of the chancellor or president of the college in question. In addition, the Community College Leadership Program at the University of Texas at Austin and other leadership programs across the country have fostered more than a dozen dissertations that employ refined versions of the original instrument first used at Miami-Dade Community College, Florida, in 1986, which was itself adapted from Likert's Profile of Organizational and Performance Characteristics.

The Six Variables of Organizational Climate

Likert's Profile of Organizational and Performance Characteristics contains fifty-one items in six subscales. Adapting the instrument for use at institutions of higher education, Roueche and Baker (1987) selected twenty-two items in five subscales—leadership, motivation, communication, decision making, and reward—for use at Miami-Dade Community College. Baker in 1988 developed the additional subscale of job satisfaction for use in the subsequent study of the Wolfson Campus of Miami-Dade. This change brought the instrument to twenty-six items. The items under each of the six groupings were selected to relate to the overall climate of an institution of higher education. After the second Miami-Dade study, Baker investigated each of the subscales and developed an adapted instrument for use in community colleges. The twenty-six-item questionnaire that was used from 1987 to 1990 appears in Figure 2.2.

Leadership. Of the six subscales, leadership is the characteristic of organizational climate most affected by the abilities of the people at the

---

Figure 2.2
Survey Items
Community College Climate Instrument
1987–1990

Following are the items as they appeared in the survey form sent to faculty. The text that appears in parentheses shows how the forms sent to administrative employees differed from those sent to faculty.

LEADERSHIP
1. How much confidence do your leaders show in the ability of the faculty (campus personnel) to do excellent work?
2. To what extent can you freely seek information from the administration (your leaders)?
3. To what extent does the administration (your leaders) encourage you to develop creative and innovative ideas?
4. To what extent are you actually assisted by the administration (your leaders) in improving your teaching (job performance)?
5. To what extent does the administration (your leaders) influence you to professionally grow and develop?

MOTIVATION
6. To what extent are your innovative ideas supported and used by the administration (your leaders)?
7. To what extent does the administration (your leaders) provide support for your professional development (career development goals)?
8. To what extent does the administration (your leaders) inspire you with a sense of purpose?
9. How much cooperation exists *across* the various academic departments (areas) of the campus?
10. How much cooperation exists *within* your department (area)?

COMMUNICATION
11. To what extent does the *quantity* of information you receive support the teaching-learning process (help you to improve your job performance)?
12. How *useful* is the information you receive in supporting the teaching-learning process (helping you improve your job performance)?
13. To what extent does the administration (your leaders) *willingly* share important information with you?

top levels of administration to influence the other organizational members. Schein (1985a) argues that organizational structure is not accidental, that organizations are created by people who create culture through the articulation of their assumptions. "Although the final form of an organization's culture reflects the complex interaction between the thrust provided by the founder, the reactions of the group members, and their shared historical experiences, there is little doubt that the

---

Figure 2.2
Continued

14. To what extent does the administration (your leaders) communicate *positive* expectations of your teaching?

DECISION MAKING
15. To what extent are you involved in decisions that affect you personally?
16. To what extent are you involved in decisions that affect the *quality* of the teaching-learning process (your specific job performance)?
17. How do you evaluate the quality of decisions made by your work group?

REWARDS
18. To what extent do you feel satisfied with the respect that you receive from students (have earned in your job)?
19. To what extent do you feel satisfied with your ability to meet the intellectual needs of students (satisfied with the intellectual demands of your job)?
20. To what extent do you feel that you are rewarded in relationship to the quality of your teaching (work)?
21. To what extent is excellent teaching (performance) *expected* at the campus?

JOB SATISFACTION
22. To what extent are you satisfied with the security of your present faculty position (present position)?
23. To what extent are you satisfied with the expenditure of energy necessary to accomplish your job?
24. To what extent do you feel your present faculty position (present position) is satisfying your professional goals and aspirations (your goals and aspirations)?
25. To what extent do you believe that your personality/temperament matches the professional demands of your job?
26. To what extent have you been able to accomplish many worthwhile things in your present faculty position (present position)?

initial shaping force is the personality and belief system of that founder" (pp. 319–320).

Leaders externalize their own assumptions and embed them gradually and consistently in the goals and structures of the group. Whether these basic assumptions are called the guiding beliefs, the theories-in-use, the basic principles, or the guiding visions on which a founder operates, there is little question that they become major elements of the emerging culture of the organization (Argyris, 1976; Pettigrew, 1979; Bennis, 1983; Donaldson and Lorsch, 1983; Dyer, 1983; Schein, 1983; Davis, 1984).

Through the years, our view of what leadership is and who exercises it has changed considerably. Not all managers are leaders. Leadership is a "process of creating a vision for others and having the power to translate it into a reality and sustain it" (Kotter, 1988, p. 25). From this perspective, leaders are people who are effective in relating a compelling vision of a desired state of affairs—the kind of vision that induces enthusiasm and commitment in others. Lee Iacocca established a reputation as a leader because he succeeded in guiding people to accomplish his new vision for Chrysler. Although it is difficult to summarize the many viewpoints of leadership phenomena presented in literature, some key leadership concepts emerge from this research.

Stodgill (1974) concludes that it is the function of leadership to define objectives and maintain goal direction, provide means for goals attainment, provide and maintain goal structure, facilitate group action and interaction, maintain group cohesiveness and member satisfaction, and facilitate group task performance. Similarly, Hollander (1978) contends that leadership is a process providing structure for helping the group to achieve performance goals and member satisfaction.

Other researchers have stressed the importance of the situation of the group being led as a major factor in sound leadership (Fiedler, 1976; Tannenbaum and Schmidt, 1973). A large amount of research shows that leadership styles are appropriate to specific kinds of situations in which the leader operates. Tannenbaum and Schmidt define seven different leadership styles on a continuum from "boss-centered leadership" to "subordinate-centered leadership," with the styles between representing different degrees of leader versus subordinate contribution to decision making.

Argyris (1964) describes the interrelationship between organizational structure and leadership. He notes that "if the participants do not trust their leaders (as well as one another), it is doubtful whether any suggestions...will have a respectable probability of being achieved." He concludes, "Organizational leadership will be the foundation" on which the organization will be built (p. 220).

Motivation. The current literature contains a number of definitions of the second subscale, motivation. The term was originally derived from the Latin word *movere*, which means "to move," and an up-to-date definition of work motivation might be "a set of energetic forces that originate both within as well as beyond an individual's being, to initiate and move forward work-related behavior, and to determine its form, direction, intensity, and duration" (Pinder, 1984, p. 8). An analysis of such a definition indicates that motivation is primarily concerned with three factors: what energizes behavior, what directs or channels such behavior, and how this behavior is maintained or sustained. Each of these three components of motivation is important to understanding human behavior at work. "The first component points to energetic forces within individuals that drive them to certain types of behavior. Environmental forces often trigger these drives. The second component refers to goal orientation, with behavior being directed toward something. The third component is concerned with forces within the individuals and within their environment that reinforce the intensity of their drives and the direction of their energy" (Steers and Porter, 1983, pp. 3–4).

Two types of motivation theory, content and process, attempt to explain the level of motivation to work. Content theories such as Maslow's hierarchy of needs (1943) and motivation/hygiene theory (Herzberg, Mausner, and Snyderman, 1959) focus on the unsatisfied needs of the employees because these needs influence what rewards they will value. Herzberg, Mausner, and Snyderman (1966) conclude that people have two different categories of needs that are essentially independent of each other and affect behavior in different ways. Their findings revealed that when people felt dissatisfied with their jobs, they were concerned about the environment in which they were working and extrinsic rewards. When people felt good about their jobs, their behavior had to do with intrinsic satisfaction associated with the work itself.

On the other hand, process theories such as expectancy theory (Hampton, 1978) focus on the degree to which employees believe their efforts will result in performance and how instrumental that performance will be in securing a personally valued reward. Another process concept, equity theory (Adams, 1963, 1965; Adams and Friedman, 1976), explores the motive power of the internalized norm of equity, defined as the shared belief that fairness in treatment, including reward of individuals, is right and should be sought.

There is evidence that an individual's need for achievement, affiliation, and power determines how he or she should be managed (McClelland, 1962). The behaviors associated with each need can be instrumental in motivating subordinates to successfully perform particular kinds of jobs.

People who seek to achieve enjoy situations in which they can take personal responsibility for finding solutions to problems, tend to set moderate achievement goals and take calculated risks, and want concrete feedback on how well they are doing. People with a high need for affiliation tend to think often about the quality of their personal relationships. Individuals high in their need for power spend more time thinking about how to obtain and exercise power and authority over others than those with low motivation toward power; they need to win arguments, to persuade others, to prevail, and to obtain positions where they can exert influence. They feel uncomfortable without some sense of power and are dependent on this sensation in order to feel a sense of well-being.

In summary, motivation is concerned with what energizes a person to action, with the forces that direct behavior once it is energized, and with the ways in which leaders sustain desired behaviors in their subordinates. When we understand that how well an individual performs is often related to his or her perception of the organizational climate, we begin to understand how important this concept is to successfully accomplishing group missions.

Communication. The third variable used in the organizational climate instrument relates to communication. A number of observational studies of the work activity of managers document that communication is the heart of management. Although communication patterns vary from job to job, most managers spend large amounts of time communicating. A number of studies suggest that distinctive characteristics and problems attach to managerial communication depending on its direction: up, down, or across the organizational hierarchy (Athanasiades, 1973; Roberts and O'Reilly, 1974; O'Reilly, 1978).

Upward communication, for instance, often carries information such as work progress and news of problems for decision making. The information is often filtered, however, so that the subordinate appears in a good light (Glauser, 1984). Managers need to communicate down the organization to inform, direct, and control their subordinates. But filtering also occurs in downward communication. Supervisors sometimes do not realize what information subordinates need to carry out their work or how to tell them what is expected of them. Superiors sometimes do not trust subordinates, do not want to overload or upset them, or may withhold information as a way of keeping subordinates dependent. Lateral and diagonal communication by managers—that is, communication with people in other departments who may be at higher, lower, or equal levels of the hierarchy—is often necessary for coordination or problem solving (Landsberger, 1961; Simpson, 1959). For some managers, this kind of communication occupies the major portion of their time (Sayles, 1964).

Wheetten and Cameron (1984) stress the importance of supportive communication in every organization and the impact of the message on the sender-listener relationship. It is important not only to communicate a message accurately, but also to ensure that the communications process strengthens the relationship between the participants. This skill includes the ability to send messages in a supportive way, to listen supportively, to empathize, and to respond appropriately to others' messages. Adequate and accurate information must be available to all employees in order to ensure good decision making (Roueche and Baker, 1986).

Decision making. Decision making, the fourth subscale, is a complex process that begins with an awareness of problems and concludes with an assessment of the consequences of actions taken to solve those problems. Managerial decision making, however, is often quite disorderly and becomes complex as it unfolds.

All decisions are steps into the unknown. Decision makers at all levels choose or refuse a plan of action, a job candidate, or anything else in light of their understanding of the chosen option and their knowledge of current circumstances, past experiences, and an extrapolation of the consequences of the choice (Heller, 1989). At all stages of this process, it is easy to be utterly wrong.

Dressel (1981) identifies six reasonably distinctive areas of decision making, varying from the routine with little or no significance beyond the immediate specific decision to those effecting major changes in institutional character and individual careers. The six areas are routine decision; decisions involving administrative or managerial responsibility for monitoring and correcting deficient performance; innovation; personnel policies and practices in appointment, promotion, reward, fringe benefits, and retirement; decisions having to do with institutional mission, role, purpose, and scope; and personal involvement. He states that this model provides one way of looking at the range and complexity of decisions faced in higher education, yet each situation also involves other factors or dimensions that must be considered before the final outcome can be resolved.

Although much of the social interaction of managerial decision making takes place in committees and other groups, there are important differences between individual and group decision making. The evidence indicates, for example, that groups make more accurate decisions when solving structured problems, but they are slower than individuals in reaching solutions (Miner, 1984).

In spite of their advantages, group decision processes are often thwarted by the groupthink phenomenon, which prevents high-quality thinking and dissident ideas because of an excessive desire for consensus to preserve the warm, cozy atmosphere of a cohesive group (Janis, 1982). Fortunately, however, groups can employ procedures such as the Delphi technique (Dalkey, 1969) and the nominal group technique (Delbecq, Van de Ven, and Gustafson, 1975) to combat these obstacles to effective group decision making. Unlike the Delphi technique, where the participants usually remain anonymous, never meet face-to-face, and communicate only in writing, in nominal group techniques participants know each other or become acquainted because they meet face-to-face and talk to one another, but their interaction is carefully controlled.

Rewards. Employees are able to evaluate their organization's culture through the final subscale adapted from Likert, the reward system. The rewards attached to various behaviors convey to employees the priorities and values of both individual managers and the organization. However, it should not be assumed that organizations will use rewards effectively. Although organizations may utilize rewards to reinforce the organization's culture, they may not use them consistently. In any event, the reward practices of an organization are an important aspect of its culture (Kerr and Slocum, 1987; Sethia and Von Glinow, 1985).

"Formal and informal reward systems...can become tools used by enterprising managers to encourage others to get on board more often than it is an incentive for them to begin their projects" (Kanter, 1983, p. 152). Thus, the reward system often tends to promote participation in planning more than participation in innovation. Ideally, rewards occur throughout the accomplishment process rather than just at the end. When rewards are administered carefully, they become a powerful means of motivating followers.

Reward power comes from the leader's ability to provide something desired by followers in return for the follower's desired behaviors. Reward power can influence people through hope, if rewards are logically and consistently applied, and the individuals perceive that granting the reward is within the power of the leader. Nonetheless, it is not certain that reward power will work in all situations and with all people. Whether an influence process will motivate a person to behave in the desired way depends on whether the individual perceives and judges that effort will lead to the reward offered, and whether the reward will satisfy a fundamental need (Behling and Starke, 1973).

Reward systems can be designed in ways that reinforce motivation theory. Links between pay and performance are important, and individuals need to understand that better performance leads to better pay. Rewards can be either formal or informal, intrinsic or extrinsic. Leaders must learn to vary rewards based on the situation in order to satisfy the needs of the various groups of employees.

Job satisfaction. Job satisfaction, a sixth subscale added by Baker, has been shown to be related to rewards. Lawler and Porter (1967) have summarized this relationship: satisfaction with a reward is a function of both how much is received and how much the individual feels should be received; satisfaction is influenced by comparisons with what happens to others; people differ with respect to the rewards they value; and some extrinsic rewards are satisfying because they lead to other rewards.

Managers can affect job satisfaction through appropriately structuring the rewards and the ways that these rewards will be viewed by employees. The extent to which the employee perceives the reward to be equitable has been found to be important; if the reward is perceived as not being consistent with rewards that others are receiving, dissatisfaction will result.

In the most general sense, job satisfaction is "a pleasurable positive emotional state resulting from an appraisal of one's job or job experiences" (Locke, 1983, p. 1300). This positive assessment seems to stem from the extent to which the job and everything associated with it meets the needs and values of the individuals performing the job. Most attempts to measure dimensions of job satisfaction involve studying needs through questionnaires and interviews. Job satisfaction is best considered as a collection of related job attitudes that can be divided into a variety of job aspects. For example, the Job Descriptive Index (JDI), a popular measure of job satisfaction, measures satisfaction in terms of five specific aspects of a person's job: pay, promotion, supervision, the work itself, and co-workers (Smith, Kendall, and Hulin, 1969). The manner in which an individual responds to the specific groups is dependent not only upon the conditions themselves, but also upon how the individual perceives them.

Job satisfaction is reflected in employee behavior, as well as in questionnaires and interviews. Numerous studies have shown that a simple, direct linkage between job attitudes and job performance often does not exist (Iaffaldano and Muchinsky, 1985). General attitudes best predict general behaviors and specific attitudes are most strongly related to specific behaviors (Fishbein and Ajzen, 1975). Overall job satisfaction, as a collection of numerous attitudes toward various aspects of the job, represents a very general attitude. Performance of a specific task cannot generally be predicted on the sole basis of one's general attitude.

Many personal characteristics affect how an employee perceives a particular job. Supervisors must, therefore, consider these personal factors in assessing the satisfaction of their subordinates. It is equally important to examine the characteristics of the work environment. In a comprehensive review of empirical studies of job satisfaction, Locke (1983) reveals seven working conditions that lead to job satisfaction for most people:

"(1) mentally challenging work with which the individual can cope successfully; (2) personal interest in the work itself; (3) work that is not too tiring physically; (4) rewards for performance that are just, informative, and in line with the individual's personal aspirations; (5) working conditions that are compatible with the individual's physical needs and that facilitate the accomplishment of his work goals; (6) high self-esteem on the part of the employee; and (7) agents in the workplace who help the employee to attain job values whose basic values are similar to his own, and who minimize role conflict and ambiguity" (p. 1328).

Job satisfaction has been shown to be closely related to turnover and absenteeism. The higher an employee's satisfaction, the less likely resignation will occur. In view of the high cost of turnover, the importance of this finding should be apparent to managerial personnel. The effect of job satisfaction on absenteeism is similar to but not as strong as its effect on turnover. The employee with high job satisfaction is less likely to be absent frequently (Locke and Latham, 1984).

The "key ingredient of the climate of effective schools is its health as an organization" (Roueche and Baker, 1986, p. 31). Organizational health is determined by strong leadership, staff involvement, systematic evaluation of instruction, and rewarding and recognizing faculty and staff. Strong community support and involvement are other signs of organizational health. Taken together, all six elements combine to create organizational health, a professional atmosphere for employees, and a strong organizational climate (Roueche and Baker, 1986).

Organizational Climate Profiles of Three Typical American Community Colleges

Climate and organizational health were examined in a college climate study known as the Commitment to Excellence Survey, conducted by the author and John E. Roueche in 1986 and 1987. The aim of the process was to promote open and constructive communication among faculty, staff, and administration through employees' sharing their perceptions concerning the campus climate. The focus was on quantifying the value of delegating and empowering others within the organization through an effective "transformational" leadership style.

Five groups of employees participated in each study: top management, administrators, full-time faculty, part-time faculty, and classified staff. Employees attended one of three sessions held to discuss and complete the Commitment to Excellence Survey. Respondents were asked to rate each of the twenty-six climate items on a five-point Likert-style scale, "one" being most satisfactory and "five" least satisfactory. Each item contained two components. Part A of each item asked the respondent to rate the item on a five-point scale, and Part B obtained a rating of the importance of the concept expressed in the item. Thus, the two-part question allowed the researchers to assess the difference between what the respondents, individually and in groups, perceived to be their actual work climate versus how important that particular item or concept was to them. The survey also allowed respondents to provide written comments after they completed the quantitative questions. These written responses were synthesized with the numerical answers to provide a complete view of the colleges.

Figure 2.3 shows the rank order of all twenty-six items as a composite for all groups at a single college. Approximately 265 individuals completed the survey. The data are shown in terms of averages for "is" and "should be" importance to the individual. The "Delta" score is the difference between the "is" average and the "should be" average. In the report submitted to the college, data are displayed for all groups and for all items.

To exemplify the complex mixture of feelings, attitudes, perceptions, and values of administration, faculty, and staff as they relate to the total organizational climate, profiles of three American community colleges (a large multicampus college, a medium-sized technical college, and a medium-sized single-campus college) are outlined in the pages that follow. The colleges themselves are not identified but are typical of the more than forty community colleges that have participated in climate studies conducted at the University of Texas at Austin since 1987.

A Large Multicampus College

The Commitment to Excellence Survey, when administered at a large, multicampus college in the northeastern United States, generally portrayed a healthy campus climate. It was found that administrators and other professionals were, in general, most satisfied with the climate at their various campuses, and career employees (classified staff) were, in general, least satisfied. Faculty were more satisfied than classified staff, but generally less satisfied than administrators and professionals with the existing climate.

The composite results from the climate survey shown at Figure 2.4 indicated that the college as a whole was functioning totally within a System Three (Consultative) management style on all subscales, with the overall average on twenty-six "A" items being 3.35 on a one-to-five scale. None of the composite ratings fell outside the consultative category, identified as a mean from 3.00 to 3.99.

Observations concerning the degree of satisfaction or dissatisfaction respecting each of the five climate factors are listed below and expressed

Figure 2.3
Rankings of Importance
Composite

Item No.	Item Description	IS N	Avg.	SB N	Avg.	Delta Avg.
10	Cooperation within department	256	3.88	258	4.77	0.89
18	Satisfaction with respect from students/peers	264	4.12	264	4.74	0.63
2	Freedom to seek information or assistance	265	3.80	264	4.72	0.92
21	Expectation of excellence in teaching/performance	261	4.12	263	4.69	0.57
19	Ability to meet intellectual needs	264	4.14	264	4.68	0.54
25	Personality/temperament matches job demands	265	4.49	267	4.67	0.18
20	Rewards relative to quality of work	261	3.29	260	4.66	1.37
1	Admin. confidence in ability of staff	263	3.81	263	4.63	0.83
24	Satis. that job is meeting prof. goals	265	3.63	265	4.61	0.97
26	Ability to accomplish worthwhile things	261	3.86	260	4.59	0.73
17	Quality of decisions by work group	242	3.73	244	4.58	0.85
22	Satisfaction with job security	265	3.69	265	4.56	0.86
16	Involv. in decisions affecting teaching/performance	261	3.31	260	4.55	1.24
15	Involv. in decisions w/personal effect	258	2.96	258	4.52	1.56
3	Encouragement to be creative	265	3.58	265	4.47	0.89
13	Admin. willingly shares important information	255	3.24	256	4.45	1.21
23	Satisfaction with expenditure of energy needed	265	3.37	264	4.44	1.07
14	Admin. communicates positive expectations	259	3.58	256	4.42	0.84
6	Support for innovative ideas	252	3.26	250	4.35	1.09
7	Admin. support for professional development	255	2.93	256	4.31	1.37
9	Cooperation across departments	246	2.96	251	4.23	1.27
8	Admin. inspires with sense of purpose	258	3.21	256	4.21	1.00
5	Admin. influence to grow professionally	263	2.88	263	4.20	1.32
4	Assistance to improve job performance	262	2.81	262	4.12	1.31
12	Usefulness of information supporting teaching/job	256	3.10	254	4.02	0.92
11	Quantity of information supporting teaching/job	255	3.08	254	3.92	0.84

diagrammatically in Figure 2.4. (The job satisfaction subscale was not employed in this study.)

Leadership. There was relative satisfaction with college leadership, reflected in the responses of all types of employees on items relating to the extent to which they could seek information and/or assistance from leaders. The most dissatisfaction registered with leadership by all employee

Figure 2.4
College Climate of a Large Multicampus College As Rated by
All Employee Groups Combined Using Composite Averages

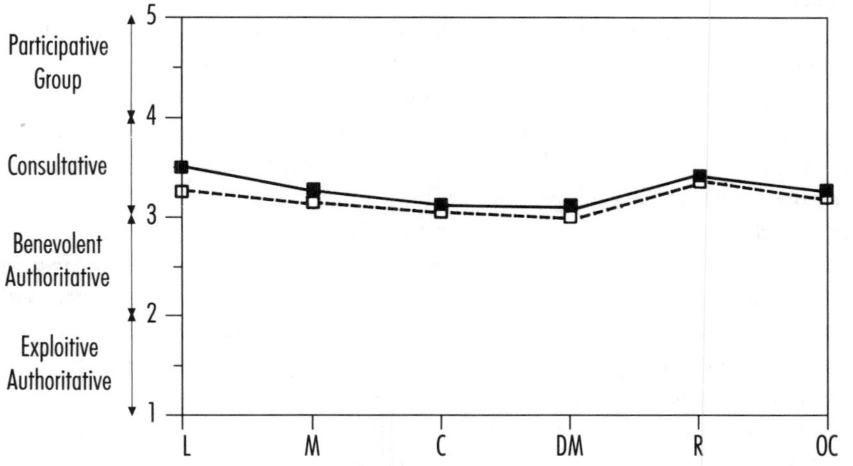

	L	M	C	DM	R	OC
■ Group Averages	3.50	3.36	3.32	3.13	3.46	3.35
□ National Averages N = 35 institutions	3.35	3.31	3.19	3.07	3.43	3.31

L = leadership   M = motivation   C = communication
DM = decision making   R = rewards   OC = overall climate

categories was with the level of assistance provided for improving job performance. Top management were relatively satisfied, compared to classified staff, with the president in terms of his expression of confidence in the staff and his encouragement of innovation and development.

Motivation. Faculty and administrators/professionals were relatively satisfied with the support received for personal career development goals. All five employee categories felt that a lack of cooperation across college/campus areas decreased motivation, but a higher level of satisfaction existed in all employee categories with the level of cooperation in their own work areas. With the exception of top management, classified staff and faculty at all levels expressed dissatisfaction with the support they received for their innovative ideas. Classified staff and faculty were also dissatisfied with the degree to which they were inspired with a sense of purpose by those who led the college.

The composite perception, when all groups were considered, was that the college was operating in a consultative environment as far as motivation went. In general, people were motivated by rewards they received and were satisfied with their involvement in the college.

Communication. There was relative satisfaction among all employee categories with the quantity and utility of information received relative to job performance. In their comments, some respondents indicated that the quality of communications is more important than the quantity. Some respondents noted the quantity of "junk" communication distributed within the college. Faculty and administrators/professionals were relatively satisfied with the extent to which positive expectations were communicated. College A needs to pay more attention to sharing information more willingly with faculty and with career employees: both these groups registered dissatisfaction in this area.

Decision making. In the collective minds of the participants, decision making fell into the System Three area—a consultative environment. Employees felt they were consulted about decisions important to them but would have liked more participation. The greatest degree of dissatisfaction registered on any survey item by faculty and by career employees concerned the extent to which they were involved in decisions having a personal effect on them. Moreover, there was dissatisfaction on the part of these two employee groups with the extent of their involvement in decisions having an effect on their performance.

Rewards. The composite score for rewards also fell into the System Three area of the model. Respondents felt strongly that rewards were related to performance. Yet, while satisfied in all areas, they would like to see more rewards available to them. Of all survey items, administrators/professionals registered the most satisfaction with the intellectual challenges of their job, and they described this as a very important area. Both faculty and career employees considered themselves underrewarded commensurate with their work quality—the item that registered the second-highest level of dissatisfaction. Comments by career employees also referred to a disparity in the distribution of the workload at the college. Both top management and faculty were relatively satisfied with the respect they received from students and their ability to meet their students' needs.

The overall college climate compared very favorably with the national averages of other similar community colleges. While they were most pleased with the quality of leadership, the perceptions of respondents supported the view that the climate could be improved in all areas. Although the college seems to be in a good position, there were still some improvements that needed to be made.

Twelve areas in need of improvement were identified for each of the three personnel groups. Each group had a slightly different set of priorities, with the three groups agreeing on six areas that needed change. These areas, in descending order beginning with items of greatest concern were: involvement in decisions that affect you personally (decision making); rewards in relation to quality of work/teaching (rewards); interdepartmental cooperation (motivation); involvement in decisions related to the teaching/learning process (decision making); information sharing (communication); and usefulness of information (communication). The items identified represent all areas addressed in the survey instrument. The communication and decision-making dimensions received somewhat more attention, with two items in each of these dimensions emerging as high priorities for improvement.

A Medium-Sized Technical College

Overall results from the Commitment to Excellence Survey for a medium-sized technical college in the Midwest portrayed a healthy campus climate. Generally, part-time faculty held the most positive perception. The responses of top management, administration, and full-time faculty were similar to each other—all three groups held positive views on most categories of the climate survey. The job satisfaction category received the highest composite rating, and communication received the lowest overall rating.

The composite results from the climate survey indicated that the college is functioning closer to a System Three (Consultative) than a System Four (Participative Group) management style, with the overall average on the twenty-six "A" items being 3.24 on a one-to-five scale (See Figure 2.5). All composite ratings fell within the Consultative range (System Three). All groups indicated that job satisfaction was the most satisfactory dimension. The groups also consistently indicated that they would like to see improvement in the area of rewards.

Observations concerning the degree of satisfaction or dissatisfaction respecting each of the five climate factors reflected a generally healthy organization with some areas identified for improvement.

Leadership. Only two groups, part-time faculty and top management, were relatively satisfied with the extent to which leaders encouraged innovation and development. The most dissatisfaction registered with leadership by all employee categories was the lack of assistance provided for improving job performance. With the exception of part-time faculty, the other four groups expressed dissatisfaction with the extent to which information and/or assistance could be sought from leaders. Leaders' lack of confidence in staff was another area of dissatisfaction registered by administration, top management, full-time faculty, and classified staff.

Figure 2.5
College Climate of a Medium-Sized Technical College Campus
As Rated by All Employee Groups Combined Using Composite Averages

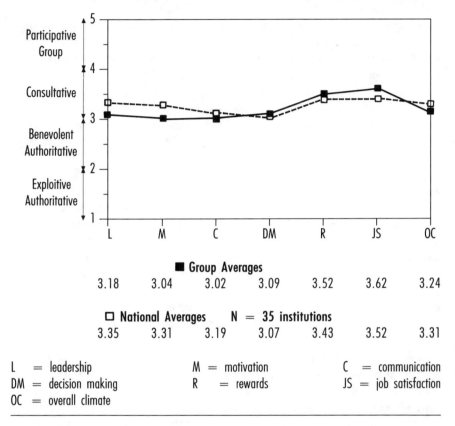

	L	M	C	DM	R	JS	OC
■ Group Averages	3.18	3.04	3.02	3.09	3.52	3.62	3.24
□ National Averages N = 35 institutions	3.35	3.31	3.19	3.07	3.43	3.52	3.31

L = leadership	M = motivation	C = communication
DM = decision making	R = rewards	JS = job satisfaction
OC = overall climate		

Motivation. Top management and part-time faculty were relatively satisfied with support received for innovative ideas, while only the top management group expressed relative satisfaction with the support received for professional development and with intra-departmental cooperation. All five employee categories were most dissatisfied with the lack of inter-departmental cooperation. None of the five groups was satisfied with the degree to which they were being inspired with a sense of purpose.

Communication. General dissatisfaction with the level of communication by all five groups indicated that attention needed to be given to two areas: sharing information more willingly and communication of positive expectations. There was, however, relative satisfaction by the top management group with the quality of information that was received relative to job performance. Administrators were relatively satisfied with the usefulness of the information received.

Decision making. The greatest degree of dissatisfaction registered on any survey item by all groups except part-time faculty was with the extent of their involvement in decisions that affect them personally. Part-time faculty expressed greatest dissatisfaction with respect to being involved in decisions relating to the teaching/learning process, but expressed satisfaction in terms of the quality of the decisions made.

Rewards. With the exception of the classified staff, all the groups expressed satisfaction with respect to meeting student needs. Top management, full-time faculty, and part-time faculty expressed relative satisfaction with the respect they received from their students. Of all survey items part-time faculty were most satisfied with the rewards they received from the quality of their teaching/performance and the level of excellence that was expected of them.

The overall college climate compared very favorably with the national averages of other similar community colleges. The greatest difference between "A" and "B" ratings was in the categories of leadership, motivation, and communication. Scores on decision making, rewards, and job satisfaction were higher than the national averages. Although the college seems to be in a good position, there were still some areas for improvement.

The top twelve areas in need of improvement were identified for each of the five personnel groups. Each group had a slightly different set of priorities, with all five groups agreeing on six areas that needed change. These areas, beginning with items of greatest concern, were: involvement in decisions that affect you personally, interdepartmental cooperation, leadership that inspires followers with a sense of purpose, assistance by administration to improve work, communication of positive expectations, and information sharing. The items identified for improvement represent four of the six dimensions of the survey instrument, with two items associated with the portion of the instrument related to motivation and two other items associated with the portion of the instrument related to communication.

A Medium-Sized Single-Campus College

Results from the Commitment to Excellence Survey for a medium-sized single-campus college in the West portrayed an ambivalent campus climate. Generally, administration held the most positive perception. Full-time faculty held views that were similar to classified staff on most categories of the climate survey. The job satisfaction category received the highest composite rating, whereas leadership received the lowest overall rating.

The composite results from the climate survey indicated that the college is functioning on the boundary between a System Two (Benevolent Authoritative) and System Three (Consultative) management style, with the overall average on the twenty-six "A" items being 3.03 on the five-point scale (See Figure 2.6). None of the composite ratings fell within the least favorable category, identified as Exploitive Authoritative (System One). Sixteen items were perceived as falling into the Benevolent Authoritative range (System Two), and two reached the most favorable level of management style, identified as Participative Group (System Four).

Leadership. All groups expressed dissatisfaction with leadership in terms of expressing confidence in staff, providing assistance for improving performance, and encouraging development. Only administrators were relatively satisfied with the extent to which leaders encouraged innovation and were approachable. Administrators were most satisfied with the extent to which they were able to provide assistance and/or information when needed. Compared to mean scores of other groups, classified staff were the most dissatisfied with receiving encouragement from their leaders in relation to development. Compared to other groups, faculty were the most dissatisfied with the lack of assistance from the leaders in terms of improving their performance.

Motivation. Relative satisfaction was expressed by administrators with respect to receiving support for innovative ideas and professional development, and cooperation among co-workers. The most dissatisfaction registered by classified staff in the motivation dimension was with interdepartmental cooperation. Faculty were most dissatisfied with being inspired with a sense of purpose and least dissatisfied with intra-departmental cooperation.

Communication. Administrators were relatively satisfied with the quality of information and information sharing but expressed dissatisfaction with the utility of information and their ability to communicate positive expectations. The greatest dissatisfaction expressed by both classified staff and faculty was in terms of information sharing. Classified staff were most satisfied with the leader's ability to communicate positive expectations, while faculty were most satisfied with the quality of information received.

Decision making. The greatest degree of dissatisfaction registered on any survey item by both classified staff and faculty was being involved in decisions that affect them personally. In contrast, compared to other groups, administrators were satisfied as far as this item was concerned. Administrators were also relatively satisfied with being involved in decisions relating to the teaching/learning process and the quality of the decisions made. Both classified staff and faculty were most dissatisfied with being involved in decisions that affect them personally.

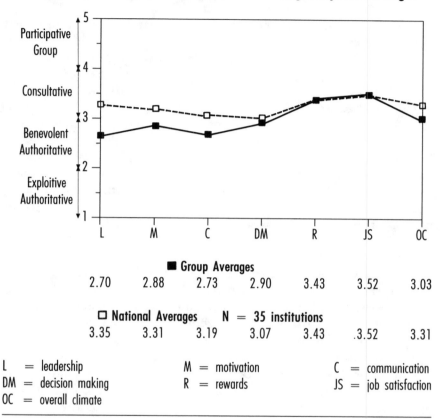

Figure 2.6
College Climate of a Medium-Sized Single-Campus College
As Rated by All Employee Groups Combined Using Composite Averages

■ Group Averages

	L	M	C	DM	R	JS	OC
	2.70	2.88	2.73	2.90	3.43	3.52	3.03

□ National Averages   N = 35 institutions

	L	M	C	DM	R	JS	OC
	3.35	3.31	3.19	3.07	3.43	.3.52	3.31

L = leadership	M = motivation	C = communication
DM = decision making	R = rewards	JS = job satisfaction
OC = overall climate		

Rewards. With the exception of classified staff, all the groups expressed limited satisfaction with respect to meeting student needs. Compared to other groups, administrators and classified staff were more dissatisfied with the respect they received from students. However, both groups were more satisfied with the level of excellence that was expected of them. Of all survey items, all groups were more dissatisfied than satisfied with rewards received from the quality of their teaching and/or performance. While administrators were most dissatisfied with the respect they received from their students, both classified staff and faculty were most dissatisfied with the rewards they received for the quality of their teaching and/or performance.

The overall college climate at this medium-sized single-campus college compared unfavorably with the national averages of other similar community colleges. The greatest difference existed in the categories of leadership, motivation, and communication. The scores produced by this college on rewards and job satisfaction were similar to the national averages. There were several areas for improvement.

The top twelve areas in need of improvement were identified for each of the five personnel groups. Each group had a slightly different set of priorities, with all five groups agreeing that six areas needed change. These areas, in descending order beginning with items of greatest concern, were allowing involvement in decisions that affect you personally, being inspired with a sense of purpose, offering assistance from administration to improve work, communicating positive expectations, expressing confidence in staff, offering rewards in relationship to quality of work/teaching, sharing information, encouraging development, encouraging involvement in decisions relating to the teaching and/or learning process, and interdepartmental cooperation. The items identified represent all six areas addressed in the survey instrument, with four items associated with the portion of the instrument related to leadership.

Conclusion

The concept of climate attempts to capture the complex and multifaceted transactions occurring between the individual and the college. The climate, or signature, of the college reflects the complete mixture of feelings, perceptions, expectations, norms, values, policies, and procedures that prevail within and are unique to a particular college environment. Measures of organizational climate produce a one-time "photograph," or image of the attitudes, feelings, and opinions prevailing in the college environment. Organizational culture is a larger, more permanent phenomenon that reflects what people believe is excellent.

Baker and Roueche's organizational climate profile can be used to obtain perceptions of employees concerning the climate of community colleges. Analysis shows that Likert's four-system theory can be successfully applied to an educational setting; the instrument has the potential of measuring not only climate, but also satisfaction with factors of leadership style; and the instrument can be used to articulate ways for improving both the climate and leadership of the institution.

One can also conclude that today's typical community colleges have, in general, developed a consultative environment. By describing the climate and culture of typical community colleges across America, this study provides a baseline for the development of subsequent research of excellent leaders, described in the next eight chapters. Unlike leaders of typical community colleges, excellent leaders have been able to move their colleges toward more collaborative and team-oriented climates and cultures.

The author has analyzed the climate standing of over forty community colleges in the past five years. In situations where the climate has been consecutively measured for two years, the trend is toward a more positive environment. For example, the collective perceptions regarding leadership become more positive, and satisfaction with rewards and decision making increases. This signals a developing culture.

According to Lacoursiere (1980), all organizations move through a life cycle consisting of orientation, dissatisfaction, resolution, production, and termination. Lacoursiere describes the dissatisfaction stage of organizational development as a decline in the morale of the organization and a gradual increase in task performance. He describes the resolution stage as characterized by increasing levels of morale and a continuing increase in task competency. In the resolution phase, there exists more comfort with the reality of the situation, a progressive internalization of goals and skills, more integration within work groups, and fewer fears of rejection and incompetence. Collegiality and mutual respect increase as members begin to assume more of the leadership functions.

Much evidence exists that the community colleges of some twenty-five years ago have evolved through both the orientation and dissatisfaction phases and are now in the resolution stage. While the typical colleges analyzed in this chapter manifested significant signs of resolution, leading-edge community colleges are moving toward the productivity stage. If this generalization is correct, community colleges are well-positioned to move toward productivity in the 1990s.

■

Chapter 3

Creating, Managing, and Transforming Community College Culture: Presidential Perspectives

By Charlotte Biggerstaff

For much of the past decade, the concept of organizational culture has captured the attention of theorists and behaviorists who have made it their business to study the formation, survival, and development of organizations. Although the concept of organizational culture remains elusive, difficult to define, perplexing to study, and a challenge to measure, it retains its fascination for theorists who continually seek to understand its influence. Recently, this fascination has extended beyond the business world and into the higher education arena. For those who wish to understand why some colleges and universities continue to thrive in times of uncertainty while others lose ground, studies of organizational culture offer valuable insights.

In their maturity, America's community colleges are facing growing challenges in both their external and internal environments. The leaders of these institutions have a fundamental responsibility to identify these challenges as opportunities and mobilize commitment around a shared vision for the future. To do so, they must find increasingly creative and artful ways of involving their constituents in this effort.

Complex issues of quality, productivity, accountability, diversity, competition, and accelerating technology require leadership of the highest order. Solving the problems of external adaptation and internal integration depends substantially upon the leader's ability to generate a shared belief system in which meaning is communicated and understood by all members of the institution (Schein, 1985a). Toward this end, viewing and responding to the organization from a cultural, holistic perspective holds considerable promise for those charged with leading others in the accomplishment of the vital community college mission. In fact, how well such institutions make the transition to maturity may depend on how fully their chief executives empower their followers and engage them in a commitment to shared vision and common purpose. The more thoroughly this sense of vision and purpose is infused throughout the institution, the more likely a supportive culture is to evolve. And, this supportive culture is the key to fulfilling the goals of maturing organizations.

The conceptual framework for cultural analysis, as described in Chapter One, captures the interactive holism of the culture phenomenon as it makes its presence felt within an organization. By identifying strategies of excellence and structures for success that are designed to optimize organizational skills, resources, and information, exceptional leaders lay the groundwork for creating, managing, and transforming the culture of their organizations. In so doing, they enable the development of shared values and beliefs that accommodate diversity, cherish creativity, and revere quality.

The Importance of Examining Leader Influence on Community College Cultures

The relationship between leadership and the evolution of an institution's culture accounts for many factors contributing to both success and failure in maturing community colleges. An understanding of this relationship can be enlightening for both current and aspiring leaders. Monitoring the organizational culture for functional and dysfunctional properties may be critical to the continued success of an institution in times of uncertainty.

As community colleges are summoned to demonstrate quality and provide evidence of student success, their leaders must take steps to reform and reshape their institutions to satisfy the needs of their changing roles. Unfortunately, the leadership process has been complicated by increasing external pressures, and many presidents have responded to these challenges at the expense of their internal environments. Cultures, however healthy and strong they may be, are not self-sustaining and tend to differentiate and ultimately disintegrate if left unattended (Kuh and Whitt, 1988; Tierney, 1988). Thus, the creative management of an institution's culture through transition is one of the foremost roles of an effective leader.

Community college leaders must begin to recognize their responsibility to create meaning for others, focusing their attention on symbolic, cultural activity in order to once again mobilize shared commitment toward a common vision. Viewing the institution from a cultural perspective can create significant insights, enabling the leader to expose and manipulate the symbolic field in the interest of all of the institution's stake holders: leaders, members, and constituents alike.

Leadership and Culture: A Study of Exceptional Presidents

Based on the understanding that creating and managing organizational culture is a primary leadership role, a study was performed to analyze how exceptional community college chief executives handle this important function. The study's primary purpose was to identify and describe examples of leadership behavior associated with transmitting and embedding culture, as revealed in interviews with a select group of community college presidents who had been recognized as exceptional and transformational in a previous study (Roueche, Baker, and Rose, 1989). By identifying and classifying examples of culturally oriented leader behavior, this study attempted to describe and clarify how forty-five effective community college presidents consider and address the cultural aspects of their institutions. The study was further motivated by a belief that rich descriptions of such behaviors would be useful to both current and future leaders who desire to analyze their own behavior for its cultural orientation.

The literature implies that such focused attention to organizational culture issues is critical to the cultivation of shared commitment to institutional purpose. As community colleges have become increasingly differentiated internally, and as external publics have introduced new pressures, much of the original holistic purpose and perspective of community college leaders has become diffused.

Guiding Studies and Principles

Interest in the cultural nature of higher education institutions is fairly recent, inspired largely by the successful application of Japanese management principles in business and industry. As Deal and Kennedy (1982) point out, the need for internal unity around common values and beliefs is now recognized as critical to organizational survival in times of change.

Over the years, anthropologists and sociologists have performed extensive research into the nature of culture and its significance for organizations of all types. The term "culture" has been defined variously (Clark, 1972; Kuh and Whitt, 1988; Sathe, 1983; Schein, 1985a); likewise, its properties of adaptability, strength, and health have been examined thoroughly (Albrecht and Albrecht, 1987; Deal and Kennedy, 1982; Peters and Waterman, 1982). Qualities and aspects of leadership have also been the focus of extensive consideration (Bass, 1985a; Bennis and Nanus, 1985; Burns, 1978) as theorists have become increasingly fascinated with organizational dynamics. Only recently, however, has attention been directed at the mutual interaction of leadership and culture.

In the past decade, Edgar H. Schein has emerged as one of the foremost authorities on this dynamic interrelationship. His research into the ways in which effective leaders create, manage, and transform organizational culture has inspired numerous related studies. Schein (1985a) identified the various levels of culture (artifacts, values, and assumptions); described the role of both founding and transitional presidents in culture creation and transformation; and developed a theory that outlines the means by which leaders create and manage the culture of their organizations. Thus, Schein's research into the effects of leadership on cultural evolution has been a major contribution to a growing body of organizational theory.

Despite increasing interest in the potential of leaders to affect the development of organizational culture, research into this phenomenon in education, particularly community colleges, is noticeably scant. What does exist is a small body of evidence that highlights the changing role of the community college and the corresponding need to position these institutions to address emerging issues. The AACJC Commission on the Future of Community Colleges (1988) claimed that, if these colleges are to fulfill their mission, they must focus on the "climate to be created" (p. 6). Eaton (1988) contended that community colleges must expand their role to include shared values for excellence, leadership, and a futures orientation. Roueche, Baker, and Rose (1989) argued that the leaders of these colleges must be able to "translate vision into understanding for followers" (p. 9), a first step toward empowerment. Clearly, the ultimate challenge for these institutions resides in the chief executive, who is charged with clarifying new goals and embedding within followers a shared commitment to common values. Taking a cultural perspective on the organization may well be the means by which this leader successfully addresses the challenges ahead.

According to Schein (1985a), leaders transmit and embed culture throughout the organization using five primary and five secondary mechanisms. Schein determined the following primary mechanisms to be extremely potent:

- What leaders pay attention to, measure, and control
- Leader reactions to critical incidents and organizational crises
- Deliberate role modeling, teaching, and coaching
- Criteria for allocation of rewards and status
- Criteria for recruitment, selection, promotion, retirement, and termination

Schein found that five secondary mechanisms are effective to the degree they are consistent with the primary mechanisms:

- Organizational design and structure
- Organizational systems and procedures
- Design of physical space, facades, and buildings

- Stories about important events and people
- Formal statements of organizational philosophy, creeds, and charters

How the Study Was Performed

In preparation for the study, it was determined that an evaluation of the cultural orientations of the forty-five community college presidents who had been identified as exceptional (Roueche, Baker, and Rose, 1989) would likely demonstrate how these leaders affect the culture of their institutions. Since the primary intent was to identify and describe examples of exemplary cultural-embedding behavior, a qualitative research design, capable of eliciting rich description, was employed.

Using the ten mechanisms identified and explicated by Schein (1985a) as the basis for a theoretical framework, research questions were developed to uncover the cultural-embedding behaviors of the forty-five participants. Taped interviews gathered for the 1989 Roueche, Baker, and Rose study were summarized to capture both behavioral and attitudinal perspectives that demonstrated a cultural orientation as described in the literature. These summaries were then reviewed for specific types of behavior as suggested by Schein's cultural-embedding mechanisms theory. As culturally sensitive behaviors and attitudes were identified, each was treated as a "unit of analysis" and was assigned a code based upon criteria developed for each of Schein's ten embedding mechanisms. (Initial criteria evolved from Schein's research and were submitted to him for verification.) Thus, in theory, if a particular behavior met the criteria for a specific embedding mechanism category, it was assigned a specific code.

However, since the process of coding narrative data is often imprecise in its early stages, the researcher performed a pilot study on six of the forty-five interview summaries using the "constant comparative method" (Glaser and Strauss, 1967), in which each unit of analysis was compared to others assigned to a specific category. Through this process, theoretical properties of each category became increasingly refined. Once the pilot study was complete, "consistency rules" were developed for each of the ten categories that enabled even more reliable coding. Since the comprehensive nature of these rules prohibits their inclusion in this chapter, the reader is referred to "Appendix D" in Biggerstaff (1990) for further elaboration.

By way of example, however, the rules applied to coding behaviors and attitudes in Category One ("What presidents pay attention to, measure, and control") include references to creating a climate for organizational success, developing a vision for the future, and realizing vision through planning. Similarly, the rules for Category Four ("Criteria used to allocate rewards and status") include remarks about behaviors presidents recognize and reward, as well as the formal and informal strategies they use to do so. Finally, in addition to the development of specific coding criteria, intra-rater and inter-rater reliability tests were also performed to further confirm consistency in the coding practice.

Once all units of analysis had been coded, the researcher compared cultural-embedding behavior across the population in order to discover the generality of emerging patterns and themes. To do this, data were clustered by common themes and displayed on large wall charts in ways that enabled patterns to emerge, as suggested by Miles and Huberman (1984). The goal throughout the process was to preserve the richness of the narrative rather than reducing it to a statistically quantifiable form in order to illuminate the ways in which exceptional community college presidents create a shared belief system and manage meaning for organizational members.

The results of the study demonstrated that exceptional community college presidents place a high value on culture and strive for shared understanding of its significance to institutional effectiveness. In the section that follows, seven of the ten cultural-embedding mechanisms are reviewed as they relate specifically to the aspects of the cultural framework described in Chapter One.

The Cultural-Embedding Behavior of Exceptional Presidents

The forty-five presidents in this study create and manage the culture of their institutions by consciously striving to strike a balance between the demands of their external environment and those of their internal constituents. They recognize the need to develop a shared belief system that considers the nature of people, the demands of the work to be done, and the importance of creating common meaning for organizational members. Furthermore, they insist that organizational culture is a phenomenon that requires their constant attention if they are to teach others what they consider to be important. And, finally, they bring together structures, strategies, and systems in ways that heighten their values for mutually interactive leadership and followership. The effects are holistic, innovative, and shared throughout the organization.

What Presidents Pay Attention To, Measure, and Control

Schein (1985a) contended that leaders form and transform the culture of their organizations by consciously attending to, systematically dealing with, and attempting to control follower behavior. Through their actions, leaders teach others about what they consider to be important. They reveal their fundamental values, beliefs, and assumptions by spending time on matters they consider significant, consistently addressing certain issues, and responding to key organizational concerns. Moreover, the more explicit and consistent their behavior, the more readily followers comprehend how the leader feels about organizational issues.

The presidents in this study demonstrated that they invest considerable time and energy in three significant types of leadership activity: creating a supportive, positive, and appropriate climate for organizational success; developing an institutional vision for the future that attends to problems of external adaptation and internal integration; and involving constituents in a comprehensive strategic planning process designed to perpetuate the desired climate and bring full realization to organizational vision. Each of these types of leadership activity is discussed more fully below.

First, to create a climate appropriate to institutional effectiveness, presidents claimed to: induce conditions that foster achievement, commitment, and pride; develop a positive, healthy atmosphere that encourages and rewards creativity; and strive for a climate of "shared visions" that challenges old patterns and embraces the accomplishment of new ones. Furthermore, these presidents' comments demonstrated that they value informality and collegiality; openness; and an environment in which tension is minimized, rapport is good, and a feeling of family prevails.

Second, exceptional community college presidents devote considerable time to envisioning where they want their institutions to go and how they want them to get there. They not only identify and focus institutional vision, but also communicate it to others and engage them in its accomplishment. Moreover, they reportedly spend a large share of their time addressing the specific needs of their community. They recognize the importance of identifying problems as opportunities, attending to diversity, understanding the significance of demographics and trends, and generally embedding a value for community responsibility within their institution. In the words of one president, "If the community is not viable, the college will not be either."

Finally, these transformational presidents asserted that comprehensive strategic planning is their primary vehicle for creating the supportive climate they seek and accomplishing their vision for their institutions. They affirmed that strategic planning is central to their focus on the future and that it is the most effective means of summoning the entire organization to attend to future issues, concerns, and directions. According to one president, "Planning is the means by which vision is translated into action." These college leaders assume primary responsibility for the planning process and exert much leadership in meaningful, organized, systematic, long-range planning activities. While they spend considerable time reviewing and revising mission, goals, and objectives, they argue that comprehensive institutional planning must also involve every-one and provide vehicles for a wide variety of input. As one president explained, "A leader who tries to refine mission independent of the rest of the college community leads no one."

Schein (1985a) claimed that leaders convey their assumptions, be-liefs, and values about what is important for their organization by at-tending to and attempting to control certain elements within it. Through such symbolic behavior as involving vested parties in planning for the future, the presidents in this study communicate their concern for creating a shared vision of what the institution is to become. Such a leadership style fosters an expectation among followers that roles, events, trends, and change will be accommodated throughout the organization.

Reactions to Critical Incidents and Organizational Crises

According to Schein (1985a), how a leader responds to a crisis will often create new organizational norms and procedures while revealing some of the leader's underlying assumptions about the importance of peo-ple and the value of the work to be accomplished. The leader has an opportunity to clarify his or her vision through reactions to critical inci-dents, because followers tend to learn more in times of heightened emo-tionalism. The presidents in this study described several critical incidents of external adaptation and internal integration that illustrate their value for both people and education.

For example, a few presidents noted that extreme controversy sur-rounded efforts to modify curricula in order to better serve their chang-ing communities. However, by involving reluctant participants in the change process and giving them the power to make decisions, and by inviting external agents to campus to discuss college/community issues, these presidents described reshaping their institution's vision over time. In other examples, patience, rather than coercion, proved to be the key to successful transformation. Several presidents described how their continued persistence over time enabled them to develop institutional awareness of community problems, particularly with regard to under-served populations. Others noted the importance of bearing in mind the values embedded in a particular community. For example, two presi-dents cited incidents in which they supported academic freedom issues that collided with community sensibilities, resulting in negative conse-quences for their institutions. In general, then, the presidents in this study attempted to identify issues in their external environment that will affect their colleges, involve vested parties in problem solving, and exercise patience and discretion in dealing with resistance to change. Such strategies for excellence imply that aligning the institution with its environment is necessary to the successful evolution of mission, purpose, and goals.

College presidents also described critical situations that clarify how they handle internal integration problems, thereby revealing their values for how people should be treated and how they wish them to behave. The presidents reported examples of how they deal with significant faculty and student concerns, reorganize structures and resources for greater effectiveness, and attempt to model the kind of behavior they wish others to adopt. They further described strategies to mobilize and empower human resources, build trust, reduce anxiety, and improve staff morale. For example, to successfully resolve problematic salary and union issues, several leaders convened task forces of well-informed individuals, while others implemented collegial "mutual gains bargaining." Furthermore, the presidents in this study acknowledged the importance of considering human issues during layoffs, soliciting the opinions of people about to be affected by significant change, and developing trust in followers by standing behind their beliefs. With regard to the latter, several presidents cited specific instances that required them to lay their jobs on the line in the service of professional and personal ethics. Presidents also discussed incidents that symbolized their value for students as partners in the educational enterprise, such as streamlining procedures for student convenience and involving them in significant campus development projects.

One can conclude that these community college presidents recognize the importance of their reactions to serious institutional problems. How they choose to manage the critical challenges presented in their external and internal environments is a matter of great concern to them. The incidents described have become symbols that clarify their vision and create meaning for others.

Modeling and Teaching Appropriate Behavior to Others

Schein (1985a) notes that effective leaders convey through their personal behavior powerful conscious and unconscious messages about what they consider to be important. Values for creativity, risk taking, commitment, and autonomy are taught as leaders act them out. Furthermore, the more consistently leaders demonstrate desired behavior, the more likely followers are to comprehend what the leaders consider to be appropriate. Consistency in behavior patterns is an important ingredient in cultural leadership style.

The community college presidents in this study hold strong beliefs and assumptions about why people are motivated to grow, develop, and behave as they do. In their interviews, presidents addressed motivational issues and the importance of valuing work, as well as their own role in inspiring followers. They also discussed the importance of holding their leadership teams accountable and teaching leader values for people, education, and quality. And, finally, they described some of the techniques and strategies they use to model and teach desired behavior.

Generally, exceptional presidents believe that educators are in the business for the intrinsic satisfaction it gives them rather than tangible rewards. They believe that people are internally inspired to grow and develop. They maintain that the more people identify with the value of the work they are doing, "buy in" to its importance, and take pride in its accomplishment, the more motivated they become. As these presidents organize their human resources, they involve people in the life of the college and its decision making, and they support what they do. In the words of one president, "The more we appreciate what people do, the more they are motivated."

The presidents in this study also recognize that strategic goals emanate from values held by those at the top of the organization and that values must be continually reflected upon and clarified for constituents if they are to become shared throughout the institution. As one president remarked, "People pick up on what a president says and does." Certain presidents specifically identified their responsibility to set the tone for the institution, to instill enthusiasm for the importance of what is being done, to inspire pride in the presidency, and to encourage leadership at all levels through empowerment. Several presidents also commented on the significance of presidential enthusiasm, energy, and personal ethics for follower motivation. Others discussed the importance of consistency between values and actions, both on and off the job. One president noted, "What I am as a college president is what I am as a person."

Interviews further revealed that these presidents acknowledge their social and ethical responsibility to set an example for their followers. Reportedly, they expect that their followers will demonstrate commitment to certain basic human values like integrity, truth, honesty, fairness, trust, and patience. The presidents value hard work, excellence in teaching and education, creativity, and risk taking. And, finally, they recognize that their behaviors are perceived by employees and constituents as representing the standards of the institution.

The presidents in this study described hundreds of behaviors, strategies, and techniques commonly used to model expected behavior. Some of these strategies imply awareness of the symbolic character of the presidency, such as attending student and faculty events, socializing with staff and students both on- and off-campus, talking about excellence in education, and participating in community affairs. Other strategies serve as examples of the kinds of behavior they wish their followers to adopt. Through modeling, presidents try to convey their beliefs that people should be treated fairly and with respect, open communication and enthusiasm should be a priority, decisions and authority should be delegated, and work standards should be of the highest quality.

This select group of community college presidents care a great deal about their roles as mentor, coach, and teacher in the service of their profession. As primary institutional leaders, they acknowledge not only their responsibility, but also their actions in this regard. They work hard to create a powerful, symbolic presence for their institutions within the community, while transmitting and embedding their values to their followers.

Criteria Used to Allocate Rewards and/or Status

According to Schein (1985a), leaders often use rewards and punishment to reinforce desired behavior. The more consistently and frequently they do so, the more likely followers are to comprehend what the leader considers important and to adjust their behavior accordingly. Furthermore, Schein argues that an organization with a systematic reward process is more likely to achieve desired behavioral outcomes in its members. The conceptual framework for cultural analysis supports these notions, suggesting that a feedback process is critical to improved performance and enhanced internal motivation.

Although a number of the chief executives in this study addressed the importance of rewards, only a few specifically delineated their criteria for allocating them. Generally, they were more inclined to discuss the ways in which they recognize achievement; they claimed to reward creativity and innovation, risk taking, overall performance, and effort. Rewards are granted both formally and informally.

Formal reward strategies include giving credit in public, holding symbolic reward and recognition programs, publishing booklets of outstanding faculty contributions and accomplishments, granting release time for leadership activity, and implementing merit pay programs. Several leaders use tangible, symbolic tokens of appreciation, such as gold lapel pins or inscribed coffee cups.

Positive behavior is reinforced in less obvious, more informal ways as well. Presidents express their appreciation by telephone or in short handwritten notes when faculty members publish books or articles, receive professional awards, or make special presentations. Some presidents use their reward systems to "push others out in front." For example, one president makes sure faculty members receive recognition for their innovations by inviting them to make presentations to other staff members.

Another president uses "we" when discussing institutional accomplishments in order to give others credit.

Using both formal and informal strategies, the community college presidents in this study recognize and reward both personal and group performance in their followers. By doing so, they reinforce valued behavioral outcomes, inspire motivation, and encourage productivity.

Criteria Used to Recruit, Select, Promote, Retire, and/or Terminate Employees

If, as Schein (1985a) and Pascale (1985) assert, one of the most powerful ways organizational culture becomes embedded is through the selection and socialization of members, leaders must clarify their expectations for membership in the organization. Those leaders who are content with their present culture are more likely to hire new members who support it, while those seeking change tend to select new members who identify with emerging problems and are willing to help socialize existing members in new directions. Thus, the criteria for selection, promotion, and termination of members evolve from these basic assumptions about the need for organizational stability or change.

The leaders in this study are concerned about whom they select and hire to fulfill the mission of their institutions, as well as how they socialize new members and develop existing ones. As one president commented, "Who we hire to replace ourselves is the most significant thing we are likely to do in the future." Presidents referred to hiring "good people," "the best qualified people," and "the right people for the right jobs." They also look for "competence," "potential," and a "sense of the college vision." The selection and organization of these "human resources" is essential to the accomplishment of collective vision and mission.

Although these presidents made few comments about why they terminate particular employees, it is apparent that they are concerned about alignment to suit the needs of the culture and the demands of the external environment. One president maintained that he refuses to "keep people who aren't quality," and another contended that an employee who fails to improve inadequate performance is subject to reassignment or termination. Furthermore, excellent presidents regard the socialization and development of their followers as essential to achieving required alignment. As one president noted, "When the community need changes, faculty must be retrained for the new emphasis."

In summary, the community college presidents in this study value the selection, employment, and renewal of well-qualified people in accord with their vision of what the organization is to become. They hold high standards for performance and manage the human resources of their college in ways that embed and transmit their values throughout the institution.

Designs and Structures Employed to Control the Organization and Its People

The design of an organization reflects the leader's underlying assumptions about the nature of tasks, the means to accomplish them, and the nature of people (Schein, 1985a). All three types of assumptions must operate in harmony if an organizational structure is to serve its purpose and function effectively. Such "structures for success" are ways in which a college does its business, that is, how it is designed so that optimal teaching and learning can occur.

The chief executives in this study hold values, beliefs, and assumptions about tasks and people that contribute to the overall design and structure of their institutions. They describe their organizations as groups of people working together in the service of others and as a collection of functions that arise from values, history, and context. Believing that their colleges should reflect how they feel about people and the functions to be performed, they attempt to organize the work that must be done in keeping with these values.

Clearly, how people treat each other is very important. In the words of one president, "Concern for human values should come before all else." These presidents see their institutions reflecting this belief, often referring to them as "congregations," "large classrooms," or "families." As one chief executive commented, "A college is not a machine, but a group of humans who respond spontaneously."

Concerns for openness, involvement, flexibility, and empowerment are manifested in structures designed to ensure accessibility, communication, and participation in decision making. Presidents' doors are open, and communication systems keep people informed. Colleges are decentralized to ensure decision making and problem solving at the lowest possible level, thus giving people some individual control. Members have both the responsibility and the authority to act on certain ideas and carry out tasks. Such institutions are flexible to encourage the "lateral entry of timely ideas" and the use of "common sense on non-routine matters." One president argued that, "When decisions are made at an inappropriate level, the leader becomes only a caretaker." Exceptional presidents structure their colleges to foster involvement and team building in order to ensure "pride in participation" and to enhance "the sense of community." And, finally, collegial governance structures at all levels further ensure that "everyone with a legitimate complaint gets heard" and "there is a vehicle for everything that needs attention."

In summary, the college presidents in this study structure their institutions in ways that demonstrate their values for how people should be treated and work should be accomplished. In the best colleges, communication is enhanced, participation is encouraged, decisions are made by those nearest to the problem, and all organizational members know they are valued.

Systems and Procedures for Managing the Organization and Its People

As the most overt manifestations of what a leader believes and values, systems and procedures reflect an organization's fundamental assumptions. According to Schein (1985a), these manners of operation create meaning for members and, when formalized, must reinforce underlying values about what is important if they are to be effective. Such arrangements are identified as applications of "structures for success," that is, theories in practice.

The presidents in this study identified a number of ways they envision and plan for the future that support their notions about the importance of member participation in the accomplishment of shared vision and common mission. Spending considerable time and effort on strategic and long-range planning, they annually review their college missions and goals in order to incorporate new environmental information and adjust their responses in a way that will gain commitment from others. As one president expressed it, "Goals must be continually and collectively reset during maturity if an institution is to move forward." Presidents also elaborated extensively upon the ways in which they try to involve their constituents in the service of their educational enterprise. Planning processes emphasize "grass-roots," "bottom-up" participation for greater creativity and motivation. For example, several presidents claimed to select individuals to serve on task forces and committees because of their "motivation rather than position," their expertise in certain areas, and their reputation for being innovative.

A variety of specific strategies are employed to cause followers to invest in the vision and participate in the vital institutional planning process. For example, presidents take board/administrator retreats, hold workshops and charettes, bring in guest speakers, develop position papers, and rely heavily on community advisory groups. One president takes the time to develop "management themes" over a two-year period, so that ideas can become absorbed, vested, embellished, and acted upon. Another has developed what he calls a "6-4-2 Plan," in which the college looks at trends and directions six years ahead, determines institutional implications four years out, and implements a "management-by-objectives" procedure for the next two years. Such planning strategies address key participation, stake holder, and ownership issues. Believing that "buy-in is critical," the presidents in this study attempt to design comprehensive planning processes that involve all constituents in order to serve "multiple property interests." As one president remarked, "Everyone should be a planner, not just a soldier."

Several presidents mentioned that students are considered equal partners in the planning process. To involve them, presidents meet regularly with student organizations and representatives; some presidents invite students to legislative meetings, board meetings, and cabinet sessions; and others discuss the minutes of student government meetings at executive staff meetings. These transformational presidents employ similar strategies with staff and faculty. For example, they use meetings of various types to solicit input and communicate their expectations for desired outcomes. While some hold open forums without specific agendas, nearly all the presidents claimed to meet regularly with their management teams, faculty councils, and/or representatives of these organizations.

Presidents described other "success structures" implemented to clarify expectations, create common understanding, and align resource and relational concepts. For example, in order to demonstrate their value for high standards and reward acceptable behavior, some presidents annually negotiate goals with staff and evaluate performance based on how well these goals have been achieved. One president mentioned conducting annual "mini-accreditations" with departments in order to "leverage" them for improved performance. Thus, it seems that excellent presidents initiate evaluation procedures that reflect their beliefs about how work should be accomplished and people should be treated.

The presidents in this study described a variety of systems and procedures that overtly represent what they believe to be important in a community college environment. Through such processes, these presidents achieve goals related to participative planning, effective communication and idea exchange, and quality performance.

Conclusion

The exceptional community college presidents in this study understand the significance of cultural embedding activity to solving the problems of external adaptation and internal integration. They are ever mindful that their institutional climate should support their vision for the future by engaging followers around shared values. They demonstrate consistency in their reactions to critical events in order to clarify meaning for others. And, finally, these presidents model and reward desired behaviors, select new members who share their vision, and organize their institutions to reflect their values for people and work.

This study of a select group of exceptional community college presidents suggests that college leaders must assess their organizational cultures for functional and dysfunctional qualities. As institutions demonstrate increasing accountability and measures of success, many of the solutions to problems of external adaptation and internal integration surface. By attending to an organization's culture, presidents can discover the reasons why styles, structures, and strategies work well in some situations and fail in others. If community colleges are to continue to respond and adapt readily to changing circumstances, presidents must attend to institutional culture and its potency to inspire commitment around shared values and beliefs.

■

Chapter 4

Culture and Communication

By Tessa Martinez Tagle

L eaders of community colleges remain acutely perplexed about their systems of communication. While communication technology continues to advance, demands for adequate and accurate information have escalated as a result of budget crises and social ills that challenge the community college mission as well as its day-to-day work.

Although technology can enhance organizational output, it can never fully replace the two-way social process of communication that is essential to collaborative problem solving, the coordination of work, and the pursuit of quality. How community college leaders sustain the human relationships that are a precondition for effective communication was the subject of a study conducted by the author in 1988. To be more specific, if a social relationship between two people is the basic unit of communication, how do America's best community college leaders cultivate a climate for relationships across their institutions? This chapter provides a brief summary of the findings of the study, deriving from it and other sources communication strategies for creating cultural change.

Background Research

In order to understand communication, it is necessary to isolate its various components. To limit the review of an abundance of literature, this section focuses only on that which addresses communication in relation to leadership behavior and its social consequences.

Stout (1984), for example, spoke to the role of the leader's self-concept in interpersonal communications since it enables leaders to be open as well as to facilitate openness in the organization. According to Stout (1984) and Barnard (1968), the effective leader has a high tolerance for complexity;

is flexible; and avoids manners, speech, and attitudes that create threat, defensiveness, and a restricted flow of information. In his description of the open organization, Ouchi (1981) further added that what he called Theory Z leaders, in particular, were observers and example-setters. These interpersonal qualities, Stout (1984) would argue, are rooted in all that a leader is—physically, socially, and psychologically—from an organismic-holistic point of view.

Some Basic Principles

While the literature identifies various levels of communication, it is at the interpersonal level (two-person communication) and systems level (communication between more than two people) that some understanding of basic principles is useful. For example, the focus at the interpersonal level is on the relationship of the individuals involved, their intentions and expectations for each other, and the "gaming" rules, defined by Thayer (1968) as the rules of protocol. At the systems level, Havelock, et al. (1973) describe interpersonal communication between people within an identifiable subunit of an organization. Related to this are the networks of data and information systems that link people across social systems so that the organization may relate to the environment, make task-related decisions, and perform with efficiency and effectiveness.

In a similar vein, Barnard (1968) defines a cooperative system as "a complex of physical, biological, personal, and social components that are in a specific systematic relationship by reasons of the cooperation of two or more persons for at least one definite end" (p. 81). No formal organization can exist efficiently without cooperative relationships, shared values, common purpose, and the interpersonal and systems communication to achieve them.

Moreover, Katz and Kahn (1978) believe that each subsystem will respond to the same input in different ways and seek out particular information to meet its needs. Hence, since "the exchange of information and the transmission of meaning is the very essence of a social system," there may need to be adequate translation of messages across subsystems and coding schemes (p. 428).

In their study of leadership effectiveness in colleges, Astin and Scherrei (1980) made a helpful distinction between proximate (those with a direct connection) and distal (those with a remote connection) outcomes of behavior. That is, some leadership behaviors, such as articulating values, expectations, or commitments, have a direct effect on communication and relationships. Other behaviors have outcomes that indirectly, yet instrumentally, affect communication and relationships. Pierce, Dunham, and Cummings (1984), for example, studied the effects of environmental structure (i.e., job design, technology, and work unit structure) on employee attitudes and behavior, such as job satisfaction, internal motivation, involvement in their jobs, overall job performance, and absenteeism.

Other Aspects of Communication

Argyris (1962) argued for "authentic" relationships—those in which individuals reciprocally give and receive non-evaluative descriptive feedback; own one's own values, attitudes, ideas, and feelings; and take risks with new values, attitudes, ideas, and feelings. Kelly, et al. (1983) proposed "close" relationships—those in which mutual impact and interdependence is high.

Language, Thayer (1968) stated, is a social precondition for communication. Not only must people share a common language, but the form of that language affects the ways people will communicate. Filley (1975), for example, suggested that a language of conflict often elicits feelings of threat or defensiveness, closing people off from each other, whereas the language of problem solving is culturally sustained by trust and a high regard for openness. Put another way, there is greater problem-solving potential within a social system when information is plentiful and feelings of threat or defensiveness are absent.

Finally, Ouchi (1981) offered suggestions on how to achieve effectiveness in the informal communication system. Describing the Japanese organization, Ouchi (1981) upheld the concept of inclusive relationships as opposed to partial relationships. Unlike Western institutions, the groundwork for formal and informal communication in Japanese organizations is achieved by employee participation in multiple relationships to the work environment, not merely in those that connect them to a task. For instance, Japanese employees have a say in the rewards they receive and the social structures that exist in the workplace.

The Study

The purpose of the author's study was threefold. In part, the study described ideal communication system characteristics and the leadership behavior characteristics associated with communication and relationship strength. Second, the study analyzed and explained how these behaviors are associated with communication and relationship strength at selected colleges. In other words, the study showed why—in terms of frequent, similar, strong, or commonly perceived administrative behaviors—communication functions as it does at those colleges. Finally, the research explored selected communication behaviors previously studied by Roueche, Baker, and Rose (1989).

Assumptions

Following are assumptions made in the study about the nature of administrative behavior, the conditions under which administrative behaviors occur, methodology, and the relationship of the study to other situations. First, it was assumed that administrative behaviors affect employee attitudes. Although employees may not perceive discrete effects from administrative behaviors, they do hold general beliefs and attitudes about the people who lead them. To be more exact, employees can describe their leaders as being effective or ineffective, influential or weak, open or closed, and so on. Ultimately, employees will also perceive these administrative behaviors as facilitating or restraining individual and collective goals.

Second, it was assumed that while people in different positions of leadership may demonstrate diverse behaviors, there are, nonetheless, a set of observable leadership behaviors that have some set of outcomes common to excellent colleges.

Third, while there were many possible research designs for the study, a nonexperimental, qualitative study was deemed the most appropriate for arriving at answers to the stated research questions. Such an approach provided the broad evaluative insight essential to understanding the complexities and richness of communication and relational strength. Specifically, because this was a descriptive study, an analytical study, and an ex post facto study, it was assumed that the theoretical domains identified as a framework of this study were adequate and accurate; the chief executive officers whose colleges served as the sample were, indeed, highly effective leaders; respondents openly and to the best of their knowledge provided the data sought; the instrumentation used was valid and reliable; and data analyses were appropriate to the questions posed by the study.

Finally, it was assumed that community colleges, by nature of their mission, share some common institutional concerns, challenges, and characteristics. From this assumption, it was expected that the research design would be sensitive to these common traits, other community colleges would be able to use the findings to study themselves, and administrative behaviors perceived to enable communication and relational strength could be applied by those who aspire to lead exemplary institutions.

Methodology

The study analyzed leadership behaviors associated with communication at twenty-three community colleges. Specifically, twenty-three colleges were identified in a study conducted by Roueche, Baker, and Rose

(1989) as a group whose chief executive officers expressed strong communicative behaviors. The colleges that participated in the study were from a larger group of fifty designated by Roueche, Baker, and Rose (1989) as having highly effective transformational CEOs.

Where the Roueche, Baker, and Rose (1989) reputational study began with a much larger participant sample comprised exclusively of CEOs from 256 colleges, this study's sample was composed of fewer participants from two strata of administration at only twenty-three community colleges. The sample included members of the top management team and a limited number of their subordinates so the study would be focused and manageable. To be more exact, the sample of leaders for the new study was drawn from those who scored high on ten communicative behaviors out of a total of thirty-four more general behaviors identified by Roueche, Baker, and Rose (1989).

A review of the literature produced several communication instruments, none of which, unfortunately, was totally adequate to the purpose of the research. As this study sought to identify leadership behaviors that enable communication and relational strength in selected colleges, three instruments were used for gathering data.

The first of these instruments was the Index of Interpersonal Communicative Competence (IICC) developed by Bobby C. Vaught (1979) at Southwest Missouri State University. The second was a menu-type instrument titled Communication and Relational Strategies Inventory (CRSI), which was developed and tested by the author in 1988. The third instrument was the Organizational Communication Questionnaire (OCQ) (also called "Communications in Your Organization") developed by Karlene A. Roberts and Charles A. Reilly III at the University of California-Berkeley.

The IICC was constructed as a self-report instrument. It measures the capability of a supervisor to effectively solve a series of simulated employee-related problems seen as important to both the subordinate and organizational life. Based upon the literature of humanistic psychotherapy, the IICC renders measures of interpersonal communicative competence on a five-level scale: judgmental; advisory; empathetic; confrontational; and problem-solving. Each of these levels is derived from varying dimensions of responsiveness, action, time orientation, person orientation, and effectiveness.

The OCQ is a thirty-five-item instrument designed to assess thirteen aspects of perceived communication in organizations and three aspects of interpersonal relations thought to influence organizational communication. The communication facets measured by the OCQ are the desire for interaction with others in the organization, directionality of information flow (upward, downward, and lateral), perceived accuracy of information received, information summarization, information gate keeping, feelings of overload, overall satisfaction with communication in the organization, and the degree to which written, face-to-face, telephone, and other modalities are used in transmitting information. The noncommunication facets of organizational behavior examined by the instrument include trust in one's superior and mobility aspirations of the respondents.

The CRSI is composed of elements gleaned from the literature. The framework for organizing communication methods and techniques prepared by Thayer (1968) and Havelock, et al. (1973) guided the construction of the instrument. Following is a description of the seven categories of communication strategies in the framework.

- *Linkage*: collaboration; two-way interaction
- *Structure*: systematic planning of efforts; division of labor; coordination
- *Openness*: willingness to help and to be influenced by feedback and new information; flexibility; accessibility
- *Capacity*: ability to summon and invest diverse resources such as people, dollars, and equipment
- *Reward*: distribution of rewards (e.g., dollars, recognition, knowledge) for communication or collaboration
- *Proximity*: ready access to diverse information sources and users
- *Synergy*: the number and diversity of persons who provide continuity, persistence, and synchronization of effort

The rationale for the development and use of the CRSI was twofold. First, while the literature contained a myriad of strategies associated with communication and relational strength, there was no instrument to detect the presence of such strategies in organizations. Second, as has already been suggested, it is the sum of a leader's perceived actions that may be the most observable and confirmable, and possibly the most valuable to a climate for communication.

Findings

The following is a summary of the findings of the Tagle (1988) study:
- When compared to a standard, the selected group of community college leaders were considerably more proficient in their ability to display higher levels of interpersonal behaviors in their individual supervisory capacities.
- In most cases, the behaviors declared by the leaders as those they used matched those their subordinates perceived them to use.
- For both leaders and subordinates, linkage-type strategies were among the most frequently used for cultivating an environment for communication.

- Communication at the colleges of highly effective transformational leaders showed networks of information flowing upward, downward, diagonally, and laterally.
- There was a positive association between interpersonal competence and organizational communication, between all strategies and organizational communication, and between commonly perceived behaviors and organizational communication.
- There was no correlation between organizational complexity and organizational communication. Single-campus colleges exhibited the same characteristics as multicampus colleges.
- Highly effective, transformational leaders displayed behaviors that appeared to be critical to increasing information for the coordination of human effort.

By and large, CEOs and their immediate management teams viewed themselves as using linkage, synergy, reward, structure, proximity, openness, and capacity strategies, in that order. Subordinates within the selected colleges viewed their leaders as using linkage, synergy, reward, structure, proximity, capacity, and openness strategies, in that order. Both groups agreed in their perceptions of strategy types used except capacity and openness. Leaders saw themselves using those strategies with greater frequency than did their subordinates.

Conclusions

One might conclude from the findings of the IICC that, along with their conceptual understandings of empathy and confrontation, highly effective leaders would naturally transform their colleges using highly interactive, personal, and collaborative strategies to achieve adequacy, accuracy, trust, and influence.

One management team member stated: "My approach to communication is very personal. I try to talk to people on a one-to-one basis, usually in their office or space. I also believe strongly that the organization depends on individuals—individual human beings—and that the organization needs to do a lot to help them adjust, to establish an ambiance of trust and cooperation." As congruence of perceptions was highest among linkage strategies, it can also be concluded that these leaders spend a great deal of time and effort shaping the organization so that they and others can give and receive feedback, facilitate negotiation processes, and share in the ups and downs of organizational life.

Readers are cautioned against making hasty conclusions about the classifications rendered by the IICC. As Vaught (1979) explained, each classification subsumes characteristics of those at the lower levels. Consequently, although transformational leaders and their teams may display interpersonal behaviors at Level Three (emphatic understanding) and Level Four (confrontation), they sometimes act at the advisory and judgmental levels. This, after all, is the range of imperfect behavior leaders bring to social systems.

Creative Cultures

Responding leaders confirmed and expanded the list of over 100 strategies identified in the literature with what they believed to be tried-and-proven techniques for generating, disseminating, processing, and acquiring information. The study found many in this group of transformational leaders who consciously attempted many of the strategies described in the literature.

Communication and Relationship Strategies

Though the use of linkage strategies prevailed, other strategies should not be overlooked. Such a discussion, however brief, would seem required in light of the identical prioritization of five of the seven strategy categories by both leader- and subordinate-participants. Synergy, the second most-preferred and most-perceived methodological type of communication, seems especially relevant to the cultivation of relationships for communication. It is not truly possible to say whether synergy develops from linkage or vice versa. It is possible, however, that by properly assembling and using task forces, considering the individual frame of reference in communication, rewarding collaborative rather than competitive behavior, and giving importance to member contributions and group products during an institutional task, these leaders are creating conditions for linkages to flourish.

Rewards structure and proximity are also important aspects of community college leadership behavior. The group of leaders examined in this study was highly consistent in its distribution of rewards, not only for a job well done, but also for jobs well done as a result of communication or collaboration. Similarly, the leaders systematically planned and coordinated effort (structure) and ensured closeness and ready access to diverse information sources and users (proximity). Effective leaders do not leave communication to chance. It is planned, never easy, and as one respondent noted, always evolving from both a personal and organizational perspective:

> We have a lot of contact with each other and an opportunity to discuss important issues and recognize people for their contributions to the college. Within each division, vice presidents do a lot of team building with their staff members. So I believe we

have a strong informal communication system. We have newsletters, staff meetings, and other mechanisms to help keep people involved and informed. In spite of it all, people still think there are things going on that they don't know about.

Climate for Organizational Communication

In keeping with the literature (Porter, Lawler, and Hackman, 1975; Sanford, Hunt, and Bracey, 1976; Havelock, et al., 1973), climate is most adequately understood through an analysis of the social conditions of the sample colleges. In this regard, then, the social conditions at these colleges can be further described from standpoints provided by O'Reilly and Pondy (1979).

First, it was highly evident in analyzing both closed- and open-ended data that leaders from the colleges have a high concern for the performance, attitude, and group relation outcomes of the communication. That is, their behaviors lean heavily toward ensuring that the climate always sustains creativity where performance is concerned, openness where attitudes are concerned, and sharing and problem resolution where group life is concerned.

Second, leaders are highly attentive to such organizational variables as structure, job design, reward systems, and information processing needs. Their structures for sending and receiving information included many references to such formalized activities as council, advisory, and cabinet meetings. Many, as the literature also noted, attend so regularly to the informal structures that it is as though they have formalized those information sources for the importance they attach to them. One chief executive officer reported:

> In addition to that formal communication network, we do a lot of informal looping both vertically and horizontally to get a pulse as to what is happening and what are the itches of individuals or areas. We don't make decisions in this informal environment outside of the formalized organizational patterns, but it does help us, I believe, have a more accurate picture as to needs and concerns. You always run into potential problems when you have looping on an informal basis, but we feel we have been able to utilize this invaluable communication technique and not endanger or weaken our formal policy-making procedure.

Finally, from the standpoint of communication structure and process variables, colleges of this highly effective sample of leaders consist of frequent, trusting, influential, and, apparently, strong communication. Because communication occurs in all directions between a wide range of people in the work hierarchy, the environment is particularly suitable to a climate for networks, accuracy, openness, a reduction in distorted and filtered information, and specialized roles that build bridges between informal networks.

There is perhaps one area where the study was inconclusive, and that is on the role that overload may play in the climate for organizational communication. In general, where the literature (e.g., O'Reilly and Pondy, 1979) cautions against the overloads of an information society, high scores on overload among both participant groups indicate that they do not perceive themselves to be overloaded, as the following response from one CEO seems to suggest:

> Everyone within the institution must have access to all information that affects the present operation and future direction of the institution. In cultivating relationships, and in maintaining effective communication, too much information is preferable to not enough information. The free flow of information is essential to sound relationships and effective communication.

Both the immediate management teams and subordinates at these colleges received high scores on their general satisfaction with the climate for communication. It appears, then, that leaders at these colleges, by their behaviors, have shaped the structures and processes of communication in such a way to avoid injury from the unmerciful outputs of the information society in which they also live. This study focused on two aspects of overload—the amount of information received by participants and the degree to which it helps or hinders their performance; and employees' perceptions of whether they receive more information than they can efficiently use. The empirical data does not show that overload in these organizations is a problem—yet.

Creating Communication Proficiencies

The use of linkage strategies for effecting organizational proficiency in communication required individuals to come into face-to-face contact for collaboration and two-way interaction. For example, leaders limited the use of communication strategies that produced closed-circuit effects (e.g., memoranda that provide no immediate feedback), but they reported holding frequent, enjoyable, and personal conversations with faculty and staff; keeping an attentive ear to the "grapevine"; and helping members to discover and invent means of cooperation.

In generating information or communication, leaders and their management teams were particularly skilled at communicating intangible facts, opinions, and ideas that typically do not pass through formal channels but which, nonetheless, must have widespread understanding. To make gradual changes that lead to communication, these leaders designed processes that afforded opportunities for individuals to experience personal influence in the organization. They placed people in specialized linking roles, found ways to create organizational attachment, established interdependent relationships within and across systems, and modeled linkage through simple human contact.

Although the use of linkage strategies was pronounced, others were also present. Following are examples of strategies that can be characterized to create synergy in an organization:

- Securing an informal organization that fosters supportive relationships
- Cultivating friendships
- Using integrating mechanisms like task forces, teams, committees, etc.
- Managing conflict by amalgamating conflicting groups
- Allowing group members to be different
- Helping groups to grow and satisfy the needs of their members
- Helping members of minority groups integrate with members of the majority group
- Reallocating tasks to compatible people
- Redesigning tasks so they require less collaboration
- Closely monitoring incompatible people assigned to the same task
- Keeping groups engaged in meaningful activity, need satisfaction, and identification
- Regulating group conflict by reducing group size or importance

Taken together, all of these strategies create a "connectedness" that integrates what leaders, their teams, and other subordinates do independently with what they do collectively and cooperatively to fulfill a mission.

Communication Climate for Shared Values

A shared vision must have an appropriate climate of relationships and communication in which it can thrive. Several social conditions necessary to sustain the vision were apparent in the study described in this chapter. These conditions were evident from both communication and noncommunication variables.

On the variable of communication directionality, for example, the institutions of highly effective leaders were unusually interactive, showing high levels of upward, downward, criss-cross, and lateral communications. Furthermore, there was a high degree of egalitarianism in communication. These climates were particularly conducive to the open sharing of both individual and collective values and the reconciling of the two.

On the basis of noncommunication variables, these colleges showed high levels of trust, a desire for interaction, satisfaction, accuracy, and summarization. Summarization relates to the appropriate emphases of information when transmitting information to others.

Communication as a Symbolic Behavior of Self-Renewal

In order to assess the symbolic behavior patterns that leaders use when they are working through and with followers, the study used the Index of Interpersonal Communicative Competence (IICC). Of 116 respondents, all subjects fell into only three of the five levels of communicative competence: the advisory, empathetic, and confrontational levels. No one fell at the extremes of the judgmental (the lowest) or problem-solving (the highest) level of communicative‍competence.

Since the judgmental level indicates a complete disregard for the subordinate, such a finding among this sample of CEOs and their teams appears quite reasonable. As in an earlier study by Vaught (1979), there were no scores at the problem-solving level. A clear majority of the leaders at the selected colleges, however, scored at the second-highest level— empathetic. In fact, this study showed a much higher percentage (76 percent) at the upper levels than did the Vaught study (52 percent).

In approaching the upper levels of interpersonal communication competence, this group of leaders has, as Argyris (1962) stated, created "a way of life" in the institution where the "emphasis then becomes one of continually diagnosing, modifying, and making more effective" individual and collective behaviors (p. 237). The institution is, in effect, in constant self-renewal to skillfully and symbolically propel its members toward its goals.

The following response from one CEO captures his ability to recognize the opportunities and potential problems of working with diverse personalities within the organization—all of whom need to accurately perceive the goals as their own from the special positions they occupy:

I try to get different individuals involved in new, exciting projects working as a team on a nonthreatening topic, issue, or area. My feeling is that if people will get to know each other personally, have to work together and talk, both have success as a result of a joint project—that they will be more willing to pick up the phone to communicate as time goes on. Also, it builds up a team approach and breaks down potential ill-conceived barriers to communication. I try to get individuals in one job area involved with people in another job area so they begin to see a different perspective, get to know more people, and experience other people's problems and frustrations. In my mind, creating situations where people can laugh together, win together, lose together, and know more about each other is a key to better communications.

The strategies implicit in the preceding paragraph are important to achieving the organization's mission. They also reflect the value of symbiotic relationships that nurture that mission.

Staffing and Skills Building

Generally, the literature suggests a three-pronged approach to organizing the college setting for strong organizational communication. The first part of such a strategy deals with the leader's design of the formal system; the second emphasizes the people's attitudes toward communication (typically called climate); and the third develops or supports the people's abilities to communicate (typically called interpersonal skills).

Any strategies aimed at modifying institutional communication must, therefore, focus on improving employee skills, attitudes, and motivational levels. One strategy includes developing what Berger and Roloff (1982) later called the "interstitial men and women" of the institution. Some of these people are gate keepers who have a wide range of contacts and through whom information enters and travels in a company. Others are knowledge seekers who position themselves physically and socially to gain knowledge. Still others are variance sensors, a type of gate keeper who identifies and reconciles discrepancies between what the organization ought to be doing and what it is actually doing. In summary, Berger and Roloff say these people "connect several worlds and can provide excellent information" across the organization (p. 62).

To truly examine what staff ought to know about building interpersonal relationships, it is first necessary to define the essence of a relationship and its function in the social system. Thayer (1968) stated that a relationship is a reciprocal connectedness between two people. Furthermore, he believes that relating is an absolute prerequisite to dealing with another individual conceptually and, hence, communicatively. Whether one chooses to analyze a relationship from a perspective of authenticity or closeness is academic. What seems clear is the need to recognize the conditions that bring about the psychological binding found in relationships and created by certain social conditions and shared norms and beliefs.

One CEO believed that the first step in bringing people together is to assure "fit" between the person and the job—either by redesign of the job itself or by attentive employee selection:

I start the relational and communication process by hiring persons who are capable and highly motivated, even though they may

not be experienced. I then give them as much freedom in performing as they are capable of handling, increasing freedom as
experience and judgment are shown.

Capacity was a common factor identified by leaders, their management teams, and their subordinates as important in the dissemination
and utilization of information. Capacity-type strategies included assembling and using task forces, involving senior staff who are able to authorize
use of institutional resources, providing other resources for more effective group action, assessing communication networks through the use
of communication audits, developing a common information base, facilitating bargaining processes, and encouraging learning communities for intellectual and creative exchange.

Strategic Behaviors that Enhance Social Bonding

The position people occupy in an organization influences their perception and interpretation of incoming information and their search for
additional information. Among the categories of communication and relationship strategies, capacity-type strategies predominated as one means
of enhancing social bonding in the community colleges studied.

Respondents reported generating information or communication through
the use of committees, assigning those who are able to authorize the use of
institutional resources to group problem solving, and creating means for more
effective group action. In disseminating information, respondents reported
such strategies as overcommunicating, especially in times of flux, and recognizing opportunities to identify issues and create solutions. To acquire information, respondents assessed communication networks with communication
audits and developed a common information base for problem solving. Finally, to ensure gradual changes that would lead to communication across
all human-resource levels, leaders created opportunities for broadened career
paths; facilitated bargaining processes; reinforced informal channels that were
congruent with goals; conducted periodic checks on processes by which groups
solved problems, performed research, and teamed up; and analyzed individual
and collective communication competence.

Excellence Through Communication

The most commonly debated issues concerning excellence deal with
how to define, identify, and measure it. Though a variety of terms are
frequently substituted for it, the concept of effectiveness is one worthwhile measure of excellence.

Effective human relationships, Argyris (1962) stated, are those that
get the job done. In an observation of effectiveness-related practices, one

study ("Organizational Characteristic...," 1985) of colleges characterized more successful schools as having high levels of: communication on
teaching practice; useful conversations following the observation of teaching; and planning, designing, researching, and preparation of materials
by teachers working collaboratively.

Having defined and characterized it, how does one assess the effectiveness of organizational communication? In analyzing the percentage
of time both leaders and their subordinates spend in the activities of the
Organizational Communication Questionnaire, the sample reported 55
percent of its time engaged in diagonal/criss-cross communication. That
is, they spent over half their time engaged in interaction with people at
a job level other than their own and other than with immediate supervisors. The high levels of communication with people in a different job
level are repeated in the receiving and sending of information. People
were spending much time on adaptation and/or socialization, and communication was highly egalitarian.

Overall, members of the immediate management teams felt more open
to discuss problems with their CEOs, more comfortable with the CEOs'
decisions even when they seemed against the interests of subordinates,
and more confident in the general fairness of the CEOs. Subordinates
of the immediate management teams, on the other hand, felt that their
supervisors desired them to interact more. Rightfully, this desire for interaction may have been projected to the subordinates by their superiors as a means of improving communication through human relationships.

Structure and Process for Communication Success

To understand formal communication in an organization, one must
understand the organization's structure. Steers (1977) has defined structure as the "unique way an organization fits its people together to create
organization...[including] the extent to which interpersonal interactions
are formalized" (p. 7). Organizational structure is coterminous with the
formal communication structure. That is, the authority relationships
represented on the organizational chart form the primary network for
sharing information, making decisions, and achieving organizational
objectives.

Furthermore, the information capacity of the primary and ancillary
networks must be equal to the information requirements of the organization. For example, Galbraith (1979) proposed that as the uncertainty
or newness surrounding a task increases, the coordination of work must
be increasingly achieved by rules and programs, hierarchy, and planning.
It is the manager's choice of balance among these that, consequently,
determines the formal shape of the organization.

Process, defined as a series of changes that lead to a particular result, is an equally important factor of structure. It is by process, after all, that open systems allow for such activities as curriculum development, shared governance and decision making, and participatory planning and goal formulation.

As Steers (1977) explained, goal formulation is a three-part interrelated process that results from: a bargaining process among system members; the prior commitments, policies, and agreements communicated by the system; and modification by group members. In the final analysis, goal formulation and planning processes enable the many systems within an organization to communicate, coordinate, and collaborate to ensure adaptation to the environment.

Feedback processes can satisfy both organizational and individual needs. For instance, developing the interpersonal skills necessary for effective group decision making helps achieve organizational goals as well as provide members with socialization, a feeling of belonging, and a sense of responsibility for the achievement of the group goals. Like Steers (1977) and O'Reilly and Pondy (1979), Ouchi (1981) reported that managers who provide their subordinates with more feedback, autonomy, and task and goal identity contribute to a more achievement-oriented climate.

Chief executive officers in the selected colleges demonstrated a high level of skill as "architects" of their institutions, designing systems for the four basic processes of communication—generating, disseminating, acquiring, and processing information. For example, in generating information, they focused on facts, figures, and trends that would facilitate the formulation of goals and evaluation of the institution's performance. In distributing information, they stated goals clearly and combatted information overload and random communication. In acquiring information, they read, reviewed, or received briefings on the steady stream of correspondence, memoranda, newsletters, and formal reports that seem to inundate the desks of decision makers. Finally, CEOs demonstrated a consistent interest in process as a means of making gradual changes that lead to improved communication and relationships. Those strategies included, but were not limited to:

- Formalizing structures and/or mechanisms by which innovation can be explored and implemented
- Designing indoctrination systems
- Minimizing excessive political cliques
- Building collegial planning structures
- Building governance structures
- Formulating policies for human growth and commitment
- Formalizing feedback mechanisms

- Emphasizing lateral and diagonal relationships
- Adapting the work to be done to the social groupings of the organization
- Structuring groups in accordance with the objectives of the subsystems

The foregoing strategies suggest, at least in part, how CEOs structure the day-to-day operations of their institutions. To corroborate this theoretical perspective, two of the leaders studied, when asked how they structure communication and relationship strength at their colleges, answered:

> Though there are a multitude of approaches, fundamental to everything is the internal respect felt for every individual in the institution and the important role they play to make the college the fully functioning entity it is. I feel this deeply, and I attempt to follow through with actions to demonstrate it.

> A key to building communication and relationship strength is the chief executive officer's need to value dissent, to remember the absolute indispensability of dissent both in posing alternatives and checking either the tyranny of authority or the tyranny of the majority.

Within the complexities and constraints of human organization, there is no one best way to structure communication. Any well-thought-out structure, however, must include consideration of who the communicators are, how communication structures and processes will reinforce the worth of individuals, and how communication and relationships will be honored toward achievement of that mission.

Postscript on Technology and Communication

Though conclusions have been integrated throughout the preceding sections, several findings deserve summary. In an aggregate analysis of the data, highly effective leaders appear to possess behavioral competencies that are perceived in a range of forms by the people they lead. Moreover, there appears to be an association of those behaviors with the quality of communication and the climate for communication at the selected colleges.

The results of the study tended to support the tenets of theorists in the fields of leadership, communication, organizational theory, and social systems theory. Specifically, the results support the concept that communication—the application of a range of knowledge dissemination and utilization strategies—helps leaders plan, organize, direct, and control an organization.

Moreover, leaders aspiring toward effective personal and organizational performance should examine their own institutions for evidence of the behaviors explored here. Clearly, one must consider that the communication behaviors of leadership shape the achievements of community colleges.

Technology continues to pose formidable challenges to the structure and climate of community colleges. It can bring people together in learning and speaking communities, or it can reduce the need and opportunity for the face-to-face social contact that is so essential to building relationships for communication.

As far as teaching goes, it is important to view technology as an instructional tool and not a replacement for a caring, responding teacher. Furthermore, even as technology, particularly interactive technology, can significantly reduce the costs and hazards of live work or laboratory experiments, it is essential that students sometimes move from interactive modes with technology to interactive modes with people. It is among people—in the real world and its human-intensive contexts and challenges—that students must ultimately perform and communicate.

Managers must constantly re-examine the appropriateness, the cost, the ownership, and the politics of a piece of technology. These factors must all be evaluated for their impact on the relationships that are a prerequisite for healthy organizational communication. Just as a command of language and facial expressions can bind individuals, so too can the possession and command of technology either bind or isolate people within an organization.

Chapter 5

Empowering the Leadership Team

By Mary Ann Roe

The constant variable of change facing our society is nowhere more evident than in education in general and the two-year college in particular. The preparation of community, technical, and junior college leaders must address a variety of critical issues and new challenges, including increased student diversity, creative resource allocation, institutional effectiveness, increased government regulation, and the complexities of information processing resulting from technological change. Understanding the role of effective leadership within the context of institutional effectiveness can also help to enhance successful student outcomes.

Expanding student diversity, for example, demands exceptional leaders. Early research in this area suggests that a direct and positive relationship exists between behaviors of community college leaders and successful programs for students with diverse backgrounds who attend community colleges (Cohen and Roueche, 1969; Roueche and Snow, 1977; Klemp, Huff, and Gentile, 1980; Roueche and Mink, 1980). Klemp, Huff, and Gentile (1980) found that the success of underprepared learners is associated closely with behavioral competencies exhibited by the president and the executive leadership team.

Further, American productivity is dependent upon the successful development of our human capital. A world-class work force that can support private sector employment needs while enhancing economic development and mitigating socioeconomic problems has increasingly become the responsibility of colleges (Roe, 1989). In addition to their internal leadership role, enlightened educational leaders realize the significance of their external role in leading others in private industry, education,

79

and government at the local, state, and national levels toward the creation of alliances that can dynamically reshape the nation.

However, the projected retirement of significant numbers of community college presidents is creating an ever-increasing need to identify and develop outstanding leaders. A Career and Lifestyles Survey conducted by Vaughan (1986) revealed that 37.4 percent of current community college presidents in 1986 were between the ages of 51 and 60, while 11 percent were over the age of 60. Founding community college presidents are retiring at a time when their expertise, gained from years of building these institutions, could be an advantage in solving salient problems (Roueche, Baker, and Rose, 1989). These problems require a radical transformation of the assumptions surrounding our institutions.

Transformation and change in organizational culture as well as within the individual is accomplished, to a great extent, through the empowerment and development of a leadership team—a cohesive group of people who have accepted the vision of the president and are working and moving together in the same direction. Through this acceptance, followers are transformed into leaders, communicating and infusing the shared vision throughout all parts of the college.

The president is the director, coach, and delegator who enables and empowers cultural transformation for the individual, the leadership team, and the college. Quality time spent by the leadership team with their followers as well as with the president is essential for cultural change and for the development and identification of readiness skills for leadership. When nurtured through planned education and training, an individual can be transformed from the readiness state to a quality leader of people to share a new and dynamic vision for the community college.

Vaughan (1986), Fisher (1984), and other researchers have produced excellent studies profiling leadership and the community college president. A need for more research on the domains of effective leadership in the community college, combined with the imminent retirement of many presidents, signals not only a need for increased and directed leadership training, but also for effective selection of leaders for training.

LeCroy (1984) suggests that there is a developmental process involved in becoming a leader and that, through this process of skill development, it is possible to effectively assume and share power. Without planning and without training, the potential of many who could become excellent leaders is either underdeveloped or lost completely. No longer do we have the luxury of such loss. It is crucial to identify and develop future leaders for outstanding educational leadership.

What appears to be missing from the research on leadership is a process for the identification of readiness for leadership; that is, the identification of qualifications that enable one to undertake roles of leadership and successfully lead others. Readiness implies the ability to lead effectively in a given situation and unite the situation, task, and followers. Readiness is also evidenced by an accommodation of the leadership styles of others, the capacity to follow and support leadership, and the capacity to lead.

The first step in the development of such a process requires a clear perception of the parameters of leadership and an understanding of the significance of the interaction between leaders and their followers.

Leading and Following: A Dynamic Relationship

Burns (1978) suggested that "if we know all too much about our leaders, we know far too little about leadership" (p. 1). Because leadership is generally considered one of the crucial ingredients in creating a culture for excellence in community colleges, educational researchers and practitioners have tried to respond to the current trends of constraint and uncertainty with a clear definition of the term. They have not found it an easy task. The problem stems, in large measure, from the uncertainty of the leader's intent. Given this uncertainty, should leadership be considered to be essentially based on behavior, influence, and power? Or is it essentially a process, taking the lead to direct, to control, and to be master of the situation? Behavioral science has attempted to clarify that which separates a leader from a nonleader and to determine differences between effective leaders and ineffective leaders.

One construct that has come out of all this research is the gestalt of leadership—the idea that the existence of leaders implies the existence of followers, and the interaction between the two is greater than the sum of the two parts. Zaleznik and Moment (1964) interpreted leadership as a relational attribute, including the behavior of the leading person and the behavior of the followers, rather than viewing leadership as an attribute of an individual functioning alone. They defined leadership as an "interaction in which the conscious intentions of one person are communicated in behavior, verbal and otherwise, with the consequence that the other person wants to and does behave in accordance with the first person's intentions" (p. 414). Factors that are focused on specific leader attributes and leader behavior have been identified as contributing to effective leader-follower interactions. Calder (1977) suggested that while leadership is a disposition or trait, this trait must come alive in the perception of others, particularly followers. Of and by itself, leadership is not a viable construct or variable for study; rather, we should examine the process by which people conclude that real or imagined leadership qualities exist in another person.

Yet most research has been unilateral in nature, focusing on the leader, and sometimes the leader and the situation, but seldom focusing on issues that relate to follower involvement and responsibility. Leadership studies have characteristically focused on deficiencies, or on the short-comings of individuals in leadership roles that interfere with effective leadership. Leader behaviors such as the abuse of power, injustice, and indecision are generally identified in the literature without reference to the other half of the relationship—the follower.

George Simmel, a contemporary of Max Weber, observed that fol-lowers have about as much influence on their leaders as leaders have on followers. Simmel purported that leaders cannot maintain authority un-less followers are prepared to believe in that authority (Gardner, 1987). Moreover, Gardner speculated that one reason bureaucracies stagnate is an assumption by executives that, given their rank and authority, they can lead without taking timely and positive actions to influence the be-havior of followers. He believes they cannot. They can be given subor-dinates, but they cannot be given a following. A following must be earned. This observation is especially appropriate for those leaders in a profes-sional bureaucracy like the community college. Effective leaders maximize follower expertise and knowledge in tandem with follower acceptance of responsibility and commitment.

From a cultural perspective, leadership of human beings is exercised when persons with specific motives and purposes mobilize others so as to arouse, engage, and satisfy their motives. This activity is undertaken in order to realize goals mutually held by both leaders and followers (Burns, 1978). Burns argued that the leader-follower relationship is the interac-tion of individuals within the same culture who function with common purposes and goals in mind, but operate with varying degrees of motiva-tion and power potential. He sees this interaction as following one of two alternate paths: transactional leadership and transformational leadership.

Transactional and Transformational Leadership

Burns defines transactional leadership as one person's taking the in-itiative in making contact with others for the purpose of an exchange of valued things, such as paying wages to employees for their efforts and skills. An agreement is reached between the leader and the follower regard-ing the need to attain a specific goal, objectives are developed to reach the goal, and the leader and follower come to an understanding about the reward for successful completion of the task or punishment for non-completion of the task. Thus, transactional leadership is one of exchange with a positive or negative payoff from the leader to the follower for a task completed or not completed as defined. Once the exchange is complete, there is no further need to interact unless another process of contingent reward is introduced. This leadership style focuses on the transaction and often includes an assumption by leaders that they must use the power of their position to reinforce the accomplishment of tasks.

Extrinsic rewards are frequently the payoffs in an exchange and occur generally in the forms of praise, recommendations, public recognition, promotion, and increases in pay. If handled correctly these rewards can lead to personal satisfaction and enhanced self-esteem for the follower, stimulating the follower's motivation to attempt another exchange with the leader. In reality, however, contingent exchanges that result in positive rewards are underutilized (Bass, 1985a).

Burns believes that the transformational leader also recognizes needs for structure and direction in potential followers, but persists beyond these basics, seeking to arouse and satisfy higher needs. The transformational leader seeks to engage all aspects of the follower's motivation and succeeds in elevating those influenced from a lower to a higher level according to Maslow's hierarchy of needs (Burns, 1978).

Maslow identified self-actualizing people as those who are becoming what they can become, that is, a person's potentiality and desire for self-fulfillment becoming actualized. The self-actualizing person may be a good candidate for transformational leadership. Increased awareness and the arousal of higher-level needs that transcend self-interest can produce extraordinary effort. Bass (1985a) suggested that it is the transformational leader who raises consciousness about higher considerations through articulation and role modeling.

One transformational factor identified by Bass is charismatic leadership. Charismatic leaders enjoy a high degree of esteem, value, and popularity from others. In a college setting, the charismatic leader is able to project a shared vision of a possible and desirable state for the college. Painting a picture for followers of the potential outcomes that their efforts could achieve, such leaders provide more meaning for the work of the organization. Individuals learn to believe that their effort "makes a difference" (Bennis and Nanus, 1985) and as a consequence the goal of "making a difference" can become a top priority.

Bass identified consideration for others as a second transformational factor, characterized by familiarity and contact, informal communication, attention to differences among followers, and skills in counseling and mentoring. Consideration for others contributes to follower satisfaction with the leader and in many cases leads to followers being motivated to be more productive and deriving pleasure from productivity. Leadership studies suggest that transformational leaders tend to be friendly, informal, and close while giving support and encouraging self-development. Yet, Bass (1985a) noted that consideration for others is not mandatory for transformational leadership and that not all transformational leaders display exceptional qualities of individual consideration.

Intellectual stimulation is the third transformational factor identified by Bass, focused on arousal and change in followers' attention to problems and how they may be solved. Intellectual stimulation by transformational leaders is viewed as a discrete leap in the followers' conceptualization, comprehension, and discernment of the nature of problems and possible solutions (Bass, 1985b). Thus, an essential factor in transformational leadership is the capacity to influence and organize meaning for members of the institution.

Although the research and literature on transformational leadership is rather limited at this time, early evidence suggests that the transformational leader must vary style and behavior to fit the situation. Blanchard (1985) suggested that as the development level of followers increases, leadership should empower followers to perform on their own by reducing direction and support. An individual or group at a high developmental level can get by and will even flourish with less supervision and more delegation by the leader as an indication of trust and confidence. This suggests that the truly great leader is the one who can "get the job done" in the way that empowers others to the maximum extent. At the same time, the transformational leader understands that it may not be possible in every situation to lift people toward higher levels of self-development. However, transformational leaders usually understand the tasks that need to be accomplished and the means to accomplish them and can lead others through the tasks while raising them to higher levels of self-actualization and development.

Following

Knowing how and when to follow is an integral part of leadership. Within the organizational framework, leadership is viewed as an interactive process involving leaders and followers (Hollander, 1987). Thus, leaders must recognize, accept, and comprehend how to lead followers and how to follow leaders, and be able to function both from above and from below. In the environment of our changing world with its colliding systems, lateral and boundary-crossing leadership skills are essential. Those who can exercise transformational leadership from wherever they happen to be in the organization are priceless (Gardner, 1987).

The transformational leader understands the relationship between leadership and followership. From this perceptual foundation, the leader recognizes the intrinsic motivational reward the follower receives from "doing it myself" and encourages followers to "run the show" whenever possible. Much more importantly, such a leader does not confuse leadership with authority and understands where leadership and followership reside in any situation. Achieving balance in the situation is a necessity for successful outcomes and often requires a tolerance for ambiguity. In essence, the understanding and acceptance of situational leadership and followership allows the development of a relationship that is trusting, candid, and even critical when the situation demands.

These relationships are affected by the perceived competence, motivation, and personality of the leader, and by the needs, motivation, and personality of the follower. Followers need their leaders to have a sense of direction and a concern for the future health of the college, and also expect leaders to be enthusiastic, energetic, and positive toward their shared future. In order to satisfy these powerful needs, the leader must be able to communicate his or her vision in ways that uplift and encourage followers to follow (Kouzes, 1988).

Leading and Following: Cultural Symbiosis

While followers have needs and expectations of their leaders, the interactive nature of the relationship predicates similar needs and expectations of followers by leaders. The myriad writing about leadership leads us to conclude that accomplishment of the task is the responsibility of the follower, and the direction of how, when, and where to achieve the task emanates from the leader. It is conceivable, however, that this interchange may not be fully understood by leaders and followers. In reality, it is not only leaders, but also followers who have the power to determine how and when task completion will be culminated. The positive or negative response to leader direction is in direct correlation to followers' commitment to the successful consummation of the task. Expectations of followers are extremely important, for if these expectations are not met, followers are likely to become unmotivated and leaders to become abusive.

During the past thirty years researchers have recognized that followership is vital to leadership (Hollander, 1987). Moreover, when followers truly accept the influence of the leader and allow themselves to be led, they often tend to seek a greater role in shared leadership. Because organizations require both leadership and followership from individuals at all levels within a hierarchy, the follower who shows the quality of being responsive will call attention to his or her "leadership potential." Behaviors that are seen to represent effective leadership include attributes of good followership (Hollander, 1987). Thus, the relationship between the influence of the leader on the follower's behavior and the influence of the follower on the leader's behavior becomes the important variable in determining who leads and who is led. In the final analysis, the key to successful leadership and followership is the mutual recognition and acceptance of these interchangeable roles.

Readiness for Leadership: Current Research

One recent and significant approach to leadership in the community college has been the effort of the Community College Leadership Program at the University of Texas at Austin. *Shared Vision* (Roueche, Baker, and Rose, 1989) sought to identify and study community college presidents who were perceived as exemplifying excellence by authorities in the field. Central to this approach is the belief that the best place to look for attributes that contribute to success in leadership is among those who are successful.

A follow-up study by the author focused on the identification of a group of exceptional followers functioning in the role of executive administrators in the community college, and evaluated their skills as well as readiness for leadership (Roe, 1989). The purposes of this study were to: (1) replicate the research of Roueche, Baker, and Rose (1989); (2) use those findings as a baseline for the investigation of readiness for leadership; and (3) provide direction for identification and training of future community college leaders.

Transformational Themes

The study examined "blue-chip" presidents—fifty CEOs who were nominated as "exceptional" by a panel of peers and selected for study in *Shared Vision*. These presidents articulated five themes that are the essence of effective community college leadership. The transformational theme of vision is the centerpiece of leadership, illuminating the other four transformational themes—people, motivation, influence, and values. Vision, the leader's conceptualized view of the future, is the light by which a leader can move others beyond routines of the past, through the security of the present, and down the path of change required by the future.

A shared vision is achieved by the understanding, acceptance, and internalized use of the other four transformational themes. An orientation toward people is predicated upon knowledge that leader/follower interaction is a living system in which the strengths of each are maximized, resulting in a united team focused upon organizational success. An orientation toward motivation is based upon the understanding that motivation binds leaders and followers, emerging from within each individual, and developing into a bond that helps achieve the shared vision. An orientation toward influence can be achieved only through the acceptance of one's own individuality and the empowerment of oneself. Self-empowerment is a necessary precursor to the empowerment of others, because it enables both leaders and followers to transcend self-interest and make an extraordinary effort for the betterment of the institution. Finally, an orientation toward values is an ethical orientation that up-lifts followers and permeates the values of the living system of the insti-tution, resulting in an individual playing out his or her values within the context of organizational life. The community college leader who has the ability to mold and blend these transformational themes for the good of the individual, the institution, the community, and the larger society is functioning in the higher-order dimensions of self-actualization described by Maslow (1950).

Summary of the Findings

Not only can these individuals lead others to higher levels, but they provide a model from which we can learn and toward which we can strive. The Roueche, Baker, and Rose study (1989) indicates that the generic skill of effective community college leadership can be defined and described and that many of these skills can be taught and learned. Present and future situations demand that the human potential of those who cur-rently serve in leadership positions and those who aspire to do so are maximized at the highest possible level.

The five transformational themes and the fifteen attributes of trans-formational leaders developed by Roueche, Baker, and Rose and expanded on by the author appear in Figure 5.1, along with the two themes devel-oped specifically for this study—Followership and Readiness for Leader-ship—and their four behavioral descriptors. In order to generate the dom-inant discrete behavioral competencies profile, a telephone interview was employed. These interviews were then analyzed for evidence of competency thoughts and actions. A "hit" process was used—each time a competen-cy was expressed the interviewee would recieve a "hit." Scores were de-rived from the frequency of hits each interviewee received, and ranged from zero to ten. Score averages are shown in Figure 5.1.

The current study revealed that a wide variance exists among thirty executive administrators in relation to the seven transformational themes and the dominant discrete behavioral attributes found within those themes. This variance is even more marked in the between-group com-parison of the executive administrators and the "blue-chip" presidents. In other words, those who have held many community college leader-ship roles or have spent a long time in leadership positions are not neces-sarily ready to become exemplary two-year college presidents. It may be worthwhile to re-think assumptions held by many trustees and executives

Figure 5.1
President and Executive Administrator
Dominant Discrete Behavioral Competencies

CLUSTER Discrete Attribute	PRESIDENT	EXECUTIVE ADMINISTRATOR
VISION	MEAN	MEAN
Concept of Future	4.54	
Ability to Shape Future	4.14	2.03
Committed to Specific Action	4.72	2.33
Causes Followers to Share Vision	6.10	
Committed to Student Access and Success	4.23	
PEOPLE		
Understands Character of Followers	4.00	2.26
Respects Individuals' Differences		2.53
Values Students and Their Needs	4.32	2.06
MOTIVATION		
Enhances Development of Followers	2.06	
INFLUENCE		
Empowers by Delegating	4.83	
Causes Followers to Work Together	4.32	2.46
Builds Network of Communication	5.41	3.80
VALUES		
Commitment to Self-Intellectual Development	5.40	
Commitment to Quality Development of Others		2.06
Builds Openness and Trust		2.13
READINESS		
Accommodates Leadership Style of Others		2.50
Demonstrates Enlightened Self-Interest		3.49
Demonstrates "Builder" Characteristics		3.00
FOLLOWERSHIP		
Able to Give Others Opportunity to Succeed		2.86

Scores derived from frequency scores.
Frequencies ranged from zero to ten.

that length of service and specific positions correlate positively with readiness for higher-level leadership.

If readiness for leadership can be viewed as a process of becoming, the behavioral attributes and themes listed in Figure 5.1 can be useful for leadership career development. Leadership development may be conceptualized in a systematic fashion with each potential leader moving along an individual continuum in various stages of leadership readiness.

Through the statements of many of these executive administrators, the study identified two additional themes, followership and readiness for leadership. Of these two themes, readiness for leadership emerged in a more defined form: confidence in one's ability to lead through acceptance of the challenge of leadership. Those who spoke with quiet authority about confidence in their ability to lead others are the executive administrators who formed the High Readiness group in the study. An expectation that a leadership role with more authority should be the reward for years of service was not voiced by those in the High Readiness group; rather, they appeared to be intrinsically motivated by leading and serving others.

Their ability to seek and accommodate the leadership style of others, not only leadership from above, but also leadership from followers below, is very often the result of self-confidence and inner security. This accommodation is represented by behavioral attributes of the followership theme identified in this study: understanding the dichotomy of leadership and followership, knowing who is leader and who is follower in any situation, and extending the opportunity for others to succeed.

In this study, many of the executive administrators revealed confidence in their ability to lead followers to task completion. The study also discovered confidence in the ability to lead followers in tandem with the desire to "build" systems, people, teams, and relationships. Leaders that possess the skills to build successful interactions between people must understand followership and the need for a reciprocal flow between followers and leaders. Thus, self-confidence and the knowledge of how to build relationships appear to be essential to a readiness for leadership.

Perhaps the most indicative behavioral attribute of readiness for leadership is enlightened self-interest. Block (1987) suggests that although genuine, long-term self-interest typically is defined as doing those things that will move one to the top, it should be defined as serving the organization first and making personal ascent the second priority. This is the better, more practical path to empowerment. Self-empowerment results from acting on enlightened self-interest and can be achieved through engaging in meaningful activities, contribution and service, integrity, the ability to have a positive impact on others, and mastery of the task at hand.

The totality achieved by combining all of these attributes is inner control and autonomy in the midst of a dependency-creating institution (Block, 1987). Thus, it would appear that confidence in ability to lead is indicative of Readiness for Leadership and can be linked to a flow process (Figure 5.2).

This study revealed not only the stages of readiness for leadership shown in Figure 5.2, but also several important facts about leadership readiness and time. Some feel that longevity in a certain position obligates the college to promote an employee, and experience is seen as a wonderful teacher. That is true if experience teaches the right lessons. However, those who linger may not be learning and, more to the point, may not possess the vision necessary to take appropriate risks to bring about change. If these potential leaders do not risk to bring about change for themselves, will they be able to risk to bring about change for others?

Figure 5.2
Readiness for Leadership

ENLIGHTENED SELF-INTEREST
Meaningful Activities
Service
Integrity
Positive Impact on Others
Mastery of Task at Hand (Block, 1987)

SELF-EMPOWERMENT
Creating Vision
Leading Followers
Releasing Need for Dependency
Finding Courage to Live Vision (Block, 1987)

CONFIDENCE
Positive Self-Regard
Confidence in Self
Challenged to Lead

LEADS EFFECTIVELY

"BUILDER" OF PEOPLE/SYSTEMS

TIME UTILIZATION

Drucker (1967) suggests that one of the major predictors of exceptional performance by executives is their ability to systematically manage their own and their employees' time. The high and low stages of Readiness for Leadership that evolved in this study were significantly differentiated by the time spent with constituent groups. While both groups spent an equal number of hours per week on campus in their administrative roles, how they spent that time appears to be a crucial factor in leadership development. Those who spent more time with constituents appeared to be at higher levels of readiness for community college leadership.

Executive administrators must follow their leaders and lead their followers, and time that they spend doing both appears to be time well spent on their own leadership development. Exploration of how their time is spent demonstrated that group-oriented functions included processes as well as constituent groups, providing researchers with an opportunity to observe quality of time utilization as well as quantity. The executive administrators in the High Readiness and High Followership groups who spent more time with each of their presidents learn leadership skills and better understand the roles of leaders and followers. Good problem-solving skills and decision-making processes may, in fact, have more opportunity to develop when more time is spent in interaction between presidents and executive administrators.

Those in the High Readiness and High Followership groups report spending more time with their followers than do those in the Low Readiness and Low Followership groups. It may be hypothesized that those in the High Readiness and High Followership groups who spend more time with their followers have integrated to a greater degree the leadership skills learned from their presidents, have made the transfer of these skills from their role of follower to their role of leader, and are leading in a more participative style than those who spend less time with their followers.

The thirty executive administrators who were the subjects of the Roe study are in distinct and definable stages of readiness for leadership. Many need identifiable and specific leadership training, while those in the High Readiness/High Followership group appear ready to move into community college presidential roles. It must be noted, however, that as leadership is a state of becoming, leadership development is always ongoing.

The Leader-Follower Interchange

It is understood that leadership is situational and training cannot prepare leaders for all of the unique demands encountered in the community college. Yet there is a lack of adequate leadership training for many involved in two-year college leadership at all levels. Without directed and individualized leadership training, it is questionable whether future community college leaders will have the skills to influence, shape, and embed values, attitudes, and behaviors in their followers.

A key role for current presidents is the development of future leaders. To this end, Bucholtz and Roth (1987) offer three maturational stages of followers that can be used as informal tools to analyze leadership development. The first stage is the dependent stage where the follower is dependent upon the direction of others, particularly the leader. Growth and development produce the independent second stage in which followers perform on their own, manifesting behaviors of maintaining relationships with leaders and with others in the organization, being responsible, contributing, and desiring independence. Leadership in this stage consists of giving more responsibility, influencing, listening, engaging in mutual goal setting, and making feedback a two-way process.

The third stage is one of interdependence with the role of leader shifting to collaborator. Followers at this stage are cooperating, assisting, supporting, uniting, caring for, and leading as necessary. In this stage, it is the way that the leader and followers relate to each other that allows the team to use each member's strengths and minimize each member's weaknesses. The leader's role in this stage is that of mentor or helper, empowering followers by soliciting feedback, establishing parameters, allowing input, giving more responsibility, and switching roles from leader to follower if necessary. If a leader has moved the follower to this stage of interdependence, higher-level transformational leadership skills could be taught and learned by both the leaders and the follower through the interaction that occurs between the two parties.

Blanchard (1985), in defining the development level of followers, refers to the competence and commitment to perform a particular task without supervision. He suggests that competence is a function of knowledge or skills that can be gained from education, training, or experience, while commitment is a combination of confidence and motivation. Blanchard views the development level of followers as a task-specific concept and offers four development levels for the successful completion of any task, based upon the fluctuation of follower competence and commitment. This fluctuation of competence and commitment varies with the directing, coaching, supporting, and delegating of the leader.

The wise leader who can lead followers to interdependence is often content to stay in the background, facilitating the growth of the followers. The Leader-Follower Interchange (Figure 5.3), adapted from Bucholtz and Roth (1987) and Blanchard (1985), illustrates stages of follower development in conjunction with actions by both leaders and followers. It must be noted that some of the most important things a leader does

Figure 5.3 Leader-Follower Interchange		
Follower Development	**Leader Action**	**Follower Action**
Dependent **D1:** Low Competence Variable Commitment	**Directing-Telling** Assignment of Duties Provide Specific Information Orient to Philosophy Set Goals Provide Feedback	Develop Competence Demonstrate Commitment Enhance Philosophy Accept Goals Seek Feedback
Independent **D2:** Developing Competence **D3:** Variable Commitment	**Coaching-Supporting** Increase Follower Responsibility Actively Influence Values Increase Two-Way Communication Mutually Set Goals	Accept Increased Responsibility Become Committed to Values of Leader and Institution Seek Opportunities for Face-to-Face Communication Negotiate Goals
Interdependent **D4:** High Competence High Commitment	**Delegating-Sharing** Share Responsibility With Followers Seek to Be Influenced by Follower Values Share Decision Making Empower Followers to Perform	Accept Responsibility Demonstrate Increased Competency Become Skillful in Shared Decision Making

Adapted from Blanchard (1985) and Bucholtz and Roth (1987).

are likely to be unnoticed; because the leader does not push or shape or manipulate, there is no resentment or resistance.

Training and Preparing Leaders and Followers

Due to the multifaceted demands upon community college presidents, such training and development are not often viewed as priorities, but where modeling behavior is lacking, leadership development is thwarted throughout the institution. To recognize worthwhile traits and merit in others, today's presidents must have the ability to recognize and accept merit in themselves. Historically, people have been selected for administrative positions in community college leadership based largely upon their intellectual and cognitive prowess and longevity in the institution. Typically, this process begins with an individual's first administrative appointment in a move from a faculty position to one of department chairperson and often culminates years later in the role of president. The author suggests that this laissez-faire process is not appropriate for the challenges of the future and does not take into account the ability of a good leader to affect the behavior of followers (Roe, 1989). It is clear from studies of transformational leaders that this ability is the critical variable in successful leadership.

A process for identifying future leaders and providing for their training through planned mentoring should be an immediate priority of responsible community college presidents. The process should be established by these leaders through self-assessment of their own leadership capabilities as well as the status of their transactional and transformational leadership. According to Bass (1985a), transformational aspects of leadership are more oriented to change, and transactional behaviors are more oriented to the status quo. Leaders will typically use a combination of transformational and transactional behaviors in any given situation. A fallacy often exists that the attainment of the top position precludes the need for further professional development. No one is free from life-long learning in this day of ever-increasing knowledge and continuous and rapid change. Therefore, a self-assessment of knowledge and leadership will have little value for the community college president without a commitment to the ongoing nature of such an endeavor.

Self-assessment is a valuable tool to plan leadership growth opportunities offered by universities, the American Association of Community and Junior Colleges, the AACJC Presidents Academy, the League for Innovation, and individual consultants. Planned professional development for current and future leaders is the key in developing good leadership into excellent leadership. Professional development for community college presidents should enhance their expertise in understanding the components of excellent leadership and transferring this knowledge to potential future leaders.

The practical application of this expertise includes modeling professional development for the administrative leadership team, long a weak area in the staff development plans of most community colleges. Moreover, the enhanced ability to recognize potential leaders by their behavioral attributes is definitely needed in leadership development. This identification can help foster an orderly process of development for future leaders through assistance and mentoring by the president. Further, another benefit of this process will be the intrinsic reward for presidents who enjoy teaching and mentoring roles. This process has the capability to develop two-year collegiate leaders who have been trained in a systematic fashion and who can maximize their own potential for the challenges ahead.

Conclusion

The tremendous workload of current community college leaders is a hindrance to the process of leadership development, and the suggestion of additional responsibility may be regarded by some as an imposition. Nevertheless, America must have qualified leaders for the future. Clearly, community college leadership is crucial for the education, training, and retraining of the nation's work force. The direct involvement of current presidents is critical to the successful identification and development of high-quality future community college leaders. While the leadership development process may appear to consume valuable presidential time, involvement in the leadership development of executive administrators will benefit not only the present culture of the organization, but also national community college leadership for the future.

Clearly, the community college is not alone in addressing the parameters of leadership; the need for outstanding leaders is not restricted to education. It is imperative that colleges provide the framework for the emergence of outstanding leaders to confront ever-increasing challenges and changes in a chaotic world. Nationally, the two-year college effort has established these institutions as essential components in the health and well-being of America. It is time to recognize the significance of well-defined processes to identify those individuals who exhibit readiness for educational leadership and act to empower and enable their development as leaders for the future.

■

Chapter 6

Instructional Leadership: Building a Culture of Excellence in the Teaching-Learning Community

By Rosemary Gillett-Karam and Eli Peña

The demographic, cultural, political, and economic changes that are sweeping our nation demand dynamic leadership. Politicians and business leaders must respond swiftly to problems in this turbulent environment. Stability is desirable and even critical, but the issues that are revolutionizing our nation demand new solutions, resources, and policy. Perhaps no other institution of higher education responds as sensitively to societal change—including environmental, demographic, economic, and political change—as the American community college. These forces for change have always had and probably will always have an important impact on the American community college. Because of this, the community college reflects the American climate and culture better than many other institutions. As law makers and political leaders respond to financial exigencies and environmental upheaval, so too must the community college leader respond to the crises of the American community college.

One such modern crisis of the community college involves teaching and learning. The changing face of America requires that community colleges alter their curriculum and teaching styles to fit a more diverse constituency and yet maintain stability and tradition. This requires a close look at the relationship between college leadership and college culture.

This chapter seeks to address how college leadership can respond to the crisis in the teaching-learning component of the community college. Specifically, we suggest two critical points: one, that CEOs should recognize and facilitate the role of the teacher as leader, thus empowering faculty in the classroom and cultivating the teaching-learning community; and two, that the strengths of exemplary college teachers, or teachers as leaders, become focus points for college teaching. In short, the CEO must create a climate for excellence that promotes exceptional behaviors and qualities of administrators and teachers and builds a community for learning.

Setting the Stage

Research supports the idea that community college presidents must take the lead in improving teaching and learning and in encouraging faculty to assume leadership roles. Some researchers call for greater participation by college presidents in directing quality education; they claim educational leadership must determine those changes that will promote teaching excellence. In this view, the role of the president includes helping faculty become better teachers (Cross, 1983); maintaining academic standards (Richardson, 1985); recognizing and encouraging curricular, instructional, and research ideas (Lilly, 1987); establishing an environment conducive to learning (Loyd, 1983); initiating and guiding faculty development (Bush and Ames, 1984); inculcating values for teaching excellence (Roueche and Baker, 1987); influencing the institutional climate that stimulates the overall learning process (Roueche, Baker, and Rose, 1989); and recognizing faculty leadership and teaching excellence (Baker, Roueche, and Gillett-Karam, 1990).

Peña (1990) summed up this research with a survey that asked community college presidents what they believed was necessary to build a teaching-learning community. The survey revealed four areas that lead to such a community: vision and influence, culture and climate, support and development, and quality and community.

• *Vision and Influence:* CEOs must have the vision to recognize change and to influence the vision of faculty. CEOs and other college leaders must serve as role models for faculty, encouraging teaching excellence by becoming excellent teachers themselves. By teaching and leading the faculty, CEOs can in turn promote teaching as leading by the faculty.

• *Culture and Climate:* CEOs must provide the leadership to develop an institutional culture that instills the egalitarian values of the American community college mission and creates a climate for excellence.

• *Support and Development:* CEOs must support faculty development and reward excellent teaching when identifying, hiring, recognizing, and promoting teachers. Faculty development must be continuous and formative.

• *Quality and Community:* CEOs must lead the effort to define, promote, and maintain quality in teaching and learning, including committing to innovative educational programs and curricula while maintaining educational quality. Leaders must establish a college community for teaching and learning.

CEOs cannot accomplish these things alone. Organizational success results from the ability of the CEO to collaborate with followers in such a way that the followers are provided with a sense of ownership. This, in turn, affects followers' and others' perceptions of the leader, particularly their expectations about leader competence and motivation. Although this depends on an exemplary college CEO, these behaviors can be learned.

Understanding the leader-follower relationship by reviewing contingency theories is essential if CEOs are to influence the quality of teaching. According to Hoy and Miskel (1987), "contingency theories maintain that leadership effectiveness depends upon the fit between behavior of the leader and situation variables such as task structure, position power, and followers' skills and attitudes" (p. 284). Contingency approaches examine the interaction between situation and leader behavior and define leadership in terms of behaviors instead of traits. In a situation where the CEO is attempting to influence teaching excellence it is necessary for the leader to structure the teaching task, use the powers of the assigned position, and enhance the skills and attitudes of faculty.

Expectancy theory—a type of contingency theory—"focuses on the network of ideas that people have about their jobs and how these combine with the strength of their desires to motivate people" (Hampton, Summer, and Webber, 1987, p. 17). Expectancy theory has four elements: expectancy, an estimate of what will happen if an outcome is achieved; valence, the strength of one's desire for that outcome; instrumentality, the degree to which one's actions help achieve the outcome; and probability, an estimate of what actions will be taken to achieve the outcome.

The path-goal theory of leadership used in the research reported in this chapter is derived from expectancy theory and couched in the language of leadership theory. Path-goal theory depends on two expectancies: whether a successful action will lead to reward, and whether an action will be successful. Thus, path-goal theory conveys that the CEO must not only provide goals and rewards, but must help faculty see the path they might follow to attain rewards, thus increasing their confidence and encouraging their efforts (Hampton, Summer, and Webber, 1987, p. 571).

Path-goal theory works equally well whether faculty are seen as the leaders and students the followers, or CEOs are seen as the leaders and faculty the followers. The theoretical framework that House (1971) proposed in path-goal theory application suggests that teacher behavior influences student motivation, and CEO behavior influences faculty motivation.

Leaders of vision can create a leader-follower bond that can be used to nurture a relationship with faculty and teaching excellence (House,

1971). By empowering faculty, community college presidents can inspire them to help transform the institution into a teaching-learning community. In order to build this community, presidents need to know excellent teaching when they see it and know how to motivate faculty to try harder to deliver it. This will help presidents identify, develop, recognize, and celebrate faculty committed to the community college and its needs, values, and mission, which will in turn encourage the growth of a climate for excellence.

The Teacher as Leader

Two recent studies examine community college teachers' effectiveness based on path-goal theory. Valek (1988) used path-goal theory as a theoretical base to determine which leadership behaviors of community college faculty resulted in exemplary teaching. Baker, Roueche, and Gillett-Karam (1990) developed a path-goal framework for examining the behaviors and competencies of exemplary teachers. They demonstrated how teacher behavior influences student motivation, and how influence and motivation are keys to student performance. Using both these studies as a framework, Eli Peña's dissertation, from which the remainder of this chapter was developed, sought to discover what community college CEOs thought about effective teaching, what they believed about exemplary teachers, and how the communication of these ideas can support a teaching and learning community.

Peña's descriptive and qualitative study was conducted in 1990. One hundred fifty-four CEOs of American community, technical, and junior colleges responded to a survey asking them to describe the characteristics of effective teachers. Peña sent an additional questionnaire to a selected number of faculty who had been identified as transformational leaders in the Roueche, Baker, and Rose (1989) study. These teachers had been previously identified in the Baker, Roueche, and Gillett-Karam 1989–90 study of effective teachers. The CEOs involved in Peña's study were chosen by using the presidents of colleges where these exemplary faculty taught.

CEOs were sent letters reminding them of the faculty that they nominated for the *Teaching As Leading* study. The questionnaire listed characteristic behaviors of award-winning instructors. The CEOs were asked to think "in general" of the excellent teachers they had nominated and to note whether the competencies were "present" and whether they "should be present." This process yielded a CEO perception of what competencies award-winning instructors possess and should possess.

The study was designed to validate the competency profile developed by Baker, Roueche, and Gillett-Karam (1990) as well as the study conducted for *Access and Excellence* by Roueche and Baker (1987). From Peña's study, an image of the role of college president in instructional leadership emerged.

Community College CEOs' Perceptions of Teaching

Analyses of data from almost 900 community college faculty involved in the Baker, Roueche, and Gillett-Karam study indicated these behaviors of excellent teachers: they arouse student needs, increase personal payoffs, clarify expectations and paths to success, reduce barriers, and increase student satisfaction.

The Peña study verified that American community college CEOs believe their exemplary faculty are able to play these roles. By believing, embedding, and transmitting these elements of a teaching and learning culture, the typical community college CEO believes he or she is able to develop and support teaching and learning at his or her institution, nurturing a teaching-learning community in the process.

The examples selected from CEOs' descriptive transcripts indicate that they believe that teachers possess a wide range of teaching behaviors. In each of the six path-goal clusters, the comments of CEOs expressed the emphases placed on different features of instruction at community colleges. Figure 6.1 indicates how often the respondents listed a behavior that had previously been identified in *Teaching As Leading*. Figure 6.1 displays two levels of behavior—clusters, such as arousing student needs, and specific competencies within the clusters, such as communicating goals. The cluster behaviors of the Teaching-Learning, Path-Goal Framework do not purport to give a full description of the characteristic teaching styles of any one individual. The framework does, however, highlight patterns that emerged from the group studied. This model of teaching competencies can be seen as a normative definition of teaching excellence from CEOs' perspectives.

These competencies help clarify the role CEOs play in defining and developing a teaching-learning culture in their institutions. Presidents must understand the faculty's teaching behaviors and the dynamics of change at the institution, and accept responsibility for both. Community college CEOs can define those behaviors characteristic of teaching excellence and use that definition to influence activities, motivate followers, build a teaching-learning community, and nurture a climate for excellence.

The Arousal of Student Needs

Teachers cannot force-feed students knowledge; before teaching can begin, students must want to learn. How do teachers recognize and engage students' desire to learn? What is the initial effort that engages both

Figure 6.1
Frequencies and Percentages Indicating "Present" Responses of Teaching-Learning Path-Goal Behaviors for Award-Winning Instructors as Reported by CEOs

| CLUSTERS | CEO Nomination Letter | |
Behaviors	Frequencies	Percentages
AROUSES STUDENT NEEDS		
Communicates Goals	25	16.23
Provides for Input	84	54.55
Is Aware of Total Student	92	59.74
INCREASES PERSONAL PAYOFFS		
Encourages Self-Worth	33	21.43
Has High Expectations	47	30.53
Encourages Responsibility	51	33.12
CLARIFIES PATHS TO SUCCESS		
Affirms Capabilities	25	16.23
Matches Needs to Plan	114	74.03
Provides Feedback	56	36.36
CLARIFIES EXPECTATIONS		
Upholds Standards	46	29.87
Is Aware: Consequences/Actions	49	31.82
Rewards Expectations	32	20.78
REDUCES BARRIERS		
Explains Alternatives	49	31.82
Personalizes Outcomes	62	40.26
Assesses Problem Situations	46	29.87
INCREASES SATISFACTION		
Motivates Learning	83	53.90
Encourages Independence	43	27.92
Rewards Appropriate Behavior	32	20.78

N = 154

teacher and student toward similar goals and aspirations? CEOs described a number of ways exemplary teachers arouse student needs. CEOs talked about the importance of teachers' helping students set their own goals. Baker, Roueche, and Gillett-Karam (1990) note that an instructor's skill for doing this "seeks to draw out from the student that which is latent or hidden" (p. 96). Good teachers also seek to communicate clearly and early their expectations and the course goals; three descriptive terms— "well-organized," "well-outlined," and "well-explained"—stand out in

CEOs' narratives of award-winning instruction. Exemplary teachers also articulate institutional goals for their students. Needless to say, faculty cannot do this unless the president of the institution articulates these goals for the entire college community.

Good teachers also allow students' desire to learn to bloom in an environment characterized by "caring," "concern for students," and "availability to students," according to CEOs. Also expressed was the "extended assistance" exemplary teachers provide to students outside the classroom, including regular office hours, sponsorship of extracurricular activities, and extra tutoring as needed. Baker, Roueche, and Gillett-Karam (1990) found that exemplary teachers spend up to six additional hours per week beyond office hours in support of students.

Finally, teachers arouse student needs by "being aware of the total student," since these teachers "understand who their students are" and "the importance of the teacher-student relationship." According to CEOs, good teachers are student advocates and recognize and respect human potential and student diversity. College leaders also said that understanding the teacher-student relationship allows teachers to make a greater difference in students' lives.

Increasing Personal Payoffs for Students

Increasing personal payoffs for students refers to increasing students' opportunities for success in college (Baker, Roueche, and Gillett-Karam, 1990). This encourages students to have high self-esteem, which increases their expectations of themselves and encourages them to take responsibility for their own learning. This, in turn, gives students an even greater sense of self-worth.

Encouraging self-worth in students begins with faculty's recognition of students' potential and capabilities. Recognition of these characteristics leads teachers to be "confidence builders." As students move beyond what they formerly believed themselves capable of achieving, their self-esteem improves, which gives them more self-control. Self-esteem and self-control feed off each other, each benefiting from an increase in the other. Good teachers can move this process along. What is essential to teaching, college leaders explain, "is the maintenance of a supportive climate that fosters student successes."

CEOs also indicated that "having high expectations of students has positive results for students toward their own success." They pointed out that students respect teachers because of "high expectations teachers set for their students." They used terms such as "exacting," "demanding," and "clearly defined" when referring to teachers' expectations of students. Easton and others (1984) reported that having high expectations for students' success supports the part of the teacher-student relationship that reinforces the creation of the learning culture that both teachers and students desire. CEOs indicated these teachers not only have high expectations for their students, but also for their peers. These findings are substantiated by the strong sense of professionalism demonstrated by the faculty, who were found to "show dedication and loyalty to the teaching profession."

Payoffs for students are also increased when "teachers delegate by encouraging the students to take responsibility for their own learning," many presidents indicated. These faculty instill responsibility and expect students to be accountable for their own learning and achievement. Having high expectations of students and giving them the support and encouragement to "take responsibility for their own learning" is expressed by one CEO of an exemplary teacher:

> This faculty member is straightforward and fair with students. In turn, they respect him and put forth their best efforts to meet his high expectations. He believes students should take full responsibility for developing their competencies, but gives them the needed support and encouragement they require.

Another CEO describes a faculty member who believes that "students must take responsibility for learning, all the while encouraging them to meet the challenges. This instructor's high expectations of students inspire student success."

Clarifying the Path to Success

One of the primary functions of effective teachers is clarifying the path to goal attainment—the essential effort to which path-goal theory refers. The leadership behaviors in this category guide students toward their own goal attainment by identifying and affirming students' capabilities, by matching the needs of students with a structural plan for their growth and improvement, and by encouraging and reaffirming students' efforts through consistent and appropriate feedback.

Teaching-learning path-goal attainment can be made easier by building students' confidence in their abilities (Baker, Roueche, and Gillett-Karam, 1990). Affirming students' capabilities begins with identifying individual skills and helping students make realistic choices. When students realize that they do have the power to accomplish much, they lose their fear of the subject and feel even more confident in their capabilities.

CEOs also see exemplary faculty helping students down the pathway of learning by creating learning situations that specifically meet the needs of students. This makes learning more significant for students by capitalizing on connections between the subject matter and the students' own interests (Schneider, Klemp, and Kastendiek, 1981). CEOs suggest exemplary teachers bring about modes of instruction that move away from the traditional practices of pedagogy, such as lecture methods, and toward a culture that better facilitates learning.

According to CEOs, one way in which effective teachers match student needs to a structured plan is in the strategy of updating programs and curricula; these are "the efforts that not only attempt, but succeed, at staying up-to-date with developments in teachers' disciplines, and at strengthening the curriculum toward providing innovations, relevancy, and reward for coursework." Other exemplary teachers "match needs to a structured plan by correlating training in laboratory or classroom activities with what happens in the workplace or the external environment." College leaders can support this connection of school activities with the external world by recognizing the efforts of their exemplary teachers to incorporate field work and other aspects of experiential learning into the curriculum.

Methods that show flexibility in planning and delivery systems (as described by Roueche and Baker, 1987) let teachers design coursework that helps students seek and attain their goals. CEOs described their teachers as "resource persons for the implementation of different teaching strategies, who package and deliver a wide variety of learning strategy materials for their students, develop appropriate software packages that facilitate learning, develop linkages between tutorial programs and curricula, and show flexibility in the planning and presentation of subject matter." College leaders speak of "facilitating the learning process" as their instructors "develop teaching strategies that specifically instill learning materials to those students with handicaps and special needs, and strengthen advising programs and curricula that . . . reinforce entry-level skills of developmental students."

Reinforcing the idea that it is easier to provide feedback to another person face-to-face, CEOs related the importance of teachers' "availability to students." This availability is combined with establishing a classroom environment in which students are encouraged to ask questions. The "person-to-person connection" is an essential component of what CEOs perceive as reinforcing the teacher-student relationship. CEOs noted that consistent monitoring of student progress strengthens the person-to-person communication between the teacher and the student. As discussed earlier, this availability to students helps give students confidence and arouse their desires to learn, but it also helps teachers provide feedback to their students and connect what is learned to their students' lives. As one CEO described an exemplary teacher:

She encourages her students to come to her office for math assistance and is flexible as to the time and place in providing the
assistance. She has developed workshops and individual sessions
to help students overcome or cope with their math and test anxi-
eties. The students feel secure and confident in her classes because of the design and overall course structure.

One CEO describes teaching strategies used by an exemplary instructor to clarify students' paths to success:

The instructor never loses sight of the fact that for every student
there is a unique approach that will be most effective. This instructor builds a wide variety of techniques into her teaching style.
These techniques include: small group discussions; opportunities
for individual student input during class; frequent written quizzes;
and in-class activities/assignments in which students apply theory. The instructor is a tireless professional who spends many
out-of-class hours meeting with students to assist them in their
development.

Clarifying Expectations for Students and Promoting Academic Standards
Students have a hard time learning unless they understand what kind
of progress is expected of them. Behaviors that distinguish the clarifying
expectations cluster include upholding standards of behavior throughout the teacher-student relationship, making students aware of the consequences of their actions, and rewarding students' expectations regarding outcomes. The exemplary teacher upholds academic standards through
a variety of behaviors, as related by this college CEO as he describes one
of his college's exemplary teachers:

This instructor sets high standards for the courses he teaches and
communicates those standards clearly to students. During laboratory sessions he is frequently huddled with a group of students—
totally involved with them, and they with him—working on a
problem or pursuing a line of inquiry related to the day's topic.
He exhibits an enthusiasm for teaching, for contributing to students' growth, and he takes pride in their accomplishments.

CEOs distinguish their award-winning instructors as "constantly communicating high academic standards to their students and maintaining
these standards." CEOs recognize that upholding standards requires knowledge in the teachers' subject areas—a strong base of academic preparation
is highly valued. College leaders also note that having quality education
demands students' attention in class and requires accuracy in their work.

Another feature CEOs called critical for effective teachers was behavior that "makes students aware of the consequences of their actions." If the ultimate goal of teaching is a mature and self-actualized learner, teachers must constantly hold students accountable for their own behavior. The student-teacher relationship must begin as a teacher-centered, teacher-in-control environment and gradually move to a student-centered, student-in-control environment. Such a strategy recognizes the maturation of the student through the teaching-learning process.

College leaders report that teachers reward students' expectations by being present at events where achievement is recognized, by structuring their course activities in a way that will reward students' achievements, and by maintaining follow-up methods that record students' successes during and after the course. Teachers can also reinforce student development activities such as counseling as a means of recognizing and rewarding student achievement. These activities serve as a conduit for praising and rewarding accomplishment. Easton and others (1984) note that effective teachers collect and use information about students' achievement and progress; this information helps teachers know how students are doing in class and provides feedback to them, and can help raise students' expectations. CEOs also talked about teachers' commitment to track graduates after graduation.

Reducing Obstacles to Learning

Often a teacher's role is not to cajole a student into learning, but to remove obstacles to learning so that the student can teach himself or herself. Effective teachers as classroom leaders understand that students may be hindered by different learning styles and personal circumstances, and they make allowances to accommodate those differences. These teachers also explore alternatives that lead to accommodation and change, personalize students' outcomes, and resolve problem situations. These behaviors not only work to reduce barriers, but they also encourage learning networks, such as integrated developmental studies programs; team teaching; and reading, writing, and computing across the curriculum.

A CEO summarizes the idea of a teacher reducing barriers for students thus:

The instructor recognizes that students have different learning styles, interests, and levels of motivation. She addresses these differences with compassion and a variety of teaching techniques; she personalizes attention to students' instructional needs; she actively listens to her students and encourages student participation in each class session.

Exemplary teachers constantly explore alternatives that reduce barriers and improve instruction. These teachers seek new methods of instruction, use a variety of methods to accommodate students' needs, and manipulate information to help students learn. In order to provide a wide variety of paths to the goal of learning, teachers must stay informed of research in their disciplines and new teaching methods.

CEOs also emphasized the importance of teachers' personalizing students' outcomes as a way of increasing motivation and reducing learning barriers. Students may be put off by the impersonal nature of the educational system, or they may have had bad experiences with previous teachers: seeing students as individuals and treating them as individuals by providing individualized instruction helps alleviate these problems. Roueche and Baker (1987) make the point that excellent teachers do not teach the subject, but teach the student. For example, excellent instructors employ the curriculum as a means to empower the student and not as an end in and of itself.

The ability to assess classroom problems rapidly and effectively also allows teachers to make appropriate decisions that address obstacles to learning. CEOs describe good teachers as improving instructional strategies immediately upon discovery of problems. Good teachers use contingency leadership theories to integrate appropriate teacher behavior and a favorable classroom situation to provide an effective leader-follower relationship (Baker, Roueche, and Gillett-Karam, 1990). A faculty member who understands the importance of adapting both the situation of the classroom and her own leadership abilities is described by her CEO in the following passage:

> This teacher's educational philosophy is that a valid learning experience can be tailored for the individual student. The teacher mixes the use of specific instructional methods with personal flexibility to constantly adapt to the changing needs and abilities of her students, by focusing on her own and her students' efforts to apply course content to daily life.

This teacher responds to her students' changing needs to reduce barriers to education.

Increasing Students' Satisfaction and Independence

Learning does not end when students receive their final grades for a class; the best teachers give students the tools to continue learning after they no longer have contact with the teacher. The ability to learn after a class has ended has two main components: a student's satisfaction with the learning process, and a student's independence from the teacher. Numerous studies can be cited to support the contention that leaders make a difference in the satisfaction of followers. To increase satisfaction in students, exemplary teachers acting in a leadership role are able to motivate students toward greater learning, encourage students to think independently, and reward appropriate behavior.

In path-goal theory, leader effectiveness is defined as the extent to which it promotes a follower's motivation (House and Mitchell, 1974). In an interesting parallel, CEOs view teachers' behaviors as the initiating structure that motivates students. The main focus of these behaviors is the teacher motivating students to meet their full potential. Besides using descriptive terms, such as "stimulating," "challenging," "inspiring," and "influencing" to describe how exemplary teachers "motivate" students, leaders also explained that teachers experienced "enjoyment from motivating students on a one-to-one basis."

CEOs' descriptions of exemplary teachers' motivating learning include phrases such as: to motivate students to do their best; to achieve success with students on an individual basis; to enjoy teaching and learning with the students; to stimulate students to think and involve them in the learning process; to motivate students to think, apply, and evaluate the knowledge they have obtained; and to use their sense of commitment as a powerful motivator to students.

Roueche and Baker (1987) describe excellent teachers as those who "foster independence in their students by giving them the tools to learn for themselves." These teachers focus on "teaching analytical skill to students." They also help students realize their goals, and they encourage students to use their abilities to "seize opportunities, harness their talents, and work arduously to understand their lessons" (p. 150). In this respect CEOs described exemplary teachers as those who develop confidence in students while leading them to independence, encourage critical thinking that leads to independence, challenge and inspire students to be success-oriented, and create an environment that encourages independence.

Recognition and appreciation of students' accomplishments is a behavior of effective teachers reported by Schneider, Klemp, and Kastendiek (1981). Effective teachers took the time to acknowledge and affirm instances where appropriate learning and achievement took place. CEOs point out exemplary teachers create a positive environment that supports recognition and appreciation of students' accomplishments whenever necessary.

One college leader describes a teacher's commitment to "increasing satisfaction in students" by focusing on this teacher's commitment to reach students' needs at three levels: motivating learning, encouraging independence, and rewarding appropriate behavior. This CEO writes:

The teacher is totally committed to teaching students and is devoted to seeing that her students receive the utmost in training so that they can be the best they can be. This teacher takes great pleasure in seeing students reach their goals and excels in being prepared to give each student what she or he needs to be successful in a chosen career.

Conclusion

For a community college to survive into the twenty-first century, it will be necessary to build a culture for both the local community surrounding the college and the teaching-learning community within the college. Most importantly, it is the CEO's instructional leadership that will guide the way in embedding a culture for the teaching-learning community. Community college leaders embed this teaching and learning community by changing the pattern of accepted habits, values, and rules and embedding a core set of assumptions and an implicit set of policies and procedures that govern day-to-day teaching and learning activities. These cultural aspects need to be "shared" at all levels of the institution.

In the new culture effective teachers will be a valued commodity. The role community college CEOs assume as instructional leaders, including the process of defining teaching excellence, necessitates knowing those characteristics that make faculty effective classroom leaders. CEOs must also articulate these behaviors to their teachers. In this way, top leaders allow teachers to become leaders themselves.

In their book *In Search of Excellence*, Peters and Waterman (1982) report that a focal point of excellent companies is "the tough-minded respect for the individual, the willingness to train him, to set reasonable and clear expectations for him, and to grant his practical autonomy to set out and contribute" (p. 239). This statement by Peters and Waterman supports a CEO's instructional leadership role toward producing an excellent college and a community of learning dedicated to teaching excellence. Or, as Robert McCabe, president of Miami-Dade Community College, Florida, puts it:

It's fundamental that I value and convey the definition of teaching excellence to my followers. I take an active part in this educational endeavor, but I also give people lots of room to grow and then let them grow. People want to feel good about what they are and what they do (personal communication, 1990).

Community college CEOs must take the lead in improving teaching and learning and empowering followers. CEOs' insights into defining teaching excellence are an essential component of being an educational leader. These insights also illuminate the path for creating an institutional culture that values excellence in teaching and its most important product—successful students.

What has been suggested in this chapter is only the first step in establishing an effective teaching-learning culture. Leaders cannot embed a new culture unless an understanding exists of the attitudes, values, and behaviors that will make up the paradigm. Our argument is that if a majority of the CEOs of American community colleges can articulate what good teaching is, they ought to be able to lead in such a way that these aspects of exceptional teaching can become the norm. This change will directly relate to their ability to make a new culture the reality.

■

Chapter 7

An Organizational Culture Consciously Shaped to Foster Creativity and Innovation

By Michele Nelson

C ommunity colleges, like all other organizations and institutions, move through organizational developmental stages (Schein, 1985a). Advancement of an institution or organization through these predictable life-cycle stages accelerates when the external environment is changing rapidly. Today's end-of-the-century external environment is chaotic (Peters, 1988), reflected in transforming demographics, accelerating global political and economic interdependence, rapidly evolving technology, an underprepared work force, and the United States' diminishing ability to compete worldwide.

Leadership strategies that were appropriate during an organization's establishment, expansion, and maturity are anachronistic and inadequate to revitalize organizations and to propel them beyond maturity into organizational renewal. Without conscious intervention, organizational decline will follow the stage of organizational maturity (Tierney, 1988). This decline can be replaced by renewal if an institution commits to a process of revitalization through creativity and innovation, a process that requires conscious shaping of the organizational culture. Community colleges, as well as institutions and businesses nationwide, must therefore rethink and restructure their organizational cultures to avoid the pitfall of organizational decline (Deegan, 1989; Peters, 1988; Guy, 1989; Kozmetsky, 1988).

Schein (1985b) describes the processes of embedding culture and shaping values within the organization. Both Schein (1985b) and Trice and Beyer (1984) demonstrate that embedding culture is, to a great degree, synonymous with leadership and results in an organization-wide understanding of the correct way to think in relation to issues confronting the institution. Similarly, Kozmetský (1986), Kuhn (1985), and Peters and Waterman (1982) emphasize management of culture to foster creativity and innovation and to provide the organizational flexibility that enables institutions to respond to external demands and environmental uncertainty and turbulence.

Bennis and Nanus (1985) assert that leadership, by its attention to ideas and deeds, sets the tone for the distinctive identity of an organization. Peters and Waterman (1982) stress that leaders mold socially integrating frameworks that contribute to organizational harmony by providing followers with a unified sense of mission and purpose. The mission is reinforced as values are shaped and becomes institutionalized as these continuing tasks are achieved. Leader-follower commitment reflected in daily decisions is based on shared values, which in turn create precedents, alliances, effective symbols, and personal loyalties. Commitments to shared values grow as institutional decisions are made (Bennis and Nanus, 1985; Peters and Waterman, 1982; Roueche, Baker, and Rose, 1989).

Chafee and Tierney (1988) and Kuh and Whitt (1988), addressing leadership and management of the community college from a cultural perspective, stress the importance of the role of leadership in consciously and conscientiously shaping the culture. Owens (1987) defines organizational culture as the "study of the wellsprings from which the values and characteristics of an organization arise" (p. 167). Schein (1985a) urges an organizational life-cycle perspective to stress the importance of the role of leadership in strategic planning and organizational renewal.

Organizational cultures that were appropriate and effective in an era of growth and relatively abundant property have become anachronistic in today's environment. The following case study was undertaken to provide insights into an effective community college culture, especially those variables that foster creativity and innovation as catalysts for organizational revitalization and that contribute to an institution's adaptability and responsiveness to its external environment.

Innovation and Creativity in Community College Cultures: A Case Study

California's Santa Barbara City College (SBCC) exemplifies a dynamic, responsive community college organizational culture. SBCC was selected as the subject of study based on two apparently dichotomous elements in its organizational culture. First, the institution has a reputation for creativity and innovation (MacDougall and Friedlander, 1989), with a nationally recognized president as leader, and has been recognized for teaching excellence (Roueche, Baker, and Rose, 1989). Secondly, the institution's age would indicate that it is functioning in the organizational stage of maturity. SBCC was founded in 1909, making it one of the oldest community colleges in the nation. The SBCC faculty, like faculty across the nation, is aging and has few career ladder options, a problem endemic to community colleges. Therefore, Santa Barbara City College would seemingly be vulnerable to organizational decline.

A case study approach was employed in the collection and analysis of the data, since researchers in the area of organizational culture (Trice and Beyer, 1984; Schein, 1985a; Chafee and Tierney, 1988) strongly advocate qualitative, in-depth, observational methodology to provide a systematic, detailed assessment of the nature of the institution. The study proposed to add a new dimension to understanding the role of creative and innovative management by focusing on the challenge of guiding a community college from the maturity stage into a renewal stage. By rethinking and restructuring, leaders can prevent their organizations from drifting into the predictable stage of organizational decline.

The structure for inquiry into the organizational culture included examination of primary and secondary cultural embedding mechanisms (Schein, 1985a), which focus on: organizational structure; leadership; decision making and strategic planning; and organizational rites and ceremonies related to motivational activities and incentives. Research addressed questions relating to: the level of strength of the SBCC culture and of cultural congruence within the institution; the degree to which cultural values and assumptions are shared throughout the institution; the elements of core dimensions of culture; and the role of leadership in the intentional shaping of the culture.

The case study format was critical to the inquiry since it provided the only path to access and explore the experiences of organizational participants and to illuminate their patterns of action, the organization's unifying symbolic traditions, and deeply embedded nuances of the organizational culture. Thirty-one interviews were conducted using the Critical Incident Technique, as originated by Flanagan (1954) and further developed by Stanley (1974) and Lincoln and Guba (1985). Additional data were collected by examining institutional records and other archival sources, as well as by direct on-site participation-observation.

Data revealed the presence of a deeply embedded organizational culture with shared values evident in organizational rites, rituals, and symbols, which transcend the more temporal influences of organizational climate. The institutional structures and processes of governance, strategic planning, and decision making have been shaped by the leadership and reflect the institutional mission and values. Creativity and innovation appear to be components of a positive organizational energy that is propelling the eighty-year-old community college into a vital and expanding stage of organizational exhilaration, fueling organizational transformation and renewal.

A review of the interviews, combined with the examination of institutional records, evaluation of archival sources, and direct on-site participation/observation, strongly indicated that: (1) the Santa Barbara City College organizational culture is exceptionally strong and congruent throughout the institution; and (2) the culture remains relatively constant even with shifts in organizational climate.

Differentiations between climate and culture are blurred, with culture consisting of shared assumptions, values, or norms, and climate consisting of perceptions of behavior. Organizational climate is subject much more to temporal factors and to the current satisfaction level of the organizational participants, whereas organizational culture is viewed as being far more deeply embedded (Schein, 1985a; Ashforth, 1985). A profound example of the distinction between climate and culture occurred in early fall 1989. With faculty expressing dissatisfaction over salary negotiations, the climate grew more and more turbulent. Posturing and strategy that accompanied the collective bargaining process appeared to dramatically affect the college climate. The value of collegiality, universally expressed by all thirty-one interviewees, was temporarily eroded. Behavior rapidly degenerated into adversarial confrontations between administration and faculty.

At the same time that the salary negotiations were taking place, the Santa Barbara City College Office of Planning and Research (1989), as part of the preparation for an accreditation self-study, administered the College Climate Survey (CCS), a Likert-type scaled instrument adapted by Roueche and Baker (1987) to describe campus climates. The results of the survey indicated that SBCC's overall composite rating, based on all employees in all categories, was 3.48 out of 5.00. This is slightly above the national average of 3.31 for all colleges that have administered the instrument. Using the CCS system, SBCC was rated Consultative, "with occasional excursion by individual groups into the Benevolent/Authoritative and Participative/Group ranges" (Santa Barbara City College Office of Planning and Research, 1989). Such a positive climate would seem counterintuitive unless the clear distinction between deeply embedded culture and temporally influenced climate is kept in mind.

Environmental Stimulants to Creativity and Innovation

Data collection processes additionally revealed the following themes, indicating the presence or absence of environmental stimulants to creativity and innovation in the organizational culture: freedom and control over one's work or ideas; supportive, communicative leadership; challenging and meaningful work; access to sufficient and appropriate resources; encouragement of innovative ideas; recognition for creative work; and sufficient time to develop innovative solutions to problems (Amabile and Gryskiewicz, 1987).

Freedom and Control

Freedom and control are characterized by the freedom to decide what to do or how to do it and a sense of control over one's work or ideas, as contrasted with constraint.

Because the organizational culture's values and mission are so deeply and widely embedded, most organizational participants are focused on similar goals. Individuals are actively encouraged to be innovative in every aspect of the college operations. This all-pervasive support for innovation was exemplified at SBCC by projects of varying extent and sizes, such as the Hotel, Restaurant, and Culinary Program coordinator's vision of a college-operated hotel and restaurant, the Study Abroad Program, and the 2+2+2 Nursing Program.

The Study Abroad Program is an innovation that has now become institutionalized and reflects a collegewide philosophical commitment to global awareness and cultural diversity. At the time the program was begun at SBCC, no other community colleges in California were pursuing full semester abroad programs. The fact that John Romo, as a division dean in 1983, could conceive of the possibilities and work with the English Department chairperson to develop a proposal, and have the project implemented by spring the following year, demonstrates the level to which members feel a sense of control over their ideas. Romo, now vice president of the college, stated:

> . . . the power of the program continues to be affirmed. Students still describe it as a life-changing experience. We run really high quality programs, and now we are negotiating to send students to Russia. We have tried to be creative with the disciplines, sending the biological sciences [students] to New Zealand, and sending students to China. We have never canceled a program for lack of interest. We do very little marketing. It is primarily internal, and it is mostly based on word of mouth. It is also a wonderful, renewing experience for the faculty.
>
> With the Soviet Union we are moving in entirely new directions. More emphasis is being placed on Soviet students coming here. Additionally, we're working with a Japanese representative to bring their students here. It is a commitment to global awareness, which is our thrust for the future. We have institutionalized

the program by establishing our International Advisory Committee and by formulating policy. The ad hoc approach of the early programs has been replaced by clear policies and procedures through which we are now able to share information with others in similar situations. These programs take a lot of attention. These programs are a reflection of the positive ideas here at this college. That is what I like about working here. (Interview, 1989).

The 1986–87 college year exemplifies the growth and comprehensive nature of the Study Abroad Program; 148 students and six faculty members studied in Cambridge, England. Students spent the spring semester studying art, drama, literature, history, and political science and visiting theaters, political events, and historical sights. The thirty-nine students taking part in the China/Japan program completed coursework in anthropology, Chinese history, and political science, while developing an increased appreciation of the language and customs of the countries. The twenty-five students who went to Salamanca, Spain, received seven weeks of intensive Spanish language instruction while living with Spanish families.

Faculty leader John Kay, reflecting on the Study Abroad Program, reiterated Romo's assessment:

The international programs are wonderful. These programs are not junkets. You see kids grow, more than you would in a normal classroom, because you are there in close proximity, seeing them every day. You see their academic agony and their excellency. You see them developing. I could give you innumerable stories about kids who came out of isolated and insulated backgrounds who blossom when they go to libraries, Parliament, and Shakespeare. I am always surprised to see how well they can do when they take a Shakespeare class with all the metaphors and analogies and references—but they begin to see it. And there is a sense of cohesiveness that is not present in the beginning of the semester. When you come back there is that extra look, an extra smile, an extra wave to students with whom you share the program. It is truly a bonding. It truly is. My face lights up to a Cambridge kid or a China kid more than to just another student from a class. Those are really good programs, and City College has really offered an opportunity to students. (Interview, 1989).

Roueche, Baker, and Rose (1989) stressed that transformational leaders set the tone for the organization, creating an environment where the capacity for leadership is enhanced and followers are empowered to lead in their own right. SBCC President Peter MacDougall is a leader who comprehends the essential nature of the leader-follower relationship and the critical need to establish the tone for the organization in order to shape the culture. He recognizes that he is most effective when he and his team collaborate to deal with an ever-changing external environment in an ongoing process of shared vision. He has surrounded himself with a team of equally committed, facilitative transformational leaders who also employ creative and innovative management techniques to empower their own divisional cadres of leader-followers.

Good Leadership

Good leadership communicates effectively, sets clear direction without managing too tightly, and supports the group, as opposed to poor leadership, which lacks effective planning, communication, and personal skills and is unclear about goals.

MacDougall has demonstrated a clarity of vision that facilitates adaptation to changes in the external environment. It is especially noteworthy that he is effective in articulating his vision in a fluent and symbolic way to his followers. Their shared vision, operationalized throughout the institution, has allowed SBCC faculty members and administrators to assume statewide leadership roles in a number of areas, particularly institutional research, matriculation, and student transfer.

SBCC relies heavily on its extensive, adeptly crafted, and thorough institutional research program as the basis for a powerful strategic planning process that is integrally linked to the delivery of academic and student support services. The overriding goal of the strategic planning process is to constantly improve and refine the teaching and learning process. The Institutional Research Committee, with members from both student services and instruction, provides vital data used in institutional planning and quality control analysis. When appropriate, SBCC joins with other community colleges to extend its research base and provide SBCC's research committee with additional funds and resources.

In summarizing this project's research findings, SBCC's Cohen and Friedlander (1989) stated that the primary objective was to provide colleges with a guide for establishing well-conceived assessment procedures and fair and meaningful course requisites that are consistent with the California Board of Governors' Matriculation Plan. Specific objectives were to:

- Establish requisites for entry-level, degree-applicable courses, based on assessment outcomes and including considerations of how to ensure that the setting of the requisites does not violate students' civil rights or have other illegal discriminatory impacts;

- Identify the combination of criteria that prove to be the best predictors of student success;
- Evaluate the reliability and validity of the criteria that faculty recommends as requisites of English, ESL, mathematics, and entry-level, degree-applicable courses;
- Develop a classification system for placing all entry-level, degree-applicable courses into categories that correspond to type and level of skill required for students to pass these courses;
- Determine the validity of the criteria used for predicting grades in courses for different groups of students;
- Develop a means for communicating to faculty, counselors, and students the probability of students' succeeding in particular courses based on assessment scores and educational background characteristics.

The research resulted in important recommendations and implications for improving institutional practices in the areas of assessment, orientation, advisement, instruction, and research. Both the research and the findings from the Approaches to Predicting Student Success Study are congruent with SBCC's own guiding principle for its Institutional Research Committee, which is to determine how the information that is gathered will affect college policy and/or practice at all levels. Before a research project is undertaken, questions are asked to determine whether the information will be used to improve instructional practices and/or will be used by the student services division to help students be more successful; whether the information is available from other sources; and what will be done with it once it is gathered. By asking these and other pertinent questions, Institutional Researcher Jack Friedlander maintains the institutional research process as a productive and facilitative mechanism for institutional improvement and resource allocation.

MacDougall's powerful transformational leadership has provided his followers with a staunch sense of direction and a clarity of mission. Through modeling and by consistently expressing the goals of excellence over an extended period of time, McDougall has instilled excellence for any project or issue with which the college has been involved. Its matriculation model was in place well before the California state legislature mandated matriculation statewide. Its teaching excellence project received state funding based on very competitive criteria. Ongoing staff revitalization and recommitment have also been fostered. All community colleges lack a career ladder for teachers, which often results in faculty stagnation and frustration. However, by encouraging creative and innovative concepts and suggestion for projects, SBCC leaders provide a variety of options to the faculty while also enriching classroom instruction. Karolyn Hanna, faculty senate president (Interview, 1989), said the confidence in the Academic Services Administration is well deserved. According to Hanna, faculty perceive that access to resources and support for ideas are based on the merit of the idea and/or request. Faculty also believe in thorough preparation and documentation of needs that are presented to faculty committees or the administration. Additionally, Hanna described the decision-making process as very open and participatory, with a free flow of information among the vice president and the deans as well as between the vice president and president.

Institutional endeavors are aimed at the improvement of instruction, student services, and/or student success; each has been achieved while maintaining the highest standard of excellence. MacDougall's creative and innovative management focuses on maintaining flexibility in positioning the organization strategically in uncertain and turbulent environments. He manages change while systematically weighing decisions against the shared vision and values. Since transfer education is a primary mission of the California Community College System, and since the number of students who transfer from a community college is an indicator of student success, MacDougall has steadfastly shaped SBCC to emphasize transfer education. Ninety-eight percent of those individuals interviewed agree that during the last few years SBCC has refocused institutional values and the institutional mission by increasingly emphasizing transfer. Cross describes this type of focus on transfer as the vertical focus, a "focus that can roughly be equated to emphasizing the transfer function of the comprehensive mission." According to Cross, colleges that have a vertical focus "offer the liberal arts courses needed for transfer to four-year institutions, stress student retention, offer transfer counseling services, conduct follow-up studies of students transferring to four-year colleges to see how well they performed, accept performance on standardized academic achievement tests as a critical dimension of quality, and develop opportunities for faculty members to articulate course content with their departmental peers in four-year colleges" (1988, p. 38).

Along with seventeen colleges statewide, SBCC was awarded state funding to establish a transfer center to assist students in transferring to four-year institutions. Since the majority of new SBCC students declare their educational goal as transfer, and since SBCC has one of the highest transfer rates in the state, transfer is clearly a primary component of SBCC's mission as a comprehensive community college.

Although the institutional commitment of SBCC to transfer manifests itself in a variety of areas, one of the major elements of the transfer function is dedicated cooperation and strong articulation of a 2+2+2 concept with both local high schools and four-year institutions. This broad commitment has been operationalized at four levels within the organization:

- Educational Leadership Coalition (ELC) is a collaboration of educational leaders convened to address the continuum of educating students from kindergarten through college graduation. The membership is composed of presidents and district superintendents of community secondary and post-secondary educational institutions and is chaired by MacDougall. Many of the members of the ELC also serve on the Executive Steering Committee for the Articulation Council.

- The membership of the Articulation Council Executive Steering Committee, also currently chaired by MacDougall, includes presidents and/or superintendents of Santa Barbara High School District, the neighboring district of Carpinterial Unified School District, Westmont College (a private four-year college), and, recently, the University of California at Santa Barbara. The Executive Steering Committee provides direction for the Articulation Council, approves projects, and allocates or develops resources to support projects to be undertaken by the Articulation Council.

- The Implementation Committee is chaired by SBCC Vice President of Academic Affairs John Romo, and membership includes site administrators from the member districts, faculty representatives, a parent representative, and an SBCC student representative. The Implementation Committee meets bimonthly to address issues that affect students who are moving through the overall educational structure. The goals of the Implementation Committee are to facilitate students' transition from one educational system to the next, to generate project ideas, and to facilitate the implementation of ideas generated by faculty in the schools. Additionally, Implementation Committee representatives fulfill a liaison function, informing appropriate staff about Articulation Council activities and projects.

- Subcommittees are made up of teachers, counselors, and administrators who implement joint projects. For example, subcommittees work out specific articulation agreements between like programs in the high schools, community colleges, and four-year institutions and plan college information visits to the high school campuses.

A specific outgrowth of the commendable accomplishments of this community-wide articulation effort is the newly developed 2+2+2 Nursing Program, which allows a student to move from an entry-level high school certified nurse assistant course into the Licensed Vocational Nursing Program cooperatively offered through the high school district and adult education office, and then into the Registered Associate Degree Nursing Program at SBCC, flowing potentially into a four-year bachelor's degree nursing program offered by a state university at a local satellite campus, and culminating in a master's degree nursing program provided by a California State University branch at a local hospital site. This meticulously constructed program is the consummation of careful course articulation and active involvement and sponsorship by local hospitals and includes a component of early outreach to junior high school students, especially ethnic minorities.

Challenge

Challenge is defined as challenging and meaningful work that feels important and contributory, contrasted with *organizational indifference*, the lack of psychological support for new ideas or creative work, apathy, and low expectations.

By its very nature, community college education involves a meaningful and challenging commitment to the processes of teaching students and providing open access. However, MacDougall never misses an opportunity to stress the institutional view that what happens in the teaching/ learning environment between students and faculty is at the crux of the institution. Teaching and learning are the reasons for the institution's existence. Every college operation and function is in place to contribute to students' success. Each institutional decision is analyzed by asking how it will serve students. Therefore, every organizational participant's commitment to serving students is constantly being reinforced.

Additionally, MacDougall meets with newly hired classified as well as certified personnel to acculturate them to the institutional values and mission, stressing their personal contribution to the "team effort." The formally structured two-day faculty orientation is another example of SBCC's commitment to the teaching/learning process as an essential and valued element of the organizational culture.

Sufficient Resources

Sufficient resources refers to access to appropriate and adequate resources, including people, funds, facilities, and information.

Information flows freely both up and down the SBCC organization. Administrators work hard at keeping their constituencies informed. MacDougall sends a constant stream of articles to the faculty and administrators from a wide variety of academic literature, bulletins from the Office of the State Chancellor, and current research reports. Most of the material he forwards includes a personal note. Underlining and annotations in his own handwriting indicate that he has read the material and is aware of how it relates to the recipient.

In the mid-1980s MacDougall saw a window of opportunity for master planning. Consequently, the SBCC facilities are currently undergoing renovation and expansion. New and renovated buildings include the recently completed Eli Luria Library and Learning Resource Center, an interdisciplinary facility currently under construction on the West Campus, a new student services building, a parking structure for which working drawings have been completed, a new campus bookstore that will double the capacity of the present facility, and a proposed Business Development Center. From about 1988 through 1990 state funds and self-generated funds from the SBCC Foundation were more plentiful than they had been for ten years. However, due to a dramatic decline in state revenues, future funding looks bleak throughout the state. Because of careful timing and planning, most of SBCC's renovation and expansion projects are in place.

Resources to provide initial funding for staff innovation remain limited, although access to resources is perceived as fair and equitable. Personal interviews and direct researcher observation in this study, however, indicated that both contingency funds to cover unanticipated costs and direct and indirect expenditure funds for establishing and sustaining innovative and creative projects (particularly those incorporating new computer technology) are stretched far too thinly. MacDougall and his administrative team recognize this problem and are working with the SBCC Foundation to aggressively seek external funding to supplement state revenue.

Encouragement

Encouragement reflects leaders' enthusiasm for new ideas, a non-evaluative atmosphere, a can-do mentality, and risk orientation, as contrasted with status quo thinking, which is an organizational emphasis on keeping things the same, avoiding risks, avoiding controversy, and taking the most conservative course.

Along with a multitude of highly successful creative and innovative undertakings, SBCC has ventured into some that have not been totally positive or benefitted the institution. Every SBCC administrator interviewed cited the Hotel, Restaurant, and Culinary (HRC) Project as both an institutional crisis and a creative and innovative undertaking.

An overview of the HRC crisis as it was spontaneously shared in interviews with members of the instructional administration indicated that for many years the department chairperson of SBCC's Hotel, Restaurant, and Culinary Program had advocated strengthening instruction by operating and managing a commercial hotel and restaurant staffed by students enrolled in the HRC Program. Committed to supporting the

HRC Program, for three years SBCC actively explored alternatives including student field placement and internships, direct purchase of a community facility, management of a site, leasing of a facility, and building the college's own facility. In 1986, a local hotel/restaurant property, a 114-room hotel with a very large upscale restaurant, became available. After careful legal and fiscal exploration and counsel, SBCC decided to lease the facility and establish an auxiliary corporation in order to protect the college and run the fiscal aspects of the operation. Within the first year of operation it became apparent that the project was not working. According to Vice President Romo:

> We just said that it was a noble idea that was ill-conceived, and we had to admit our mistake and let it go. Our position was that we could not run an operation that was not educationally sound for students. We stated that we were going to walk away from it. It was met with anger and frustration by the original lease holder, who threatened further action. It never came to that, however. Approximately $800,000 in the cafeteria fund was lost, and that does not account for the astronomical costs of administrative time throughout the operation.
>
> In my first year as vice president, the HRC came under my supervision. It consumed every hour of every day. I did all other aspects of the VP job at home at night. Jack Friedlander was dean of HRC, because in his first year on the job, he too was consumed by the program. All through it, Peter never blamed, never backed off; he hung in there. I was real impressed with his tenacity and being able to deal with everyone (Interview, 1989).

Notwithstanding, failure of the HRC project has not diminished SBCC's commitment to creativity and innovation. The college practice of supporting faculty innovation is reinforced by Kanter (1983), who, when comparing highly successful and less successful American corporations, determined that high-performing organizations develop a culture of pride and a climate of success. Kanter states that a culture of pride "is emotional and value commitment between person and organization; people feel that they 'belong' to a meaningful entity and can realize cherished values by their contributions" (p. 151). Interviewees at every level, from top administrators to classified employees, consistently expressed a feeling of pride in belonging to an excellent organization with a record of achievement. They felt that they were contributing members of a team rather than mere employees of a large organization.

The diversity of creative and innovative projects, both successful and unsuccessful, attests to the institution's enthusiasm for and support of new ideas. Innovation and creativity thrive on the SBCC campus, as demonstrated by projects such as the highly visible Santa Barbara City College Foundation, the recently funded Tomorrow's Teachers Program, the Transfer Achievement Program (TAP), and the Classroom Research Project to improve teaching effectiveness.

The SBCC Foundation provides a paramount example of MacDougall's building-block concept for inculcating a can-do mentality in the organizational culture. When MacDougall came to SBCC more than eight years ago, the foundation was administered on a part-time basis by a former staff member who had taken an early retirement. During the period of this retiree's involvement, the foundation, although modest, demonstrated increasing potential. By setting aside enough funds for seven months of salary, the college was able to hire the current director, Jim Minnow, an experienced full-time fund raiser. He was appointed with the stipulation that he would have to not only generate his own salary, but also concurrently undertake a major capital campaign to raise more than $2 million. The capital campaign was intended to provide the necessary match to state funding for construction of a new library and learning resource center, as well as a new social sciences classroom building. In addition, Minnow greatly expanded the foundation's role by assisting both academic and student services departments as they attempted their own fund-raising efforts.

In the fall of 1989, the foundation began a long-range capital campaign by developing plans through the year 2000. *The Santa Barbara City College Century Campaign: Toward the Year 2000* provides an overview of the college's accomplishments, educates foundation members about budgetary matters, and compares expenditures per student with both the state and university and the state college systems. It also notes

> . . . that state budgets provide campus administrators and planners with little flexibility to enhance, expand, and create important programs, provide significant scholarship assistance to students, reward excellent teaching and develop faculty incentives, enhance existing classrooms and laboratories, and install equipment which reflects current technology (Santa Barbara City College Foundation, 1989).

Toward the Year 2000 delineates several broad categories that require increased private financial support.

(a) The college seeks to establish endowed faculty chairs in several disciplines. The suggested amount required to endow a chair is $350,000, and the Foundation Director seeks to endow five new positions over the next five years.

(b) The college will endeavor to establish endowed professorships. These professorships would require endowments of $75,000 each and would provide the necessary supplemental financial support of each selected faculty member.

(c) Due to the excessively high cost of housing within a reasonable distance from the campus, Santa Barbara City College has been working and continues to work on a faculty housing subsidy plan, since the exorbitant cost of housing impedes SBCC's ability to compete in attracting the best faculty (Santa Barbara City College Foundation, 1989).

Another innovative project, Tomorrow's Teachers, has two strands. In the first strand, students, particularly those from underrepresented groups, who are interested in pursuing careers in teaching will be identified as early as the ninth grade. Participating local high schools will foster the students' interests through a teaching club, a summer education class between the 11th and 12th grades, and paid internships as teaching assistants in elementary schools. Upon acceptance by a four-year institution or SBCC, these students will receive financial aid. The second strand of the project will encourage employed instructional aides to pursue careers as teachers by providing tutorial support and financial assistance.

The importance of the teaching and learning environment, the classroom, is a major focus at SBCC. In interview notes for the 1989 Roueche, Baker, and Rose national leadership study, MacDougall stated:

> If we are really going to make a difference in our institutions, then we have got to involve our faculty. The power of research increases our ability to do this in pointing out just how influential the faculty members can be. If we can use the research by providing feedback to the faculty members that you really can make a difference. . . then this can be tremendously motivating for the faculty. . . . If we can show through our research how pivotal their position is, and work with them in developing ways they can utilize this potential to the greatest degree possible, it is going to make a big difference in our institution.

As an outgrowth of the institutional research referred to by MacDougall, SBCC submitted an instructional improvement proposal to the state, titled "Improvement of Student Learning and Retention Through Classroom Strategies," to help ten or fifteen faculty develop classroom behaviors demonstrated in research to be effective in making a difference in teaching and learning environments. By applying those behaviors with classroom teachers, SBCC anticipated that it would be possible to see what effects a systematic application of those behaviors might have on students' retention, grades, and satisfaction with instructional faculty. The project was not initially funded by the state, yet MacDougall made good his promise "to find the money somewhere to do this because I think this can be very important to us" (Interview, 1989).

The project proposal was revised based on a first self-funded year, resubmitted, and received state funding for the following year. The overall goal of the project's second year was to increase student success and retention in selected courses through the implementation of one or more innovative instructional strategies in the classroom setting. In the 1988–89 academic year, faculty representatives from seven of the nine instructional divisions participated in the project. They reported gaining expertise in new instructional strategies, expanding their ability as facilitators of learning in the classroom, improving the level of their personal satisfaction and fulfillment from the classroom experience, and gaining a deepened sense of being a participant in the collegial community. While some of the participants' projects markedly improved retention and more productive student performance, others did not generate objective data to support participants' positive subjective experiences. However, in all cases, there was a perceptible sense of change in student satisfaction with learning, accompanied by a significant increase in faculty members' satisfaction with teaching.

Certainly the instructional improvement project warranted the institutional commitment of initial start-up funds that ultimately resulted in state funding. Literature on creative and innovative management (Amabile and Gryskiewicz, 1987; Kanter, 1988; Peters and Waterman, 1982; Kuhn, 1985) stresses the importance of providing resources to nurture and support creativity and innovation by underwriting new projects. In a time of statewide fiscal restraint, SBCC has carefully allocated budget resources to support innovation. Unlike funds for many colleges throughout the state, revenue generated from the state lottery does not all go into the institution's general fund to cover the costs of operations (including salaries). A portion of the SBCC lottery funds is set aside specifically for discretionary funding of new projects. Although resources may be limited, faculty access is perceived as fair and equitable. Allocation of resources in this manner transmits a powerful message to the organization; creativity and innovation will be supported and rewarded with resources.

Recognition

Recognition consists of the general sense that creative/innovative work will receive appropriate feedback, support, recognition, and reward, whereas inappropriate evaluation includes too much criticism of new ideas or work; work that is evaluated on external criteria, not on the value of the work itself; and lack of feedback on work.

MacDougall consistently acknowledges the efforts of everyone who contributes to meetings, events, projects, and virtually all activities on the campus. He sends personal handwritten notes as well as formal and informal memos to individual faculty members, members of the administration, and citizens of the community, expressing his appreciation for their efforts. He is visible on the campus, taking every opportunity to interact with the staff and to verbally express his thanks for their hard work and commitment. MacDougall has expanded the college's formal recognition process with numerous symbolic avenues for honoring both students and college staff for outstanding achievement. Premier among these is the college's annual report, *The Community College: A Mission of Excellence,* a beautifully illustrated celebration of instructional improvement at SBCC. The report describes innovative teaching methodology and research activities by the institution's distinguished faculty. In his introduction to the eighth annual edition, MacDougall states that

> Excellence, for an individual or an organization, persists when motivation and commitment combine with opportunities for revitalization. Santa Barbara City College is committed to assuring that the teaching/learning process is our central focus and that we strive for its continuing improvement.... With pride, the College acknowledges individual faculty members who have worked to improve the teaching/learning process at the College. These individuals exemplify the commitment of Santa Barbara City College to excellence in our educational programs and services (Santa Barbara City College, 1989, p. 5).

Sufficient Time

Sufficient time refers to adequate time to develop creative solutions to problems/challenges, contrasted with insufficient time, characterized by too heavy a workload in too little time.

SBCC has innovative projects underway throughout the campus. Personal interviews and direct observation indicated that staff at every level feel overtaxed and overburdened with an ever-increasing workload and an unrelenting demand for creative and innovative projects that contribute to the college mission. MacDougall and Friedlander (1989) stated that staff overextension, burn-out, and resentment can result from the following conditions: "(a) the same administrators and faculty members are asked to assume responsibility for an innovation year after year; (b) staff members are not provided with adequate release time and/or resources to develop and implement the innovation; (c) no additional funds are available to relieve staff members of the excessive workload they endure during the early stages of the project, or to accommodate the increased work activity resulting from the success of their program; (d) the workloads of support staff are not taken into account in decisions to add new programs at the institution; and (e) unrealistic goals are set for the innovation" (p. 257).

All of the above conditions exist not only at SBCC, but also at all ten innovative community colleges included in the MacDougall and Friedlander study.

Other Organizational Characteristics

Aspects of the overall organizational culture that are not addressed above include a cooperative and collaborative atmosphere, good organizational communication, the valuing of creativity, and systematic strategic planning and decision making. These positive characteristics are contrasted with environmental obstacles such as inappropriate competition within the organization, inappropriate reward systems, lack of support from other areas, overly formal and bureaucratic procedures, little regard for creativity, and an overly political atmosphere.

SBCC was consistently described by interviewees as an organization with a stimulating environment, one that challenged, yet supported, individuals and their ideas. MacDougall is aware that bureaucratic compliance demands from the state can create environmental obstacles to effective functioning and creative and innovative management. He has publicly pledged to advocate a reduction of unnecessary compliance documentation at the state level, and he has directed his administrative team to consolidate the workload to reduce unnecessary duplication wherever possible and to delegate decision making to the lowest level possible.

Conclusion

Leadership behaviors contributing to creativity and innovation have emerged in the literature as generative components of effective organizational cultures and organizational renewal (Kanter, 1983; Peters, 1988; Peters and Waterman, 1982; Roueche and Baker, 1987). Renewal, revitalization, and recommitment are required antidotes to the national organizational epidemic of apathy, escalating environmental turbulence, and uncertainty perniciously infecting organizations in the mature phase of their life cycles.

Studies (Cross and Fideler, 1989; Roueche, Baker, and Rose, 1989; AACJC Commission on the Future of Community Colleges, 1988) have observed that community colleges are clearly moving from the growth phase of their developmental life cycle to the maturity phase, distinguished by a slower pace of growth, ambivalence in the larger community about their role and mission, and competing internal priorities. Tichy and Devanna (1986) warned that if organizations do not consciously intervene to cultivate institutional renewal and revitalization, the next stage in the organizational life cycle is decline. Numerous studies have attempted to diagnose various aspects of the problem of reinvigorating organizations drifting toward decline, yet many merely conclude by describing the threat of impending disaster if change does not occur.

The case study of SBCC was designed to explicate the essential character, nature, and meaning of creativity and innovation as it is present in a mature community college organizational culture. The study focused on those variables that foster creativity and innovation as catalysts for organizational renewal and revitalization and contribute to an institution's adaptability and responsiveness. SBCC provides a powerful model of an organizational culture with shared values at every level. Its strong culture was evident in organizational rites, rituals, and symbols. Institutional structures and processes of governance, strategic planning, and decision making, which reflect the institutional mission and values, have been intentionally and effectively shaped by the leadership.

This study of a creative and innovative community college's organizational culture has indicated directions for consciously rethinking and restructuring organizational culture to accomplish revitalization and renewal. Yet it has raised several unanswered questions that were beyond the scope and methodology of the research design for this study. Additional research in several areas could test and expand the findings of this study and would enhance the growing body of literature on organizational culture in the community college: (1) a similar case study (or studies) of other community colleges that have been ranked among the leading institutions in creativity and innovation; (2) a study of the organizational culture of SBCC compared with the organizational cultures of other colleges with recognized institutional leaders in innovation; and (3) a comparative study of community college organizational structures as stimulants or obstacles to innovation and creativity.

Community colleges throughout the nation now must choose between organizational decline or conscious commitment to organizational renewal. This study of Santa Barbara City College, a community college that has successfully made the leap from maturity to revitalization, demonstrates the importance of creativity and innovation as forces that drive organizational vitality and renewal.

■

Chapter 8

Cultural Leadership:
The Founder

By Phyllis Barber

I
n the 1990s the need for leadership in the nation's community colleges
is especially critical as they are faced with replacing growing numbers
of retiring presidents. Many of those retiring founded the institutions
they'll be leaving—founded them during the years of stability, prosperity,
and growth in the 1960s. Their successors will face a vastly different environment—one marked by competition for scarce resources and turbulence.

In guiding organizational change, new community college presidents
of the 1990s should take their cue from effective leadership behaviors in
the corporate world. They should also study effective leadership behaviors
exhibited by founding and succeeding presidents at excellent community colleges. To that end, this chapter presents a case study of a founding
president, Richard H. Hagemeyer, at a celebrated community college—
Central Piedmont Community College, Charlotte, North Carolina—and
Chapter Nine examines his successor, Ruth G. Shaw.

The Blueprint for the Case Study

Conducting a case study of Central Piedmont and its presidential
succession provided the opportunity to chronicle and render factual information; to examine social, political, individual, and organizational
phenomena; and to engage in evaluation and interpretation (Yin, 1989).
Among the data sources of the study were administrative documentation (e.g., progress reports, annual reports; letters, memoranda, and other
communiques; agendas, announcements, minutes, written reports of
events; formal studies or evaluations of the site; and newsclippings and
articles appearing in the media); archival records (e.g., organizational
records, budgets, organizational charts, survey data previously collected

about the site, and lists of names); direct on-site observation; participant observation; historical profiles of the founding and the succeeding president; and, following the presidents' interviews, interviews of a purposive sample of individuals who had served with one president or both.

A combination of Critical Incident and Behavioral Events interview techniques were employed. The depth interviewing (Patton, 1987), pursued through a structured, field-tested interview guide, afforded the researcher the opportunity to observe thoughts, attitudes, and feelings; to note the manner in which interviewees had organized the world and attached meaning to what goes on within it; and to learn about behaviors that took place at earlier points in time.

Data were analyzed using the theoretical frameworks of Schein (1985a) and Bass (1985a, 1985b). Schein (1985a) asserts:

> Organizational cultures are created by leaders, and one of the most decisive functions of leadership may well be the creation, the management, and—if and when that may become necessary—the destruction of culture. Culture and leadership, when one examines them closely, are two sides of the same coin, and neither can really be understood by itself. In fact, there is a possibility—underemphasized in leadership research—that the *only thing of real importance that leaders do is to create and manage culture* and that the unique talent of leaders is their ability to work with culture (p. 2).

Additionally, Schein contends that leaders must develop an understanding of the organizational life cycle, the distinct functions of culture within each phase of the life cycle, and the mechanisms of change required by each phase in order to initiate and influence culture.

To assess Central Piedmont's culture according to Schein's theoretical framework, the data were examined to determine the organization's basic assumptions about its relationship to its environment, about the nature of truth and reality, about human nature, about human activity, and about the nature of human relationships (Schein, 1985a). Data were also examined to determine the use of primary and secondary mechanisms for embedding and reinforcing culture as identified by Schein (1985a) and detailed in Chapter One.

To determine the extent to which the leadership behaviors of each president influenced the development of the organization's culture and organizational change, data regarding each president's leadership behaviors were simultaneously examined from the perspective of Bass's (1985a, 1985b) theoretical framework of leadership. That framework differentiates transactional and transformational behaviors and provides an environmental milieu in which each might arise:

In a well-structured environment with clear and strong norms, sanctions, and institutions in which the social and economic status quo is reasonably satisfying, more of the leadership which occurs is likely to be transactional. On the other hand, in distressed societies, whose institutions are unable to cope with violations of expectations and need dissatisfactions, more of the leadership which emerges is likely to be transformational (p. 154).

Bass (1985a) asserts that in times of distress or rapid change—the current environment of the corporate and community college worlds—transformational leadership arises; times of stability foster transactional leadership. Tichy and Devanna (1986) posit that it is the transformational leader with an ability to recognize the need for revitalization, to create a new vision, and to institutionalize change who is best able to transform organizations in unpredictable times.

Bass (1985a) identifies five categories of behaviors: contingent reinforcement, management-by-exception, consideration, intellectual stimulation, and charisma with a subfactor of inspirational leadership. Indicative of the transactional leader is a preponderance of contingent reinforcement and management-by-exception; indicative of the transformational leader is a preponderance of consideration, intellectual stimulation, and charismatic/inspirational leadership. Bass (1985a) asserts that individual leaders can exhibit both behaviors, "but in different amounts" (p. 22).

The Founding President: Establishing the College's Culture

In writing about organizational culture formation, Ott (1989) isolates three sources or determinants of organizational culture: the broader societal culture in which the organization resides; the nature of the organization's business environment or business; and the values, basic assumptions, and beliefs of the founder or early dominant leaders—a determinant of foremost importance as articulated by organizational behavior and leadership theorists Bennis (1989) and Schein (1985a). The formation of the culture of Central Piedmont Community College reflects each of the three determinants, with the influence of the founder predominating. What became the shared values of the college were essentially the values, basic assumptions, and beliefs of the founder.

On September 17, 1963, Richard H. Hagemeyer joined a newly formed state system of community colleges in North Carolina. The state system held beliefs about community colleges that essentially mirrored Hagemeyer's own beliefs; both believed in providing each student the opportunity to learn at his or her own pace, in reaching each student in the classroom regardless of his or her level, and in meeting the community's needs.

Indeed, Hagemeyer envisioned that the concerted efforts of the right group of people could forge, from Mecklenburg College and the state's industrial education center located in Charlotte, the new educational enterprise for which the state and legislation called—a comprehensive community college, specifically, Central Piedmont Community College.

The specific vision of how to create a comprehensive community college—a new service and product in the marketplace—Schein (1983b) characterizes as entrepreneurial. As Schein (1985a), Ott (1989), and Bennis (1989) describe as typical of most founders, Hagemeyer brought his entrepreneurial vision and his strategy of excellence with him from his past.

For ten years prior to coming to Charlotte, Hagemeyer had been an administrative staff member at Henry Ford Community College in Dearborn, Michigan—a comprehensive community college Hagemeyer (Interview, 1989) called "one of the real pioneers." Although Central Piedmont was to be a comprehensive community college, Hagemeyer's vision, emanating from his Henry Ford experience, was that the core mission of Central Piedmont was to meet the articulated needs of business and industry by training students in job-related skills for the current and emerging job market. In Charlotte-Mecklenburg, Hagemeyer's vision and the second cultural determinant—the nature of Central Piedmont's "business" and the "business" environment of Central Piedmont—found a match.

Another aspect of Hagemeyer's vision resulted from his success at Henry Ford Community College in starting and coordinating the college's training program for Ford Motor Company. According to Hagemeyer, it was one of "old Henry Ford's pet projects" (Interview, 1989), replete with unique teaching methodologies and training materials. Undergirding this aspect of his vision were the beliefs that (1) educational truth in the community college came most often not from educational theories and methodologies, but from experience in business and industry; and (2) because of the nontraditional nature of the student population and the mission of the community college, traditional teaching methodologies were ineffective and the educational status quo should be challenged.

Another influence on Hagemeyer's vision came directly from the culture of the Ford Motor Company, where he worked prior to Henry Ford Community College. Hagemeyer was part of a strong culture driven by the vision of Ford Motor Company founder Henry Ford I.

Henry Ford I was the monarch of an empire that was ruled by a "bizarre combination of feudal laws, naked power" (Collier and Horowitz, 1987, p. 201) and by the man who was Ford's "other self," Harry Bennett (Collier and Horowitz, 1987, p. 157). Authority and control were centralized at Ford Motor Company because of Ford's belief that the only decisions of value were those that came from the pioneering spirit that he represented—a spirit that championed visionary innovation against safer, less exciting alternatives (Lacey, 1986). Ford paid little attention to the structure of the company, dismissing it with his heavily transactional belief in "no organization, no specific duties attaching to any position, no line of succession or authority, very few titles, and no conferences" (Ford and Crowther, 1922, p. 207).

Henry Ford I and Harry Bennett shared a view about financial reports: "You never know what someone will do with one of these" (Collier and Horowitz, 1987, p. 202). Consultants working for Henry Ford II under the direction of Charles B. "Tex" Thorton, who had been hired for his financial expertise, asked a member of the controller's office for his projection of some figures in six months' time. The consultants in turn were asked, most seriously, "What would you like them to be?" (Collier and Horowitz, 1987, p. 218). These cultural aspects had a marked influence on the vision Hagemeyer brought to Central Piedmont.

With a clear vision about what the nature of Central Piedmont should be as a community college and the kind of instructional approaches it should take, Hagemeyer began the process of culture formation. As outlined by Schein (1985a), Hagemeyer began by bringing into the college a core group that shared his initial vision, or as Ott (1989) expresses it, were "strongly predisposed to accepting it" (p. 88). Hagemeyer said he "was very fortunate because I was able to locate people, or they located us, who were really wanting to become a part of something that was different" (Interview, 1989).

The Board of Trustees was in place at the time Hagemeyer was named president, and its members, strong politically and powerful in the community, provided additional core support. Hagemeyer also sought support within the community, according to Assistant to the President Worth Campbell (Interview, 1990), by "working on public relations, spending a good deal of time talking about what [Central Piedmont] could do."

To this, he added his structure for success. From the beginning, as people were brought in to form Central Piedmont's core, a centralization of authority and control existed that mirrored the Ford Motor Company's industrial organizational culture. As Hagemeyer explained, "When we first started, I don't think we had a structure, and I jokingly remarked that I even ordered the toilet paper" (Interview, 1989).

Bill McIntosh joined Central Piedmont in 1962, when it was still the Central Industrial Education Center, as department head of data processing and electronics. He was serving as vice president of educational planning and evaluation when Hagemeyer retired, and he related that with

Hagemeyer's level of involvement "he was the architect of educational programs; he was the architect of the student development program" (Interview, 1990). Bill Claytor (Interview, 1990), a member of the Board of Trustees for thirteen years who was serving as board chair when Hagemeyer retired, indicated "he was basically the sole decision maker of most every decision that had to be made at Central Piedmont." As Hagemeyer (Interview, 1989) expressed it, "I had my fingers in everything to avoid where I had to delegate it."

Hagemeyer ensured retention of authority and control, the essence of his entrepreneurial leadership style, by fashioning the responsibilities of administrative positions after what he had observed in business and industry. The people whom Hagemeyer brought in, as he explained it, "were people who had experience in various other places, but not this kind of experience" (Interview, 1989). Recruiting people who had excellent administrative experience but no experience in the type of institution he envisioned kept his expertise and experience in the new venture paramount and authority and control centered in the office of the president.

This carefully constituted core group, composed of a Board of Trustees and a small number of faculty, staff, and administrators, under Hagemeyer's leadership and following his vision, began to act in concert, creating an organization, building a common history, and arriving at cultural elements. Cultural elements are learned solutions to external adaptation and internal integration that come through positive problem solving or anxiety-avoidance (Schein, 1984). Anxiety-avoidance plays an extremely important role in culture formation because of the anxiety created by the human need for cognitive consistency and order apparent in the cognitive maps of an established culture, and because of the anxiety associated with hostile environmental conditions that may result from something different and new and with social relationships that are unstable.

According to Schein (1984), founders and early leaders of organizations provide most of the cultural solutions in new organizations. Hagemeyer diffused for his followers much of the anxiety that accompanies doing something different: according to McIntosh (Interview, 1990), board members, faculty, staff, and administrators deferred to Hagemeyer's experience, expertise, and self-confidence.

Hagemeyer's entrepreneurial vision—a vision shaped by success in his past—became a most important facet in the acting, creating, and building processes. His goal of educational excellence, with its heavy emphasis on occupational education and service to business and industry and its challenge to traditional teaching methodologies and the educational status quo, drove what had to be done and provided cultural solutions.

The college succeeded in solving external problems of adaptation and internal problems of creating a workable set of relationship rules. For example, from 1964 to 1967 the college saw a 280 percent increase in enrollment, and the budget nearly doubled. In 1969 the college received initial accreditation (Warren, 1988) and later that year was invited to join the League for Innovation in the Community College. This invitation demonstrates that the educational status quo was successfully challenged with what were at the time considered to be innovative teaching and learning methodologies—the use of audio and video tapes that permitted individualized instruction at the student's own pace.

The college's success is directly attributable to the basic assumptions contained in Hagemeyer's vision of the organization's relationship to its environment, the nature of truth and reality, and the nature of human activity. These basic assumptions become the foundation for shared cultural assumptions or values around which a college's culture takes shape (Schein, 1985a). With their base in anxiety-reduction, the cultural assumptions that are formed possess a high degree of stability (Schein, 1984).

Embedding and Reinforcing the Culture

As he had in establishing his core group within the college, Hagemeyer made human resource selections carefully. In embedding and reinforcing culture, he used "one of the most subtle yet most potent ways in which culture gets embedded and perpetuated" (Schein, 1985a, p. 235)—the hiring process. He continued to hire those who were compatible with the organizational culture. By paying attention to, measuring, and controlling hiring, he demonstrated another of the primary embedding and reinforcing mechanisms. Criteria applied in the promotion process emphasized personal affinity with the organizational culture.

An examination of organizational charts from a historical perspective reveals that the organization of the college followed an initial mixture of models from education and from business and industry, moving in the 1970s more to the industrial model. The initial mixture gave Hagemeyer latitude in pursuing a "promotion-from-within policy" (Interview, 1989). Hagemeyer explained the relationship of the changing titles on the organizational chart, promotion, and the criteria used for promotion:

> There is a saying that I think everyone agrees to and that is, 'The person who is granting the title doesn't think too much about it, but the person who is getting the title thinks it is very important.' So, in the movement throughout the growth period, a lot of people ended up in positions that they made, that five years

before they would have never thought that they could have had. But, they had really produced. The opportunity was there, and they had grown to the point where they could fit in. And suddenly they ended up with titles that they could brag about. And that's good for morale (Interview, 1989).

Promotion of this nature led to ten vice presidents on the organizational chart prior to Hagemeyer's retirement/resignation.

While business and industry experts might have examined that final organizational chart for problems of span of control, span of control was not an issue for Central Piedmont. Selection and promotion of this nature, as posited by Schein (1985a), serve as "powerful mechanisms for embedding and perpetuating the culture" (p. 236). As Hagemeyer (Interview, 1989) reflected:

It is the concept of span of control, according to theory, which limits the number of people one leader is expected to supervise, but what happens when you have different people doing different things with different ideas? Yet, if everybody is in tune, and they all are in agreement concerning what they want to do, and they have a similar philosophy, it's not really a problem. When the same kind of people live together for a long time, you pretty much know what the other person is going to do.... The continuity that we were able to develop and maintain enhanced our program immensely.

Continuity at the managerial level can be noted in the fact that upon Hagemeyer's retirement, "of the ten or twelve top people that I had surrounding me...the least time on staff of that group was seven years, the next one was eleven years" (Interview, 1989). In essence, Hagemeyer used the primary culture embedding and reinforcing mechanisms of recruitment, selection, promotion, retirement, and excommunication; status and reward; and what a leader does or does not pay attention to, measure, and control. He combined these with the secondary mechanism, as identified by Schein (1985a), of organization design and structure to maintain within Central Piedmont a coherence in thinking, philosophy, vision, cultural assumptions, and values.

Using Organizational Systems and Procedures

Hagemeyer used another of Schein's (1985a) secondary mechanisms for embedding and reinforcing culture—organizational systems and procedures that reflect cultural assumptions. Systems and procedures for communication, decision making, college planning and development, budgeting, and staff development were generated around the organizational design and structure that Hagemeyer shaped through early hiring practices and through retention of authority and control in the office of the president. As such, organizational systems and procedures provided signals to followers regarding what Hagemeyer did or did not pay attention to, measure, and control.

Communication and Decision Making

In the early days of the college, communication as a whole was quite informal and most often oral. Hagemeyer's communication with all segments of the college—administrators, faculty, staff, and students—was informal and personal. He walked around, talked to people, and invited people to drop by his office. He established social relationships with administrators, faculty, and staff by entertaining in his home.

As Central Piedmont grew, Hagemeyer became socially distant, following the industrial model, according to McIntosh (Interview, 1990). Hagemeyer's regular visits around campus were less frequent, and invitations to his office declined except for specific matters of business, which established greater distance. However, Cindy Johnston, who joined Central Piedmont in 1976 as a part-time instructor and was serving as department head of Adult Basic Literacy Education (ABLE) when Hagemeyer retired, indicated that his communication with her and her department remained direct. As she explained, "If [Hagemeyer] was interested, I mean if he was really interested and committed to something, I think he went whole-heartedly into that" by maintaining direct communication (Interview, 1990).

Communication as a whole, despite changes promoted by the growth of the college, never lost the organizational structure and design characteristic of authority and control at the top. For example, organizational charts reflected specific vertical lines of reporting and responsibility. Research indicates that the protocol of reporting lines often was not followed. Vice presidents, directly responsible to the executive vice president, would bypass their line of reporting by "going directly to Hagemeyer," said Joe Barwick, a member of the English Department who served as president of the faculty senate during Hagemeyer's administration (Interview, 1990). According to former Executive Vice President Gayle Simmons, Campbell, and McIntosh (Interviews, 1990), vice presidents realized that Hagemeyer ultimately held authority and control and made the decisions. This condoned management activity did much to perpetuate Hagemeyer's early hands-on approach with its centralized authority and control.

When Hagemeyer asked someone for input into a decision, Barwick (Interview, 1990) reported that "what he really wanted was affirmation of the decision he'd already made." According to Barwick, most frequently input was sought from someone who would have a key role to play in the implementation of the decision.

Outside of the offices of the president and the executive vice president, the only formal collegewide structure for communicating and gathering information for decision making was, as Hagemeyer explained, "...what we called a Cabinet. It was the top people with whom I interacted on a daily basis. They reported back and forth" (Interview, 1989). Educational areas, budget responsibility centers, and departments, for example, met infrequently, if at all, reported Barwick (Interview, 1990) and Administrative Secretary Judy Smith (Interview, 1990). The faculty senate met once a month, and as Barwick commented, "Although Hagemeyer wanted a senate, valued a senate, ... he had a little bit of difficulty with it because there's no line there [of organizational reporting] so he could actually control it" (Interview, 1990). The Cabinet met weekly.

It is important to point out that a fit with the organizational culture at large does not always ensure a perfect fit with the culture of subgroups within an organization (Schein, 1985a; Ott, 1989). Such was the case with the Hagemeyer Cabinet. On occasion, some socialization of Cabinet members took place. As explained by Ott (1989), the socialization process is a learning process in which individuals learn appropriate behavior for their positions through interactions with those who have normative beliefs about the roles of those individuals and the authority to reward or punish. Commitment and satisfaction of the individuals are created by narrowing the gap between organizational and individual expectations.

Carrietta Adkins, who joined the college in 1984 as director of staff development and was serving in that capacity when Hagemeyer retired, learned from observing the interactions of the Cabinet that

> Things didn't happen in an open forum. They happened through negotiation, behind the scenes. So, if I wanted something, I was not going to risk being embarrassed publicly at the Cabinet meeting. I got it all worked out ahead of the meeting and set a time with him to discuss the issue, so that when it was presented publicly it was de facto. Hagemeyer supports it. That's it (Interview, 1990).

Hagemeyer also provided an example of socialization as it was used with the Cabinet:

> We taught people that we met every Wednesday morning and we'd talk. Again, we ran this in a very businesslike way. One or two people learned the hard way that when we said we started

at eight o'clock, we did. One particular person came in a little later twice, and everybody kind of looked at that person. I spoke to her at another time. I said, "We're starting at eight o'clock." The next morning the door was locked, and she was never late again (Interview, 1989).

Effective socialization led to effective cultural fit; people were socialized to share information rather than to question, which Ott (1989) posits can contribute to organizational rigidity and overconformance. By creating an environment where competition among staff members could flourish, the Cabinet kept Hagemeyer apprised about the activities of the college's various administrative units, infrequently raising issues for discussion or question.

The manner in which the Cabinet (and the organization as a whole) was consistently asked by Hagemeyer to determine what Schein (1985a) calls the nature of truth and reality provides additional insight into communication, decision making, and governance processes.

It was Hagemeyer's basic assumption that the people with whom he worked were rational individuals. For example, when suggesting ideas that challenged traditional teaching methodologies and the educational status quo, he believed that "people will enthusiastically support change if they are given a good rationale or they are convinced that it is worthwhile to try it and given the support to try it" (Interview, 1989). While talking about motivating members of the college community whom he attempted to influence, such as Cabinet members, Hagemeyer (Interview, 1989) noted:

> It's just communicating with them with ideas that make sense and letting their own good judgment make the decision. I think a president has to be a salesperson. You have to sell ideas, and the ideas have to be sound ideas.

He could reveal truth and sell it rather than lead others to discover it. He would "lay out the facts and say, 'Okay, now just use your common sense. Does this make sense?'" (Interview, 1989). To Hagemeyer explanations played a key role:

> Basically, if you attempt to explain, they might not agree, but if you can explain it correctly or reasonably, reasonable people will usually come up with reasonable decisions (Interview, 1989).

Not wishing to seem unreasonable, Cabinet members, for example, maintained the informative/reporting nature of Cabinet meetings, and Hagemeyer conducted these meetings taking no votes, according to interviews with Hagemeyer (1989), Dean of General Studies Dave Hunter (1990), McIntosh (1990), and Simmons (1990). As Hagemeyer expressed it:

> None of that. Democracy is wonderful, but somebody has to make the decision. So, we would have enough discussion so that you'd get a feel of how people thought. . . . You begin to feel there's logic in this over here, and that's what you base your decision on (Interview, 1989).

As Barwick (Interview, 1990) reported, "It was always clear that Hagemeyer made the decision, which affected a lot of the discussion."

In 1990 interviews, Johnston, Barwick, and Adkins said the operation of this formal structure in collegewide communication and decision making—and the lack of involvement of others at the college in systems of communication and decision making through committees or task forces, for example—created the awareness that communication and decision making were "top-down" and that all decisions were made by Hagemeyer. Hagemeyer was cognizant of the comments such an awareness created, and he countered those comments by speaking to the strength of socialization and acculturation:

> Nothing could be farther from the truth. The people who were directly around me knew how the decisions were being made. A lot of [the decisions] were exactly what [I] wanted to have done, but it wasn't because I forced them. Over a period of time the philosophies of people had to get conditioned so that we were thinking as a team. So, if they had heard me say something very strongly five years before, and all of a sudden something comes up and it's decided the way I would have decided the situation five years before, I didn't have anything to do with it (Interview, 1989).

Hagemeyer met in settings with the college at large for the purposes of information sharing, according to Smith (Interview, 1990) and Chris Buchanan, who joined Central Piedmont in 1969 as the executive secretary to the executive vice president and was serving as administrative assistant to Hagemeyer when he retired (Interview, 1990). In doing so, Hagemeyer sent what Schein (1985a) characterizes as some of the most important signals about those things to which he paid attention. Large group meetings were held, according to Hagemeyer:

> . . . when we had something that could justify calling everybody together. We didn't have meetings just to meet. For example, we had so much, as you know, of our financial situation imposed

on us by the state, and we had certain rules and regulations and policies that we followed. We had to describe these so people could understand them (Interview, 1989).

His attention at these college-at-large small- and large-group meetings concentrated on providing budgets, policies, procedures, rules, and regulations, explained Smith (Interview, 1990).

College growth increased the need for formal written communication, and to that end a newsletter, *The Communicator*, was developed. As Simmons (Interview, 1990) explained, *The Communicator* "was started as an avenue of required reading. Anything that was in it was something that it was the responsibility of all employees to read, and they couldn't excuse themselves by saying, 'Well, I didn't know.' " Its function was to explain, in writing, changes in policies and procedures at the state and college level, provide information about guidelines and regulations, furnish models for the completion of forms, and so forth, according to Simmons, Smith, and Buchanan (Interviews, 1990).

Planning and Staff Development

From the outset, most college planning and development, both short- and long-range, were done informally by individuals inside and outside of the college in conjunction with Hagemeyer. For example, no formal short-range planning documents for facilities or education were developed during Hagemeyer's twenty-three years as president, and only three formal long-range planning documents were developed.

The first formal planning document, which contained enrollment projections for the period 1964–70, was developed by Hagemeyer and presented to the Board of Trustees on January 6, 1964. The second formal planning document, *Report: College Location and Future Expansion* (1965), was a "Master Plan for Expansion" (Central Piedmont Community College, April 30, 1965)—a facilities plan. McIntosh (Interview, 1990) described Hagemeyer's role in the development of the Master Plan for Expansion as "visionary. . . . Ninety-five percent of [the Master Plan for Expansion] is exactly like Central Piedmont is now. . . . [Hagemeyer] seemed to have a real grasp of the community, what it could do, what it would do." Hagemeyer's hands-on management led him to serve as the project engineer for the first two buildings erected on the campus under that master plan: Terrell, the administration building, and Mecklenburg Hall (later named Van Every), a general classroom building. Also exemplary of his hands-on management in planning is the absence of full-board participation in formal planning sessions to discuss the recommendations of the master plan. Planning sessions were promised when the plan was introduced to the board in February, but the plan was approved at the next board meeting in April without those full-board sessions.

A third planning document also reflected Hagemeyer's hands-on management. It exhibited his affinity for the world of business and industry, his belief that the business and industrial world held educational truths for the community college, and his belief in the need to challenge traditional teaching methodologies and the educational status quo.

As Hagemeyer (Interview, 1990) indicated, the third planning document was "developed in a very unique way." Rather than have the college use what Hagemeyer described as the traditional method of planning in higher education, which was to

> bring in some other people from higher education and have them advise you as to the planning that you should do and assist you in making a plan. . . we enlisted the support of industry and business and the military. The idea was that we anticipated, at that time, that the traditional methods and the traditional ways of education would have to change in order to meet the needs of the next decade. Industry and business had already faced these problems, and we thought that we could learn a great deal from them (Interview, 1990).

The *Long-Range Planning Report*, therefore, represented more than the opinions of education. According to Hagemeyer (Interview, 1990):

> We had three consultants from the traditional areas—that is, higher education. But we also had consultant help from companies such as IBM. . . and also the military because they all had faced the problem of providing instructional services to people in ways other than just bringing them to a central location, but instead taking it to them where it was more convenient for the learner. We anticipated that would be the wave of the future; and since they had already worked in those areas, we felt that was the way we could have the soundest base for the programming or the plan that we were developing.

The opinions of the educational, business, industry, and military consultants were placed, along with the reports of three advisory committees and five steering committee members, as appendices to the report. As Hagemeyer's memorandum of transmittal of the report to the Board of Trustees indicated, the appendices material was being "presented here as back-up for the recommendations of the administration" (Hagemeyer, 1974). Faculty and staff involvement in the report was, as it had been in the previous two formal planning documents, minimal.

Hagemeyer (Interview, 1990) recounted that he considered the content of the report "significant. . .because it charted the course for the development of the institution really right to the early parts of 1980." He credited the plan with setting "the stage for our working with and involving ourselves in a leadership position in the innovative ways by which instruction is presented to students"—setting Central Piedmont's strategy of excellence based on his inculturated founding assumption that traditional methodologies and the educational status quo were to be challenged.

A formal program of staff development was a later addition to the systems and procedures of Central Piedmont. Barwick (Interview, 1990) said Hagemeyer saw staff development as "primarily a way of giving people the skills to carry out the kinds of things he wanted carried out." According to Adkins, the staff development projects that Hagemeyer assigned her did just that. They were generally narrowly defined and parochial in vision. His hands-on management was reflected by the fact that he would make a check-off list of expected behavior, she said (Interview, 1990). He would use the same check-off system for projects that she developed for which she observed a need.

Budgeting

Budget matters followed the model of business and industry. Established with the hiring of a comptroller in the first years, budgeting was controlled in the offices of the top administrators and was not altered significantly as the college grew. Budget making was in the hands of the comptroller and Simmons, the executive vice president; budget allocation decisions were in the hands of Hagemeyer.

According to Barwick (Interview, 1990), "Nobody ever knew quite where the money was; department heads, vice presidents, nobody had the whole picture." Even as vice president of educational planning and evaluation, McIntosh related that he'd "never been to a budget meeting" and "never worried about budget" (Interview, 1990). As Campbell (Interview, 1990) expressed it:

> Somehow, by some kind of magic, there would be amounts of money allocated to the various vice presidents to operate their areas. And the vice presidents were really not involved a whole lot in determining how much money they were going to get. It was some kind of ouija-board stuff that determined it.

However, according to Barwick, Simmons "maintained control of the books for Hagemeyer" and "if any single individual knew where the money was on campus, he did" (Interview, 1990).

As Barwick explained the budget process (Interview, 1990), it permitted managers of budget responsibility centers to work under an informal system with no real responsibility, no established guidelines, and little, if any, accountability:

> People who were in charge of responsibility centers received a 'check,' essentially, which they were to use, and when they ran out, they asked for another check. And they got a lecture and another check. So nobody ever knew what the limits were or anything else. Sometimes they were told 'no'; sometimes they were told 'yes.' It just wasn't clear.

Barwick continued, elaborating on the hands-on control of budget Hagemeyer utilized:

> Hagemeyer would fund the things that he valued...you got funded by convincing the right people that what you wanted was what Hagemeyer valued. He rewarded those efforts that generated the most FTEs. He made money available, pointed out and recognized people who'd been most cost-effective, who had the highest numbers at low cost.

Skills of the Organization: Challenging Traditional Teaching Methodologies and the Educational Status Quo

Hagemeyer developed the skills of the organization to challenge traditional teaching methodologies and the educational status quo through innovation. To embed and reinforce innovation within the culture, he used the primary mechanisms of what leaders pay attention to, measure, and control; criteria for allocation of rewards and status; leader reactions to critical incidents and organizational crises; and deliberate role modeling, teaching, and coaching (Schein, 1985a). Hagemeyer, like Henry Ford I, championed innovation over safe, traditional alternatives, particularly those innovations that appealed to his own pioneering spirit.

Hagemeyer (Interview, 1990) acknowledged that a "chief executive officer usually reflects his/her own background, in expressing his beliefs to others and in expressing ideas of what the future would hold." To Hagemeyer, based on his experience with the Ford Motor Company project at Henry Ford Community College, to meet the needs of contemporary society—the training of individuals for current and future job markets—education had to find ways to utilize emerging technologies in teaching. He became, therefore, the executive champion described by Peters and Austin (1985)—seeking out, facilitating for, and promoting through recognition individual faculty or small teams of innovators.

Hagemeyer made heroes out of two early innovators, Doris Weddington, a communications instructor, and Claud Hunter, an auto mechanics instructor, referred to by Barwick (Interview, 1990) as "a legend around here." Hagemeyer saw to it that both Weddington and Hunter gained national reputations as innovative instructional leaders. Peters and Austin (1985) and Kanter (1983) view such treatment as critical to encouraging more innovation.

In October 1970, it was announced that as a result of their impressive innovations in individualized instruction, Hunter and Weddington would appear in that year's edition of *Outstanding Educators of America* (Warren, 1988). In addition, discussions of Hunter's teaching techniques found their way into such national publications as *General Motors World*, *Industrial Education*, and *Popular Mechanics*.

According to Ott (1989), Hunter and Weddington served to "reinforce and maintain the culture by setting standards of behavior and providing performance role models" (p. 33). Hagemeyer's creating innovation heroes signaled what he as a leader would pay attention to, measure, and control, and established at the same time criteria for reward and status.

Innovation was a constant in Hagemeyer's vision:

> The idea was always there. And it used to be a joke, and in some ways, it was an insult. But, everybody knew that we were all working at this together. The comment that I would make is, 'Look, go ahead and try it, it can't be any worse than what we are doing now.' It was the type of attitude that if you failed, okay. It sure wasn't worse or wouldn't do the students any more harm than what we were doing to them now (Interview, 1989).

To foster innovation in teaching, Hagemeyer attempted to create an environment devoid of the fear of failing, where faculty "dare not feel that if something they try fails that is a stigma" (Interview, 1989). Hagemeyer's consistent method for dealing with questions or concerns re-enforced his desire for innovation in instruction. He coupled his influence with creating an environment that encouraged risk taking, which "could be as potent as formal control mechanisms and measurements" (Schein, 1985a, p. 225).

In creating this environment, Hagemeyer took an active, personal role in challenging the educational status quo—modeling the innovative behavior he sought, incorporating some of the key elements of the entrepreneurial spirit of risk taking, independence, and competitiveness, as described by Kotter (1988), and the entrepreneurial ethic of courage and innovation as pictured by Maccoby (1981).

Like the entrepreneur characterized by Daft (1988), Hagemeyer often demonstrated a concern for seeking opportunities rather than looking for problems. For example, Hagemeyer turned the educational status quo problem of almost every institution of higher education—parking—into an opportunity for Central Piedmont. Hagemeyer (Interview, 1989) explained:

> Central Piedmont constantly dealt with parking problems. We used the argument you had to have a parking sticker in order to park in a parking lot. But that was only part of it. The idea was to ensure that all students had parking stickers. If we put a parking sticker on the back of every back bumper, and we insisted it be seen...every time you turned around, you'd see a car with a CPCC parking sticker. People would start to talk.... and it wasn't long before CPCC was pretty well known.... People would say, "Hey, there's a place that I might be able to go and get some help."

He managed instructional innovation as he managed other aspects of the organization—hands-on. As Hagemeyer (Interview, 1989) related:

> My kicks came from what was happening in the instructional process. All of my people recognized that I was always sticking my nose in their business. I pretty much watched what they were doing. Because I grew up with it, I knew what was going on, and I knew what we were trying to achieve.

He controlled the "organizational power tools" of the innovative market of the college. According to Kanter (1983):

> organizational power tools consist of supplies of three 'basic commodities' that can be invested in action: information (data, technical knowledge, political intelligence, expertise); resources (funds, materials, space, time); and support (endorsement, backing, approval, legitimacy) (p. 159).

As Hagemeyer expressed it, "our emphasis and our push and our plea and every bit of coercion we could use was devoted in trying to teach in a way so that the individual student could profit and not waste his time" (Interview, 1989).

From the outset of his career at Central Piedmont, Hagemeyer constantly challenged traditional teaching methodologies and the educational status quo by encouraging innovation and the use of emerging technologies. He shaped the skills of the organization around innovation, and in doing so, he utilized all of Schein's (1985a) primary mechanisms for embedding and reinforcing culture. It was this focus on innovation that brought him and three other staff members the title of Innovator of the

Year in 1986. The title, awarded by the League for Innovation, went to Hagemeyer, Terilyn Turner, Cynthia (Cindy) Johnston, and Jocelyn Dienst, for the development of the Adult Basic Literacy Education (ABLE) project.

The Board of Trustees

Hagemeyer's attention to embedding and reinforcing his basic assumptions so that they became the cultural assumptions of the Central Piedmont culture was not limited to the college itself. As Simmons (Interview, 1990) stated, "He did a great deal to help the board understand its role." Hagemeyer's use of primary and secondary culture articulation and reinforcement mechanisms is apparent in his work with the Board of Trustees.

From the beginning, Hagemeyer signaled what he and the board would pay attention to, measure, and control. He did this through the development of the board committee structure, establishing at the September 24, 1963, board meeting committees on policy, finance, buildings and grounds, and personnel.

As Hagemeyer (Interview, 1990) explained, from that point "the committee structure evolved"; however, it did not actually evolve much beyond the parameters set up in the first configuration. When Hagemeyer retired in 1986, the board committees were executive, finance, buildings and grounds, and public affairs. A review of board minutes from September 1963 through April 1969—the formative years for the college, which, according to Schein (1985a) set the culture, indicates that agendas were dominated by matters of building and finance.

In the area of finance, particularly in matters of budgeting by the state, Hagemeyer established within the board a platform of disagreement with state authority, basing it on Central Piedmont's differences from the vast majority of the state's other community colleges and technical institutes—its urban service area, its size, its need to meet the sophisticated demands for training from the businesses and industries within the service area—and the failure of the state to recognize those differences. Board members shared deeply his frustration with the state and its funding practices, often embroiled in the urban versus rural politics of the state. In the latter years of his administration, however, the constant focus on conflict with the state, an insistence that cooperation would not work, and the failure to take a proactive position along other avenues was often more frustrating for the younger members of the board, according to Claytor (Interview, 1990).

Some matters of curriculum were raised by the board or reported to the board by Hagemeyer; however, they were not often discussed at length or made items of study. According to the minutes of the March 18, 1968, board meeting, Board Chairman Edgar Terrell "suggested that the trustees could take a more active role in interpreting, studying, and planning programs that the college offers." Minutes of subsequent meetings do not reveal an increase in board activity in this area, and as Claytor (Interview, 1990) commented, the board continued to be told about educational and curriculum matters on a "need-to-know basis."

The board, much like the college, therefore contributed little input and feedback in some critical areas of planning, according to Claytor (Interview, 1990). Board meetings, much like Cabinet meetings, were more informational than decision-oriented, with the exception of finance and buildings and grounds.

Albert F. "Pete" Sloan, a member of the Board of Trustees for sixteen years who served as board chair for four years with Hagemeyer, indicated that Hagemeyer "recognized the responsibility of making a sale, of giving you the same information that brought him to the point of making a recommendation and seeing if, with that information, you agreed with him" (Interview, 1990). As exemplified by the Long-Range Planning Report (Hagemeyer, 1974), the results of studies were reported to Hagemeyer. He then condensed the results and gave them to the board in the form he wanted, said Claytor (Interview, 1990). The manner, therefore, in which the board arrived at the nature of truth and reality resembled that of the Cabinet. In Hagemeyer's view board members, as rational individuals, were presented the facts and convinced of their soundness. Hagemeyer said:

I had business leaders, political leaders, educational leaders, and as a result of that, if what we were trying to do made sense, they were intelligent, they could support it, and they would say 'go' (Interview, 1989).

Although appointed and in place at the time Hagemeyer was named president, the Board of Trustees, politically strong and powerful in the community, provided a perfect base of support for Hagemeyer and the assumptions he brought with him to Charlotte-Mecklenburg about what Central Piedmont should be. Well acculturated as the years passed, boards continued to provide a base of support. As expressed by Claytor (Interview, 1990):

To his everlasting credit, during the period in which [Central Piedmont] was formed up until he left, it was good Hagemeyer was there. He was the person to push people, pull people...do whatever it took to get [Central Piedmont] from square one to where it was in 1986.

When Hagemeyer was asked about the nature of his relationship with the board, a board that did not measure the progress of the college against objectives or evaluate the leadership of its president in any formal sense, he replied, "I guess the fact that I survived twenty-three years would indicate that it must have been fairly decent" (Interview, 1989). That "fairly decent" relationship was made possible because, again, as Hagemeyer (Interview, 1989) said, "their needs and what they wanted fit what I wanted to do. Our background, our philosophies fit."

Hagemeyer's development of culture within the board replicated in many ways his development of the culture of the college. His values and strategy of excellence became the trustees', largely through the exertion of his style of leadership on the skills of that organization, its information systems, and its structure.

The State Level

The leadership that Hagemeyer evidenced in establishing the culture of the college and the board was characteristic, to a degree, of his work with the state. With his ten years' experience at Henry Ford Community College, Hagemeyer could offer experienced leadership not only as the founding president of Central Piedmont, but also as a founding president within the new state system. The basic assumptions he brought with him about the nature of a comprehensive community college matched what many community college professionals viewed as the state's "original mission" (Wiggs, 1989, p. 219) for community colleges—vocational education. As expressed by McIntosh (Interview, 1990), "there was an absolute, clear, definite link between economic development of the state and these institutions. . . . The view was that these institutions were to be there primarily to provide education and services to industry."

Hagemeyer incorporated his basic assumptions through his early active involvement in the system's development and decision making. As McIntosh recalled, Hagemeyer "tried to fashion the state into what the state ought to be doing in terms of community colleges" (Interview, 1990). The area of influence and leadership at the state level to which Hagemeyer spoke specifically during the course of an interview (1990) was instruction:

I think probably that over the years our use of individualized instruction was probably the most outstanding example of the work that we were responsible for diffusing to other programs in other community and technical institutions.

However, as explained by Simmons (Interview, 1990):

Hagemeyer had to do continual battle with the state over funding. The state was so interested in counting seat time, chair time of students for funding reimbursement, that it was very reluctant to even consider, for earnback purposes, courses taught through educational technology, courses taught through the media— newspapers, television, radio, computers, telephone, and so on.

Although "Hagemeyer was able to win some very important battles in this regard," they were never won rapidly enough "to allow a broadside movement into any of these areas at any one time," said Simmons (Interview, 1990). Yet, precedents were set.

McIntosh (Interview, 1990) commented that Central Piedmont spent a great deal of time "overcoming oppositions in points of view and circumventing" when unable to "overcome in a legal way" obstacles to do what was "best for this institution, this community." McIntosh's comment, when combined with the interview remarks of Hagemeyer, North Carolina Department of Community Colleges Full-Time Equivalency Auditor Phil Marion, and Simmons, reveals that of paramount importance to Hagemeyer was not his allegiance to or work with the state system, but his allegiance to Central Piedmont and its unique place within the system. This manner of allegiance often set Hagemeyer at odds with the state system and its other community colleges, according to board members Sloan and Claytor (Interviews, 1990). In his work at the state level, Hagemeyer combined the key elements of risk taking, independence, and competitiveness, which Kotter (1988) calls part of the entrepreneurial spirit, with parochialism, vision, and strategy, which are best for the entrepreneur but not necessarily for the entire system, and a very strong and cohesive network of subordinates that ignored important peers and superiors (Kotter, 1988).

The surfacing of these characteristics Kets de Vries (1989) refers to as "the dark side of entrepreneurship" (p. 143). In illuminating the dark side, Kets de Vries (1989) posits that the utmost desire of the entrepreneur is "to run his own shop" (p. 143), to control, and to avoid being at the mercy of others. This last characteristic leads some to be "preoccupied with the threat of subjection to some external control or infringement on their will" (p. 146). For Hagemeyer, the state and its controls often stood in the way of his vision for Central Piedmont and, in essence, posed a threat of failure.

According to Kets de Vries (1989), the highly achievement-oriented entrepreneur in response can adopt the defensive pattern of "splitting— the tendency to see things in extremes when dealing with other people" (p. 151). To Hagemeyer, the state offices in Raleigh never understood that Central Piedmont was different from other colleges in the system and, as such, needed to be treated differently. As Hagemeyer (Interview, 1989) said:

> We had a great deal of difficulty with the built-in bureaucracy. For example, those people in the state office really were not involved in what we were doing, and they couldn't hear, see, watch, and observe. They were up there in their different environment, and they wanted things done according to the book. As a result, they constituted a major barrier over the years because our methods were different, and they didn't fit the pattern.

Simmons (Interview, 1990) relayed there was sentiment in the college's administration that "in the audit exceptions that came out of the late '70s and culminated in the early '80s, Central Piedmont was not only misunderstood, misinterpreted, but was being a little bit victimized by the rules and the interpretations of those rules."

As the champion of the college's differences and what he perceived as its right to be treated differently, Hagemeyer adopted an us-versus-them posture. As expressed by Marion (Interview, 1990), Hagemeyer "was always perceived as a person who had an adversarial role with the [state] department," and the process of raising awareness of differences was often "confrontational in nature." Simmons (Interview, 1990) characterized Hagemeyer's leadership at the state level as "playing the role of the thorn." As Kets de Vries (1989) indicates, such posturing and role assumptions can lead to "insularity and factionalism" (p. 153).

The Founding President: Leadership Behaviors and Style

A close analysis of the case study data regarding the culture established and embedded by the founding president of Central Piedmont Community College leaves no doubt that "culture and leadership, when one examines them closely, are two sides of the same coin, and neither can really be understood by itself" (Schein, 1985a, p. 2). The type and strength of culture Richard H. Hagemeyer developed and the leadership behaviors and style he evidenced seem, indeed, to be two sides of the same coin.

This portion of the case study will analyze Hagemeyer's leadership behaviors along the five categories differentiated by Bass (1985a): contingent reinforcement (both positive and aversive), management-by-exception, consideration, intellectual stimulation, and charisma with a subfactor of inspirational leadership. Founding presidents generally exhibit leadership behaviors that are transactional in nature and spirited by entrepreneurialism: a preponderance of contingent reinforcement and management-by-exception behaviors. According to Schein (1985a) these behaviors work well in "institutions in which the social and economic status quo is reasonably satisfying" (p. 154). Consideration, intellectual stimulation, and charismatic/inspirational leadership work better in a turbulent environment "whose institutions are unable to cope with violations of expectations and need dissatisfactions" (p. 154).

The analysis of data from the many sources represented within the case study substantiates Hagemeyer's use of transactional behaviors in establishing, embedding, and reinforcing the culture of Central Piedmont. The transactional behaviors related to contingent reinforcement and management-by-exception are tied to an underlying relationship which, according to Yukl (1989), involves the formal or implicit social contract governing the terms of a person's expectations of what he will do for the organization and what the organization will do for the individual. At founding, these transactional behaviors established in Central Piedmont a culture that, through constant embedding and reinforcing by those same behaviors, had reached a maturity and strength that culminated in nationally recognized organizational excellence. However, at the point of Hagemeyer's retirement, that same cultural maturity and strength had also become a liability, limiting the college's responsiveness to external and internal demands.

Transactional behaviors on the part of Hagemeyer are noticeable in his hiring and budgeting practices, which he used to embed and reinforce culture. As noted earlier, he found people who wanted to be part of his vision of a comprehensive community college with an occupational focus. Hiring on the basis of a shared vision was reinforced by the development of the contingent positive reinforcement characteristic of a "goal-performance-reward cycle" (Bass, 1985a, p. 123). Hagemeyer retained strict, paternalistic control over funds and required transactional renegotiation for budget changes during the fiscal year. The goal of the cycle was adherence to and maintenance of cultural assumptions and central control.

Hagemeyer also established a system of contingent aversive reinforcement—a "manager's reaction to an employee's failure to achieve the agreed-upon performance" (Bass, 1985a, p. 122) for cases of non-promotion, excommunication, and firing. Criteria, as in the goal-performance-reward cycle, focused on employee fit with organizational culture and demonstrated what Hagemeyer, as a leader, paid attention to, measured, and controlled. The case study data indicate that contingent aversive reinforcement was used only when there were breakdowns, failures, or deviations—the practice of management-by-exception (Bass, 1985a).

Success of contingent reinforcement, whether contingent reward or contingent aversive reinforcement, is dependent on a supervisor's explicitness in giving instructions (Bass, 1985a). Hagemeyer (Interview, 1989) clearly expressed what would lead to reward and what would prevent punishment, for example in establishing his exchange relationship with Bob Hoelzel, the college's comptroller:

> If we got into a predicament where we had a program or something we wanted to change or we wanted to do this or that and so on, instead of [the comptroller] bucking, my instruction to him would be, 'Bob, I want you to figure out how this can be done, and the next thing you've got to do is remember what I tell you every week, "Your main job is to keep me out of jail." Anything you can do to help us do this, I want you to do it.'

Leader and follower accepted "interconnected roles and responsibilities to reach designated goals" (Bass, 1985a, p. 122), with the leader having the ability to provide, directly or indirectly, contingent positive or aversive reinforcement.

Hagemeyer gained influence in exchange relationships with subordinates through his abilities to protect college interests and compete for organizational resources at the state level; to gain approval for proposed changes and initiatives from the Board of Trustees; to form coalitions and alliances with local business, industrial, social, and political community groups and leaders for the purpose of supporting college initiatives; and to focus national attention on college accomplishments. He also gained influence through his possession of perceived critical knowledge and expertise from his past, an influence that increased with each success related to his consistent vision.

Hagemeyer, as a result of the influence gained, was perceived as a powerful person, and there was little doubt about his coercive power. When he would indicate something was going to be a certain way, that is the way it was; there was no questioning, said staff members Campbell, Adkins, Dave Hunter, Smith, and Barwick (Interviews, 1990).

Hagemeyer used the goal-performance-reward exchange cycle to distinguish in-group from out-group performance. As case study data indicate, those who complied with traditional educational role expectations and recognized Hagemeyer's legitimate authority—the out-group—received the standard compensations for their positions within the college. Those who distinguished themselves through performances that challenged the educational status quo—the in-group—were rewarded through three avenues, two of them highly visible.

Hagemeyer said reward was visibly reflected in "a promotion-from-within policy as we developed" (Interview, 1989), and, for those faculty members not seeking management responsibilities, visible reward was reflected by the distribution to them of the organizational power tools of innovation. Analysis of case study data indicates other forms of reward that deepened the exchange relationship for in-group subordinates with Hagemeyer. They included access to inside information through office and/or classroom, laboratory, and site visits; participation in the confirmation of his decisions; his personal support and encouragement; and assignment to desirable tasks.

One's in-group/out-group status in relation to Hagemeyer was recognized on campus. Those subordinates who gave Hagemeyer what he expected got his attention; those who didn't remained anonymous to him. With consistency of exchange the in-group relationships fostered a high degree of loyalty, support, and mutual dependence.

Also exemplary of the transactional leadership behavior of contingent reinforcement, as revealed in the case study, is a frequency of communication about job-related matters (Bass, 1985a). As expressed by Barwick (Interview, 1990), "If you talked to Hagemeyer, you talked about an educational issue." Hunter (Interview, 1990) said, "Hagemeyer lived and breathed the college. . . talked about it constantly, on campus, socially, on the golf course."

Hagemeyer's insistence on centralized authority, control, and hands-on management produced few leadership behaviors in the area of consideration. Consideration behaviors include consultation, consensual decision making, treating all subordinates similarly, delegation, participation of followers in decisions affecting work and career, informal versus formal contact, promotion of familiarity and contact, and expressed appreciation for a job well done.

Similarly, analysis indicates that the entrepreneurial characteristics of control, centralized authority, and hands-on management led Hagemeyer to evidence transactional leadership behaviors in dealing with subordinates. Subordinates, as revealed by the case study, were seldom involved in "the tasks of analysis, formulation, implementation, interpretation, and evaluation" (Bass, 1985a, p. 99), and when input was invited, it was for the purpose of confirmation of what was intended.

From the founding, Hagemeyer was confident that his vision for Central Piedmont provided the best way to achieve external adaptation and internal control. Bolstered by repeated success in that environment, Hagemeyer concentrated, as a transactional leader, "on how to best keep the system running. . . reacting to problems generated by observed deviances, looking to modify conditions as needed, and remaining ever mindful of the organizational constraints" (Bass, 1985a, p. 105) within which he had to operate. With his strong achievement orientation, an important element in his entrepreneurial spirit, he provided rationally oriented direction. Bass (1985a) characterizes such direction as emphasizing "competence, independence, and industry" (p. 110) and its leaders as "decisive" and "directive" (p. 111), requiring little information on which to base solutions. The decisions of leaders providing rationally oriented intellectual stimulation are final, and efficiency is an emphasis (Bass, 1985a). As a transactional leader, Hagemeyer used his power and energy "to maintain the status quo" (Bass, 1985a, p. 110).

In discussing the nature of charisma as a leadership behavior, Bass (1985a) points to the multiple meanings the term charisma has assumed in the popular media. According to Bass, "the competition between old and new systems of values where change to the new has not been legitimated" (p. 37) sets the stage for the appearance of a charismatic leader—an appearance made easier "in societies that seek, expect, and/or encourage their appearance" (p. 38). Hagemeyer was in such a situation at Central Piedmont's founding.

Charismatic leaders are described by Bass (1985a) as "imbued with self-confidence in their own competence, conviction in their own beliefs, and a strong need for power" (p. 40)—characteristics they use to increase follower commitment to group objectives aligned with strongly held organizational values and ideals, follower trust, and follower compliance. These charismatic characteristics enabled Hagemeyer to establish the college's culture.

The ability of the charismatic leader to focus on the needs, values, and hopes of followers through leadership behaviors of individualized consideration and intellectual stimulation moves the charismatic leader from transactional to transformational leadership and followers "into their better selves" (Burns, 1978, p. 462), converting them into leaders. Within this case study, leadership behaviors by Hagemeyer related to control dominate, and behaviors in the areas of individualized consideration and intellectual stimulation are absent. Kets de Vries (1989), in describing entrepreneurial charisma, provides the best insight into Hagemeyer's own brand of charisma, which was transactional and dominated by controlling behaviors: "Entrepreneurs convey a sense of purpose and by doing so, convince others that they are where the action is" (pp. 142–143).

A search through the case study for inspirational leadership behaviors, a subfactor of charisma, reveals that in individual instances, Hagemeyer was able to build the confidence of followers; inspire belief in "the greater cause" among constituents in the community; demonstrate an action orientation rather than a focus on constraints; and use media, coupled with persuasive language, to inspire extra effort—all behaviors Bass (1985a) associates with inspirational leadership. However, when juxtaposed with Hagemeyer's use of rationally oriented intellectual stimulation, transactional inspirational leadership behaviors predominate.

The case study indicates that Hagemeyer, indeed, exhibited some leadership behaviors within transformational leadership categories. Such is anticipated by Bass (1985a), who asserts that leaders generally do exhibit both transactional and transformational behaviors, but in differing amounts. For Hagemeyer, the preponderance of leadership behaviors were transactional in nature. Such a preponderance is also expected; Bass (1985a) posits that times of stability—certainly those times of Hagemeyer's administration—foster transactional leadership. Through the life stages of birth, growth, midlife, and maturity (Schein, 1985a) at Central Piedmont, Hagemeyer's leadership behaviors, transactional in nature and spirited by an entrepreneurialism often attributable to founders, served the college well. They culminated in that final stage as a maintenance mechanism for a status quo (Albrecht and Albrecht, 1987; Bass, 1985a)—a status quo that reached a nationally recognized level of excellence.

The Latter Years: Entrepreneurship—the Dual-Edged Sword

The college's national reputation for excellence earned it an invitation into the prestigious League for Innovation in the Community College, as well as a major leadership role in the American Association of Community and Junior Colleges (AACJC). Hagemeyer (Interview, 1990) attributed his leadership in AACJC as a board member from 1974 to 1977 and as board chair from 1976 to 1977 as reflective "of the position that the institution had in the country."

The leadership reputation of Central Piedmont was confirmed in 1985 by a study of excellence in the nation's community colleges, co-directed by Roueche and Baker (1987). In that study, a panel of community college experts placed Central Piedmont in the top five community colleges in the nation.

During the latter years of Hagemeyer's administration, however, his entrepreneurial spirit acted as a dual-edged sword, slowing the college's response to needs for external and internal adaptation.

Along with its many benefits, entrepreneurialism has a dark side that can breed insularity and factionalism. While these characteristics are helpful in periods of birth, growth, and development for a college when resources seem unlimited, after the college matures and resources become limited, homeostasis can result.

Albrecht and Albrecht (1987) explain organizational homeostasis— the tendency to maintain internal stability during times of disruption in the environment—as an organization's systemic attempt to preserve its once successful state of affairs. In essence, all the organizational systems, methodologies, procedures, processes, and value systems pull the organizational membership back to the "correct" way of doing things.

Under ordinary circumstances, because of the stability produced by internal homeostasis, it is of benefit; however, when environmental forces alter significantly to a point beyond that for which organizational norms have been optimized, internal homeostasis becomes a liability.

The analysis of data indicates the presence in the latter years of Hagemeyer's administration of homeostatic patterns of culture as delineated by Albrecht and Albrecht (1987): locally based membership, not transient; clear application of rewards and sanctions; well-fixed authority and authority figures; clearly defined norms; uniform, fixed standards of behavior; simplified values; a slow or nonexistent rate of change; and resistance to changes in configuration. As Johnston (Interview, 1990) observed: "When Hagemeyer was here, there was no organizational change. I mean, it was the same organizationally. We may have grown and expanded, but basically it was the same." As succinctly expressed by Buchanan (Interview, 1990), "Everything just rolled along, status quo."

In a similar fashion, the very nature of the individual or small group innovation that gave Central Piedmont its reputation as an excellent community college may have also kept the college from achieving Hagemeyer's goal of faculty-wide use of technology in teaching and learning. Kanter (1983) suggests that innovation is most successful where integrative thinking within integrative cultures and structures exists—where actions are viewed for the implications of the "whole" and mechanisms exist for the exchange of information and new ideas across departmental boundaries, encouraging multiple perspectives in decision making. While innovation was certainly integral to the culture of Central Piedmont, it was compartmentalized.

Despite the fact that Hagemeyer encouraged the process of innovation "by the explicit management of the after-the-act labeling process—in other words, publicly and ceaselessly lauding the small wins along the way" (Peters and Waterman, 1982, p. 74), innovations were narrow and viewed as independent of their contexts and of their connections to other campus areas. Throughout his administration, Hagemeyer did not change the manner in which he championed innovation, nor did he change the way in which he influenced innovation.

Part of the "segmentalism" (Kanter, 1983, p. 28) of the innovative nature of the college may be attributed to the segmented structure of the college: a large number of compartments lined off from one another—department from department, level above from level below—and few if any exchanges taking place except between individuals at the boundaries of segments. Individual segments, therefore, developed good, innovative ideas, but there was little impetus and no mechanism for the transfer of the knowledge from one segment to another or for examining its applicability across segments as part of the innovation process.

Kets de Vries (1989) points out that the characteristics of control and very intense hands-on management evidenced in the entrepreneurial spirit of leadership work well when a business is small and in its infancy. However, as the business grows, the need for the active cooperation and support of additional internal and external constituencies increases. For some entrepreneurs, meeting that need is not possible, and, as Claytor (Interview, 1990) recognized, the balance shifts with the once-positive spirit becoming "more of a detriment than it [is] a positive force."

Perhaps Hagemeyer, as an outstanding leader who had taken Central Piedmont to a level of national acclaim, recognized the changing requirements of the times. According to Warren (1988), and to Barwick (Interview, 1990), when recalling a conversation with Hagemeyer, as Hagemeyer reflected on his decision to retire, he commented on his enjoyment of his years at Central Piedmont and said, however, "It was a case of realizing that every institution needs new blood, new insights. Sometimes I felt maybe I stayed too long."

■

Chapter 9

Cultural Leadership: The Successor

By Phyllis Barber

An examination of the latter years of Richard H. Hagemeyer's administration at Central Piedmont Community College reveals that the strong culture he established—a culture that enabled the college to reach a level of nationally recognized excellence—was showing signs of the need for external adaptation and internal integration. The preponderance of leadership behaviors that brought the college to its point of excellence were transactional in nature, were spirited by entrepreneurialism, and served to perpetuate the established culture rather than facilitate adaptation. As Schein (1985a) asserts:

> What is correct or whether strength is good or bad depends on the match between cultural assumptions and environmental realities. A strong culture can be effective at one point and ineffective at another point because external realities have changed (p. 315).

The case study of Central Piedmont indicated that homeostasis—the tendency of an organization to maintain internal stability during times of disruption in the environment to preserve its once-successful state of affairs (Albrecht and Albrecht, 1987)—had become an organizational liability.

To reverse homeostasis as a liability, the established culture or framework Central Piedmont was using to impart meaning to and impose structure on its particular domain required reframing (Bartunek, 1988). Reframing imposes a qualitatively new framework on a domain, providing a new way of understanding and seeing it. Reframing is a discontinuous, "double-loop" (Argyris, 1982), "second-order" (Levy and Merry, 1986), qualitative shift in the understanding of a domain rather than an incremental modification of a previous understanding.

There is little disagreement about the beginning of the reframing process (Bartunek, 1988). It begins with a person, an important event, or a statement—an instigator or trigger—that "unfreezes" a particular way of understanding a situation (Lewin, 1947), either explicitly or implicitly. The challenge to current understanding, however, must be extremely strong because of the strength of developed frames and their quality of endurance (Nystrom and Starbuck, 1984).

Schein (1980) asserts that the magnitude of cultural change is dependent upon two factors: the degree to which the organization is unfrozen or ready to change as the result of internal forces for change or as the result of an externally induced crisis; and the developmental stage of the organization—growth, organizational mid-life, or maturity. At different stages of development, the forces capable of unfreezing the current culture are likely to differ, and certain mechanisms of change will assume particular relevance.

For a mature organization like Central Piedmont, in a state of negative homeostasis, Schein (1985a) recognizes that culture becomes a constraint on innovation and preserves the glories of the past, providing a valued source of defense and self-esteem. For the mature organization, therefore, there are inherent difficulties for framebreaking change.

However, according to Schein (1985a), there are two options for change: transformation or decline. For transformation, culture change is necessary, but not all elements of the culture can or must be changed; essential elements must be identified and preserved. Culture change can be managed or can simply be allowed to evolve. Within the destruction option, culture change occurs at paradigm levels and through the massive replacement of key people.

The same primary and secondary mechanisms useful for founders in creating, embedding, and strengthening culture become the mechanisms of the succeeding presidents in framebreaking and reframing. For, as Schein (1985a) points out, when culture becomes dysfunctional it is leadership's role to assist the organization in unlearning some of its cultural assumptions and learning new assumptions—a role best assumed by a transformational leader (Bass, 1985a; Tichy and Devanna, 1986; Roueche, Baker, and Rose, 1989).

Since for organizations, much like individuals, yesterday's events shape today's and constrain tomorrow's behavior, Kimberly (1988) argues that it is helpful for a successor president to know about the organization's past in order to understand and predict behavior. Tushman, Newman, and Nadler (1988), Kimberly (1988), Hambrick and Mason (1984), and London (1988) argue that leaders for organizational transformation, reframing or framebreaking must come from the outside because those who have become a part of the organization's culture and identity are the least able to precipitate major change.

For change to occur, Schein (1985a) reiterates the inseparability of culture and leadership, positing that leadership must recognize how intertwined it is with cultural formation, evolution, transformation, and destruction. In essence, "the unique and essential function of leadership is the manipulation of culture" (Schein, 1985a, p. 317).

Data sources within the case study of Central Piedmont indicate that several critical incidents at the college precipitated a readiness for change. Tushman, Newman, and Nadler posit that leadership succession "seems to be a powerful tool in managing framebreaking change" (1988, p. 126).

The Succeeding President: Influencing Culture Through Leadership

For Central Piedmont, the beginning of the reframing process—the instigator or trigger that "unfreezes" a particular way of understanding a situation (Lewin, 1947)—was not a person, an important event, or a statement, but all three.

On May 6, 1986, Board Chair Bill Claytor announced that Ruth G. Shaw would become the next president of Central Piedmont, joining the college in July. The announcement was made in a collegewide meeting in Pease Auditorium on the campus. Because of a board meeting in Dallas, Texas, where she was then president of El Centro College, Shaw could not attend the announcement. Wanting to address Central Piedmont on that occasion, Shaw sent a videotape of her remarks. In these remarks she pointed immediately to what she as a leader would pay attention to, measure, control, and reward—a primary mechanism for embedding culture (Schein, 1985a). Shaw indicated both explicitly and implicitly a qualitatively different way of understanding.

She focused on the positive characteristics of the college and its work, of the community, and of the leadership of the Board of Trustees and the State Board for Community Colleges. Indicating she was looking forward to becoming a part of the service Central Piedmont provided to the citizens of Charlotte-Mecklenburg, Shaw asserted that this was a time for "growth, opportunity, and challenge" for everyone and visualized Central Piedmont as a "great institution poised for even further greatness." Shaw recognized Hagemeyer's contributions, telling those present, "On his great foundation, we will build together still more greatness." Recognizing a fit between the values and strengths she could bring to Central Piedmont and those the college needed in a president, Shaw cited "vision, commitment, caring, and competence" and pointed to the "vigor and student centeredness," "instructional excellence," and "dedication to meeting the needs of students" she sensed at the college.

Shaw's remarks then took a personal perspective, as she referred to the important role family played in her life, mentioning each family member briefly but in a way each could be remembered. She pointed out that she enjoyed work and worked hard, found pleasure in teamwork, gained satisfaction in helping people achieve their best, set high standards for herself and those with whom she worked, enjoyed shared values, enjoyed sharing "the essence of commitment," and was "analytical, decisive."

In closing, Shaw returned to a focus on the college, holding out, as she had at the outset of her remarks, a vision of growth, opportunity, and challenge by commenting, "It is at times like these that we experience our greatest growth, times that are more conducive to opening ourselves to opportunities." As her "first official act" as president, she attached a Central Piedmont pin to her lapel, saying she planned to "wear it with pride for many, many years to come" and looked forward to her arrival on July 14 "with great anticipation."

For Central Piedmont, the announcement, the event, and Shaw's videotaped remarks signaled the beginning of the reframing process. Within her remarks was language that hinted of some new basic assumptions, for example, about the nature of reality and truth ("analytical"), human relationships ("sharing"), human activity ("teamwork"), and human nature ("helping others achieve"). It is these underlying assumptions around which cultural paradigms form, according to Schein (1985a). Because of the strength and endurance of developed frames, Nystrom and Starbuck (1984) assert that challenges to current understanding within a strong culture must be extremely strong. Analysis of the case study data indicates that this occasion provided a strong challenge.

Reinforcing the Trigger Event

Shaw's vision or strategy for excellence was a vision of "how the college would work" (Interview, 1989), a vision driven by basic assumptions that were significantly different from the cultural assumptions in place. Her strategy was precipitated by her observation of two distinct feelings on campus:

> People felt very good about the outcomes of the college. I think there was a general, strong feeling that the college was performing its work well. There was also a feeling on the part of the faculty and the staff and the board that how it was performing was not always exactly the best for the times (Interview, 1989).

To confirm her observations and gather information, Shaw made herself highly visible on campus, talking to everyone—faculty, staff, students, and administrators. What she paid attention to in the information-gathering process, her visible behavior, had, as Schein (1985a) puts it, "great value for communicating assumptions and values to other members" (p. 232). Shaw (Interview, 1989) recalled:

> Within the first ninety days, I set up a series of meetings with all the top managers. I had each of them develop written reports, and then I had long meetings with them to discuss their observations of strengths and weaknesses within each of their areas.
>
> I put on my Reeboks and walked, literally walked the parking lots, walked every building, made departmental visits, did a tremendous amount of that during the first year. And I did a lot of it in the first ninety days.

According to Shaw, the information she gathered "taught me enough to know that I had to have a much, much more action-oriented agenda than I had thought initially" (Interview, 1989).

The agenda Shaw developed had at its nucleus the involvement of people. Shaw saw an urgency in instituting "coordination and communication across areas," the lack of which "was simply stunning"; in the education area, the need for "a more evaluative approach and a more consumer-, student-oriented approach"; the necessity "to pull business and administrative services together"; the requirement to change the organizational structure for "a team approach"; the need to clean up "some of the simple systems like classification and compensation"; and the demand for a revision in the planning process (Interview, 1990).

In addition to providing her with information on which to base her agenda, Shaw's visibility on campus that first ninety days reinforced for people the spirit of openness and caring that they felt and confirmed the desire for teamwork they saw in Shaw's introductory videotape. This visibility also advanced the framebreaking process begun in the videotape. As she sought information, framebreaking was made possible by Shaw's ability to communicate her basic assumptions and values, for example about the active involvement of people in discovering truth and reality, the caring and helping side of human nature, and the collaboration and teamwork possible in human relationships. Schein (1985a) recognizes this role modeling, teaching, and coaching by leaders as one of the primary mechanisms of embedding and reinforcing cultural assumptions.

At about the nine-week mark of the ninety-day period, Shaw had the opportunity to address the college in person for the first time at its annual Fall Conference. She used the occasion to "share values":

> I talked about who I am and what's important to me. I talked about issues of trust, of responsibility, of doing away with things

like the anonymous note in communicating with each other. I talked about excellence. I talked about the recognition of the people who were stars among us. I talked centrally about students being at the heart of everything we do, and our work focusing on those students (Interview, 1989).

She reinforced the values she had mentioned in her videotape—vision, commitment, competence, and caring—and strengthened her articulation of new basic assumptions for the fabric of the college's culture. Those assumptions were related to the nature of reality and truth, human relationships, human activity, and human nature—the "how" of the work done at the college. Nine weeks of experiences, both on campus and off, gave her the opportunity to weave the threads of her videotaped remarks into the fabric of Central Piedmont.

Shaw added another value—responsibility—thus expanding her challenge to the organizational culture. With this value her Fall Conference speech addressed decision making and participation—"I believe that I have the personal power to affect the world in which I work—and I believe that you do, too. To exercise that power, we must be willing to risk and to trust each other"; communication—"We must forego the anonymous note in favor of face-to-face conversation...say straightforwardly what we think"; recognition and reward—"I want to work in a place that helps the stars shine and that recognizes and rewards its star performers"; and planning and participation—"I want a planning system for Central Piedmont that will engage all of us in developing an action agenda for our college."

In her speech Shaw also challenged the cultural perspective on the nature of innovation. She broadened the scope of innovation as an activity, saying: "We must remember that most innovation doesn't come from the administrative offices or from giant grants. It comes from that ceaseless tinkering to do the day-to-day in a better way." Her challenge was extended to technology but with a focus on building on excellence through shared values and a focus on people: "We'll build on the tradition of excellence you have started because of our shared values, not because we hop on the latest instructional bandwagon or instructional fad." She stressed that technology was "a tool, a means to an end...not an end in itself....No single technology or methodology is the answer to dealing with the diverse and wondrous challenges presented by the students of the community college."

Before Shaw closed her Fall Conference remarks she added one final value—quality, saying: "I look relentlessly for evidence of quality in my work and in the performance of our college." And, as a leader, she indicated how she would measure it:

I believe quality is not a technique dictated by the latest instructional or managerial fad. Instead, it comes from within each of us—from the care we show our students and each other, from the real passion we feel toward our work. It comes from the day-in and day-out ways in which we show that passionate caring. And, it comes primarily from looking students in the eye, hearing what they have to say, and acting to do our best.

Her final words combined her new vision of the "how," her challenges to current cultural assumptions and a sense of assurance in the implementation of those assumptions, with the spirit of the past: "These values will translate themselves in a thousand ways in the years ahead, and together we will live the commitment to continue the tradition of excellence at CPCC."

The Inaugural Address: New Cultural Assumptions Made Concrete

Slightly over six months after her arrival on campus, Shaw was inaugurated in a formal academic ceremony at Ovens Auditorium. In her speech for this occasion, she chose, as she had previously, to blend Central Piedmont's past with its future: "To imagine our future at Central Piedmont Community College, we must have a sense of the forces that have shaped us." She cited many people, including Hagemeyer, by name, noted their contributions, and emphasized the college's "tradition of quality," noting that "it is built on our commitment to open admission, our emphasis on economic development, and our devotion to educational excellence. These values will guide us as surely in the future as in the past."

As at the Fall Conference, Shaw's point of departure became the "how"; after recognizing the past, she turned to predict the change in Central Piedmont's future. She cited two environmental forces with which the college would have to contend: the educational challenges to retrieve drop-outs and to retain students in public schools in times of educational reform; and a state economy in transition with new job requirements and demands for more sophisticated skills. She predicted: "Our tomorrows will be unlike our yesterdays, and our success may depend both on doing the same things differently and on doing different things."

Each "how" that Shaw isolated was a challenge to Central Piedmont's current culture. Undergirded by concrete new cultural assumptions, the result of successful adaptations to the external environment and integration internally, in the future

- The comprehensive nature of Central Piedmont would emerge with a new philosophy; the "Learn More, Earn More" college bumper sticker issued during the previous administration would be converted to "Brainpower Training"

- The belief that technological teaching and learning systems were the method of choice for improving access would be examined for other choices
- Strengthened articulations in all educational areas would match the comprehensive nature of the college, expanding student opportunities
- The concept of building community through economic development would be enlarged by building community through service
- The past philosophy of what Hagemeyer called "the student's right to fail" (as told to 1986–87 Faculty Senate President Joe Barwick, Interview, 1990) would emerge as the student's right to succeed

For many in the college community, the inauguration event reduced anxiety about change by bringing closure to its direction. As Barwick remarked: "The inauguration showed us how strikingly different things were likely to be from that point forward."

Analysis indicates that during this speech Shaw was able to capture and convert the direction she envisioned for the college into a concrete reality. She had been able "to make conscious what lies unconscious among followers" (Burns, 1978, p. 40).

In her first six months at Central Piedmont Shaw exerted in each of her major addresses what Albrecht and Albrecht refer to as "frame-of-reference control" (1987, p. 122), a leader's capacity to build an invisible framework around the thoughts of others by offering a ringing statement, a strong metaphor, or an organizing concept. They assert that listeners respond unconsciously to this frame of reference, accepting it as a model for their own points of view.

Weick (1980) argues for the power that accrues to the leader through what he terms "the management of eloquence in language" (p. 18). For Weick (1980), as for Albrecht and Albrecht (1987), the value of such management is not in the arousal of followers but in how "it affects what followers tell themselves when they try to discover what they are thinking" (Weick, 1980, p. 18). Viewed as "a form of potency on the leader's part" (Albrecht and Albrecht, 1987, p. 122), this skilled use of language and conceptual fluency on the part of a leader earns the acceptance of listeners.

With each major event—the videotaped introduction, the Fall Conference address, the inaugural address—and the series of events characterized as "walking around," Shaw used four of the five primary culture-embedding and -reinforcing mechanisms identified by Schein (1985a): what leaders pay attention to, measure, control, and reward; leader reactions to critical incidents; deliberate role modeling, teaching, and coaching by leaders; and criteria for allocation of rewards and status.

Analysis of the case study data for Shaw's first six months at Central Piedmont indicates that through framebreaking and reframing Shaw managed the dynamics of organizational transformation through the first three phases—the trigger event, the development of a felt need for change in the organization accompanied by a dissatisfaction with the status quo, and the creation of a vision of the desired future state (Tichy, 1980, 1983; Tichy and Ulrich, 1984; Tichy and Devanna, 1986). Two phases remained for achieving active management of the organization: mobilizing commitment and institutionalizing the change by shaping and reinforcing the new culture that fits the revitalized organization (Tichy, 1980, 1983; Tichy and Ulrich, 1984; Tichy and Devanna, 1986).

Mobilizing Commitment and Institutionalizing Change

To mobilize commitment and institutionalize change, Shaw set about to change the current system of "how" the organization would function to achieve goals, targeting specifically the organizational structure and the systems of decision making, communication, planning, and reward and recognition that she mentioned in her Fall Conference address. As she made changes, she set about to instill the value of responsibility through involvement and participation. An initially paradoxical path of development was also initiated—the destruction of the existing organizational structure.

Transforming the Organizational Structure. The organizational structure Shaw inherited had an executive vice president to whom most, but not all, vice presidents reported; some reported directly to the president. Vice presidents were "at all kinds of different jobs reporting to all sorts of different people," Shaw said (Interview, 1989). As she described it: "A cultivated pattern of behavior existed" that had vice presidents routinely bypassing the executive vice president to "come to the president on an array of issues" (Interview, 1989). In addition, "there was a culture that expected the president to be calling the shots...there was a real conditioning that the main shots, and sometimes not-so-main shots, were called from the president's office" (Interview, 1989).

Shaw found the meetings of the President's Cabinet, composed of all the vice presidents, the executive vice president, and the president, very unsatisfactory and "uncomfortable" (Interview, 1989). "It was the president's agenda and the president's meeting, and...you were expected to respond in that way," Shaw said, noting, "No group ever met together, except that one President's Cabinet, and it was all just information sharing" (Interview, 1989).

Shaw envisioned instilling responsibility and improving the systems of decision making, communication, and planning by building "a structure that would encourage teamwork. . . . I wanted people to talk to each other; I wanted projects to be coordinated. I wanted people to be thinking together about implications of issues" (Interview, 1989). She began by engaging the President's Cabinet in an examination of alternative organizational structures, finding its members dissatisfied with the way the President's Cabinet worked (Interview, 1989). The result was a new structure: a five-person College Cabinet replacing the large, ten-plus President's Cabinet. The College Cabinet meets weekly and is composed of the vice president for education programs; the vice president for business and college services; the vice president for student, staff, and organizational development; the assistant to the president; and the president.

The creation of additional structures opened new communication channels and fostered teamwork. Outside of the College Cabinet meeting and meetings on an as-needed basis during the week, vice presidents meet individually with the president each week. In those meetings, information is shared, discussion takes place, some direction is given, and some check of progress toward goals is made. Communication between Shaw and the vice presidents in cabinet and in individual meetings is described as open, honest, direct, fact-finding, information-seeking, and precipitating critical thinking and thinking in options, according to vice presidents Wingate, Harper, and McIntosh (Interviews, 1990).

Communication is also facilitated through what are generally weekly meetings of the vice presidents to share information about day-to-day operations, discuss issues and matters of budget, and plan. Vice presidents also hold weekly meetings with their staffs, and some have adopted the practice of meeting individually during the week with each of their staff members.

The Formation of the College Council. To counterbalance the reduced number serving on the College Cabinet and what might be perceived as less campus involvement, Shaw created a College Council, with representatives serving from across the campus community. The council examines campuswide issues, receives committee and task force reports with campuswide implications for its comment and recommendation (e.g., mission review, futures committee), and assists in the development and review of campus policies and procedures (e.g., substance abuse, drug-free workplace, grievance). According to many staff interviewed for this study, the College Council is widely viewed as a vehicle through which Shaw has implemented her vision of the participation and involvement of all areas of the campus in decision making, planning, and communication. The relationship between the College Cabinet and College Council is facilitated by the assistant to the president.

The Use of Committees and Task Forces. In commenting about her development of a common understanding of what the college is doing, Shaw (Interview, 1989) stated she feels no need to dictate [the common understanding]. I really am a believer that the facts will speak for themselves and that what you need to do is create a vehicle and a structure that will let people be privy to those facts and reach some common understanding.

To instill responsibility for the discovery of truth or common understanding in a culture conditioned to having these things revealed or dictated, Shaw has made extensive use of committees and task forces.

She admits: "I am controlling in terms of what's the charge to the group, who's going to be on the group, and I pick the leaders...constructive, clear, hard-hitting thinkers" (Interview, 1989). Committees and task forces are often supplied, she said, with "a tremendous amount of background information" (Interview, 1989), or, according to Barwick and 1989–90 Faculty Senate President Barbara Andrews (Interviews, 1990), are encouraged to develop their own bibliographies around the topic of their charge, from the viewpoint that information is empowering. Shaw (Interview, 1989) continued: "I insist that committees educate themselves. Pooled ignorance is not a rich resource." Once a committee has received its charge, has its sense of direction, "I certainly don't control, from the point of view of being actively involved in their business," Shaw said. "Once the reports come back, if they've been well done, then I'm pleased with them. That's their role" (Interview, 1989).

The issues around which committees and task forces have been formed are varied, but all reflect what, as a leader, Shaw pays attention to, measures, controls, and rewards. The first two she established were the Futures Committee and the Employee Recognition Committee.

According to Shaw (Interview, 1989), the former served as an initial "flash point for what is happening in this community that we need to be aware of and respond to." Exemplary of Shaw's "global thinking," according to Wingate (Interview, 1990), the Futures Committee served in a strategic planning function, encouraging some Janusian and paradoxical thinking among its membership.

The implementation of the Employee Recognition Committee provided Shaw with the opportunity to immediately begin a program of reward and recognition. As she had stated in her Fall Conference address, "I want to work in a place that helps the stars shine and that recognizes and rewards its star performers." Monetary awards are given each quarter during the Faculty/Staff Forum for outstanding performances in a faculty, support, classified, and administrative role. As Shaw expressed: "Every quarter we have those forums and celebrate our excellence. It is renewing for everybody, not just the people who get the awards. They all really share in the accomplishments of other people." The annual winner in each of the recognition categories is announced during Fall Conference, along with the Innovator of the Year Award and another teaching award, the Larry B. Harding Award. Awards for service are also given at that time. According to interviews with staff for this case study, the establishment of the Employee Recognition Committee, the formation of a recognition and reward system, and the environment of celebration that surrounds each ceremony has had a tremendously positive impact on the campus community.

Shaw formed some of the additional committees and task forces as the result of an action agenda she received from the faculty senate at the end of her first year as president. The agenda pinpointed issues of faculty concern—the grading system and advisement, for example. Shaw has established committees and task forces to take a proactive stance on emerging issues such as enhancing campus diversity; others, to examine options for an area undergoing change, such as the Student Development Task Force, formed to examine student services and activities.

Analysis reveals that Shaw's use of committees and task forces incorporates what leaders pay attention to, measure, and control; leader reactions to critical incidents and organizational crises; deliberate role modeling, teaching, and coaching; and criteria for allocation of rewards and status—four of the five primary mechanisms for embedding and reinforcing culture identified by Schein (1985a). Her use also incorporates three of five secondary cultural articulation and reinforcement mechanisms identified by Schein (1985a): the organization's design and structure; organizational systems and procedures; and formal statements of organizational philosophy.

Committees and task forces are widely viewed as additional vehicles through which Shaw has implemented her vision of the participation and involvement of all areas of the campus in decision making, planning, and communication, according to numerous interviews for this study. Interviewees expressed the perception that as a result of committee and task force involvement, opportunities exist for discussion before decisions are made and that the institution of some policy initiatives and actions may move directionally from the bottom upward.

Improving Campus Communication. In addition to the improved communication that occurs from involvement and participation in the work of the Cabinet, College Council, and numerous committees and task forces, Shaw has also chosen additional avenues to improve campus communication. To foster openness and honesty in communication, Shaw "addresses the grapevine," noted Adult Basic Literacy Education Department Head Cindy Johnston (Interview, 1990). Johnston elaborated:

She knows it's there. She tries to dispel myths or rumors when they start, if they are, in fact, [false] rumors. If they are not, she's very open and honest about that as well. There are still communication problems, but when the grapevine is as strong as it is at Central Piedmont, it's very difficult to dispel it.

Shaw has instituted quarterly faculty/staff and student forums. She and the vice presidents attend and often respond to questions in their areas.

A regular monthly breakfast meeting with the vice presidents and the administrators who report directly to them has been created. While providing an opportunity for information sharing, the meeting also affords team-building experiences through, for example, brainstorming when the meeting takes an issues orientation. Similar monthly breakfast meetings are scheduled between the president and smaller groups on campus.

Shaw very capably communicates appreciation to members of the college community. As Assistant to the President Worth Campbell (Interview, 1990) expressed it, "Shaw never misses the opportunity to send a thank-you note or to recognize someone for his or her contributions." Administrative Assistant Chris Buchanan (Interview, 1990) concurred: "She thanks everybody for everything." In public gatherings, she is quick to recognize and give credit to the work of those accompanying her. In making personal introductions, she communicates respect and pride for the person being introduced.

Hiring to Influence Culture. Although a complete turnover in the cabinet since Shaw's arrival has affected the level of team synergy achieved by top administrators, that turnover has also provided Shaw with an opportunity to embed and reinforce cultural assumptions at the administrative level through hiring practices (Schein, 1985a). For example, in the hiring process for all three vice presidents, people who would work with and for the individuals in those positions participated in the search process, offering Shaw their recommendations for final selection. The individuals selected for each position are representative of the potential for teamwork and share in the vision and values of the college.

For example, Vice President for Business and College Services John Harper, the "senior" member of the vice presidential team, supports Shaw's strong student orientation and her desire "to provide as much support to the student as can be obtained within the resources available," while being ever "mindful of taxpayer stewardship and very interested in carrying out assessment or analysis to be sure that the dollars being used are being used efficiently as well as effectively" (Interview, 1990). It was in support of this student orientation that Harper introduced, at Shaw's request, control systems in budgeting, hiring, and purchasing, for example. When systems have met with resistance, Shaw has supported the systems, "sometimes even doing a little cheerleading," Harper said (Interview, 1990). Of the strong student orientation, Harper (Interview, 1990) says:

> Even when we deal with students at the VP level, it's very much a result of her direction—a 'can-do' attitude. At Student Forums, we are going to give each person there the opportunity to speak, and no issue is too small to receive the direct attention of a vice president.

Shaw has also begun to influence the culture and climate through hiring practices at other levels of the college. In a 1989–90 revision of the college's hiring policies and procedures, a confirming interview with Shaw prior to the final offer of a position became a part of the hiring process for faculty, supervisory and managerial level positions, and professional support faculty. Despite the confirming nature of the interview, Shaw retains the right of final refusal (Central Piedmont Community College, 1989a, 1989b).

Individual Development. In addition to organizational development, Shaw's emphasis on involvement and participation has assisted in the development of individuals. Because of Shaw's emphasis on activities such as fact finding, validating, critical thinking, global thinking, and discussion, College Council and committee and task force involvement has provided individuals with growth, challenges, and opportunities in learning and leadership. Case study analysis of data indicates that during 1989 and into 1990 staff development activities with a management or leadership focus increased.

According to many staff members interviewed for the case study, Shaw also encourages individuals to further their education and has expanded the thinking of several about career options. Commented upon most often by interviewees, however, is Shaw's skill at making people aware of their abilities and assisting them in bringing those abilities to the forefront and using them.

Building Community Relationships. Shaw said one of the items on her agenda when she came to Central Piedmont was "to build community relationships" (Interview, 1989). Shaw (Interview, 1990) related:

> I think, in terms of following somebody who is well-established and has been there twenty-three years, one of the first tasks is to become the president in terms of other people's views of what is going on. So, a part is building community and raising image.

Part of it is, indeed, personal in terms of who you are. Can you establish yourself as the individual in that position?

According to retired Board of Trustees Member Pete Sloan (Interview, 1990), Shaw "hit the ground running and worked very hard," demonstrating that "she was the person who was here, she could get the job done, and we're not going to miss a step." In her first year as president, Shaw took her Central Piedmont message to more than a hundred civic, social, political, and service organizations. As college foundation Director Powell Majors (Interview, 1990) remarked, "She sold herself to the community, lock, stock, and barrel."

As the 1989 Campaign Chair for the United Way of Central Carolinas, Shaw further developed her community-building role. As she spoke at the various United Way kick-offs in businesses and industries throughout the Central Carolina area, she carried her strong personal message of vision, care and respect for others, commitment, competence, quality, and responsibility. In personal conversations, Shaw describes United Way as an organization that "helps people help themselves. . . empowers people—putting people in touch with the capacity within themselves" and that is about "creating connections. . . building community." As envisioned by Shaw, the United Way is very similar to the community college, acting as an agent of transformational leadership—lifting people, through their services, into their better selves. With her leadership, the ambitious annual goal of $16.7 million was exceeded.

The Board of Trustees. As with the college itself, there is little disagreement about the beginning of the reframing process for the Board of Trustees. The process began with a person, an important event, and a statement: the hiring of Shaw as president and her expressed desire to have a contract and be "evaluated annually. . . in a systematic way" (Interview, 1990). While the board was agreeable, her expressed desire, explicitly and implicitly, brought with it a qualitatively different way of understanding. With the founding president, evaluation had been informal, and there had been no contract.

As with the faculty and administration, Shaw knew that board members thought the college was performing its work well, but they questioned whether *how* it was performing was right for the times. Mindful of the good working relationship between the board and the founding president, Shaw set to alter the "how" of her working relationship. Recognizing that the board had been "clearly administrative driven," she said she wanted to create "a better balance in that" and improve the position of the college by ensuring that the board was "very well informed and really understands what the issues are, what the directions are" (Interview, 1990). Shaw indicated:

To me the 'no surprises' dictum that is given to presidents [by boards] has very little to do with individual incidents and a lot to do with creating a context and a climate in your board in which board members really do know the issues and the directions (Interview, 1990).

As she had done with the college, her method of achieving a state of "no surprises" for the board was involvement and participation. To facilitate this, Shaw indicated (Interview, 1990) that she provides information to the board in the same manner she does, for example, to campus committees, based on the assumption that the truth of matters is gradually discovered, not magically revealed. Current Board Chair Claytor (Interview, 1990) noted that the board now receives or hears reports and studies "at the same time Shaw does for the first time, and we can react to the same extent that she can." As a result of the openness in information sharing, Claytor indicated the board "knows more about what is going on at the state level than we ever have before, and that's continuing to increase" (Interview, 1990). He continued: "We're starting to invite members of the State Board [of Community Colleges] to our local board meetings to try to encourage some communication there. And that's never been done before."

In July 1989, Shaw took another step to increase the involvement and participation of the board. She proposed to Claytor a change in the board committee structure that would have, she said, "the governance structure reflect the institutional priority" (Interview, 1990)—education. She proposed the addition of a new committee, an Education Committee, along with the Finance and Facilities, Development, Governance, and Executive committees. The previous committee structure had included only Finance, Facilities, Public Relations, Policies and Plans, and Executive committees. The proposed committee structure, in addition to reflecting the college's top priority, would provide a way for cabinet members to work in a staff role with the board and, Shaw said, "would provide a more even distribution of work that more adequately reflected our priorities" (Interview, 1990). Claytor was most receptive to the proposal and took it to the board, which approved it and began working within the new committee structure in the fall of 1989.

Claytor assesses Shaw's relationship with the board as "a partnership... and the board is another member of that team that she's created" (Interview, 1990). Such an open relationship also speaks to her effectiveness in establishing herself as a legitimate and capable president, possessing a strong base of competence, confidence, credibility, and trust.

The State. Shaw has begun to alter the historical relationship that the college had with the state using the same methodology that has been effective with the college and the Board of Trustees—involvement, participation, and information. The open, collaborative way in which she and the vice presidents deal with issues such as full-time equivalent (FTE) auditing and with questions of autonomy is credited with producing positive results. In state FTE Auditor Phil Marion's view (Interview, 1990), there is a spirit of cooperation, of making things better together. As he described it:

> Shaw has been attacking issues that we have recommended be reviewed. And those things have been changed. Her way of dealing with things is proactive, where she's trying to ward off problems rather than hoping they'll come to a head and then get to fight them.

Making the Transformation

Analysis of quantitative data generated in this study indicates that the variety of conditions specified by Lundberg (1985) as necessary for transformation within an organization—permitting, enabling, and precipitating—existed at Central Piedmont under the leadership of Ruth Shaw. All four permitting conditions distinguished by Lundberg (1985) are apparent in the case study analysis: the availability of some surplus of change resources; a system readiness for change—a willingness and ability on the part of system members to live with the anxiety that accompanies uncertainty; the existence of a minimal degree of system coupling; and the ability of transition agents to envision and skillfully communicate alternative organizational futures.

During organizational transformations, which often take three to five years (Tichy, 1980, 1983; Tichy and Ulrich, 1984; Tichy and Devanna, 1986), the leader must manage the organizational dynamics of transformation, taking the organization through five phases: (1) the trigger event; (2) the development of a felt need for change in the organization and/or a dissatisfaction with the status quo; (3) the creation of a vision of the desired future state; (4) the mobilization of commitment; and (5) the institutionalization of change by shaping and reinforcing the new culture. Tools through which transitions are shared and visions become practice are the organization's communication, problem-solving, and decision-making systems; and major levers for institutionalizing change are the human resources systems of selection, development, appraisal, and reward (Tichy, 1980, 1983; Tichy and Ulrich, 1984; Tichy and Devanna, 1986). Analysis of data sources in this case study indicates Central Piedmont is in phase five of organizational transition, and the extensive use of identified tools and major levers is evident.

Clear, also, is the effective relationship of what Schein (1984) identifies as primary and secondary culture-embedding and -reinforcing mechanisms in framebreaking and in reshaping an organization's culture. They can be the effective tools of succeeding presidents in community colleges, as they have been for succeeding CEOs in business and industry, when managing the organizational dynamics of transition.

The Succeeding President: Leadership Behaviors and Style

A close analysis of the case study data regarding the transformation of culture begun by Ruth Shaw leaves no doubt that leadership and culture are inextricably linked and that "neither can really be understood by itself" (Schein, 1985a, p. 2). Prevailing are transformational leadership behaviors—those required to effect and implement change and to manage the organizational and individual dynamics of such change.

According to Bass (1985b), it is the transformational leader who "changes the social warp and woof of reality" (p. 24). Bass (1985b) describes the transformational leader as "one who motivates us to do more than we originally expected to do. This original performance expectation is based on our original level of confidence in reaching desired, designated outcomes by means of our performance" (p. 20).

A leader achieves the transformation of followers in one of three closely connected ways:

- By raising our level of awareness, our level of consciousness about the importance and value of designated outcomes, and ways of reaching them
- By getting us to transcend our own self-interest for the sake of the team, organization, or larger polity
- By altering our need level on Maslow's (or Alderfer's) hierarchy or expanding our portfolio of needs and wants (Bass, 1985b, p. 20)

Case study analysis indicates Shaw's ability to use each.

Shaw's vision for the college, her strategy of excellence, which drives the transformational change effort, is marked by the values of that vision—caring and respect for others, commitment, competence, quality, and responsibility. Undergirding the vision and values are some basic assumptions, best expressed through her use of language in interviews for this case study and in campuswide speeches: on the organization's relationship to its environment—"I believe that I have the personal power to affect the world in which I work—and I believe that you do, too"; on the nature of reality and truth—"Pooled ignorance is not a rich resource," and valuing "analytical" truth-seeking; human nature—"helping others achieve," and "Do you know how good you are?"; the nature of human activity—"I am responsible to those with and for whom I work—but I am not responsible for them"; and the nature of human relationships—"teamwork," and "collaboration."

Shaw's assumptions represent significant departures from the assumptions that were embedded in the culture of Central Piedmont when she arrived. An outgrowth of Shaw's assumptions is her marked use of the transformational leadership behaviors of consideration, intellectual stimulation, and charisma with a subfactor of inspiration.

Caring and respect for others is an expressed value of Shaw's, and, as such, transformational behaviors related to consideration are readily identifiable in the data sources of the case study. According to Bass (1985b), consideration has two components: (1) the consideration in consultation with subordinates as a group, in consensual decision making as evidenced in regular group meetings, and in treating all subordinates alike; and (2) individualized consideration.

In regard to the first component, case study analysis points to those leadership behaviors in regard to Shaw's work with the College Cabinet and the Board of Trustees. Consideration is also revealed in regular campus group meetings and the manner in which Shaw works with the College Council, faculty senate, and the various committees and task forces she forms. Bass (1985b) asserts that consideration "is central to participative management to the extent that it focuses on the employee's needs for growth and participation in decisions affecting his work and career" (p. 82). Data from numerous interviews with staff support a general perception that Shaw's caring, sensitivity, openness, and respect, for example, are extended equally and unilaterally to all involved in the college.

According to Bass (1985b), the behaviors of individualized consideration—the second component of consideration—can take many forms. Most important is the leader's ability to express appreciation for a job well done. Case study data support Shaw's adeptness at and the energy with which she pursues this behavior. In working with individuals, Shaw is described by staff members interviewed for this study as being open, caring, nurturing, counseling, and advising in nature. This description supports Shaw's ability to constructively point out weaknesses to followers—another important aspect of individualized consideration. Case study analysis reveals individualized consideration in the form of Shaw's assigning special projects to provide learning opportunities, to promote follower self-confidence, and to bring out a follower's special talent. Case study data support the exemplary manner in which individualized consideration, seen in keeping individual followers informed about what is happening and why, is demonstrated.

A preponderance of Shaw's leadership behaviors are also to be found in the second category of behavior aligned with transformational leadership—intellectual stimulation. Bass (1985b) explains:

> By the transformational leader's intellectual stimulation, we mean the arousal and change in followers of problem awareness and problem solving, of thought and imagination, and of beliefs and values, rather than arousal and change in immediate action. The intellectual stimulation of the transformational leader is seen in the discrete jump in the followers' conceptualization, comprehension, and discernment of the nature of the problems they face and their solutions (p. 99).

By expanding involvement and participation through such avenues as the College Council and committees and task forces, the campus community as a whole has become involved in more strategic thinking, in rethinking, in thinking about old problems in new ways, and, in general, in what Bass called "the tasks of analysis, formulation, implementation, interpretation, and evaluation" (1985b, p. 99). Case study analysis additionally demonstrates Shaw's active use of proactive thinking and the encouragement of proactive as opposed to reactive thinking throughout the campus.

Indeed, as revealed by case study analysis, the College Cabinet, College Council, committees and task forces, and the forums have become symbolic of Shaw's vision of greater involvement and participation. As Bass (1985b) indicates, the new symbols "help to articulate, propagate, and recall the new ideas and beliefs, as well as to attach emotional value to them" (p. 110).

With a concern for building trust and teams, Shaw provides an existentially oriented intellectual stimulation that is aligned with transformational leadership. Bass (1985b) characterizes such stimulation as promoting integrative decision making, in which much information is used to "generate many solutions for implementation" (p. 111). Relying on informal processes, the existential leader believes that "intellectual understanding can only emerge in the human process of interacting with the environment" (Bass, 1985b, p. 111). This type of stimulation favors "creative synthesis over pure logic" (Bass, 1985b, p. 111). All activities revealed by case study data that work toward participation and involvement provide evidence of existentially oriented intellectual stimulation.

As in the categories of consideration and intellectual stimulation, case study analysis indicates a preponderance of leadership behaviors in the category of charisma with a subfactor of inspirational leadership. According to Bass (1985b), "Charisma carries with it a challenge to the old order, a break with continuity, a risky adventure, continual movement, ferment, and change" (p. 37). Such qualities characterized the texts of Shaw's speeches and activities during her first six months as president. On each of those occasions, Shaw related "the work and mission of their group to strongly held values, ideals, and aspirations shared in common by their organization's culture" (Bass, 1985b, p. 40). Bass continues:

> In organizational settings, they paint for their subordinates an attractive vision of what the outcomes of their efforts could be. This provides subordinates with more meaning for their work. It arouses enthusiasm, excitement, emotional involvement, and commitment to group objectives (1985b, p. 40).

Analysis of data within the case study indicates that Shaw demonstrates many leadership behaviors related to self-confidence/self-esteem, self-determination, and freedom from internal conflict (Bass, 1985b)—characteristics of charismatic leadership. One of the characteristics of charismatic leadership that aligns it most closely with transformational leadership—insight into the needs, values, and hopes of followers (Bass, 1985b)—is abundantly present in Shaw. She builds on the needs, values, and hopes of followers through dramatic and persuasive words and actions; conceives and articulates goals that increase optimism for the future; provides to followers a sense of overall purpose; transmits a sense of mission to followers, appealing to achievement, affiliation, and power motives; works toward mutual enhancement of effort; inspires loyalty in followers to the organization and/or to her; inspires; structures problems for followers, providing for easier comprehension and more effective problem solving; displays individual consideration; creates enthusiasm about assignments; and assumes the role of mentor, coach, and teacher.

Within the charismatic leadership subfactor of inspiration, the case study reveals Shaw's strong use of the leadership behaviors described by Bass (1985b); in particular, Shaw inspires followers by emotional supports and appeals, transforming their levels of motivation beyond original expectations; uses symbols, images, a vision of a better state of affairs, and persuasive language to inspire extra effort; inspires belief in "the greater causes" (p. 70); builds confidence; utilizes the Pygmalion effect; possesses an action orientation; creates a climate of openness and trust; has a vast, open, informal communication network; encourages volunteerism; and employs or adds non-intellectual, emotional qualities to the influence process.

Close analysis of the study's data sources indicates that Shaw's leadership behaviors clearly fall within three of the five categories identified by Bass (1985b)—consideration, intellectual stimulation, and charisma with a subfactor of inspiration. The absence of significant behaviors in the remaining two categories—contingent reward and management-by-exception—is not surprising. The former encompasses behaviors contrary to Shaw's valuing, emphasizing, and facilitating higher order goals. The latter, which involves the use of contingent aversive reinforcement only when there are breakdowns, failures, or deviations, embodies behaviors contrary to Shaw's forward, proactive thinking.

Conclusion: Culture at Founding and in Change

The case studies of the founding and the succeeding presidents of Central Piedmont Community College do much to inform emerging leaders about the relationship of culture and leadership. Obvious is the manner in which the values, basic assumptions, or beliefs and the leadership style of each president, as exerted in either founding or changing the culture of the college, shape shared values, organizational structures, communication, decision making, and planning.

Three conclusions can be drawn from the case study. First, the leadership behaviors of the founding and the succeeding president have both been appropriate, in their times, for the college. The leadership of founding president Richard Hagemeyer, transactional and marked by an entrepreneurial spirit, was well-suited to the college during its birth, growth, and mid-life and into its years of maturity—years of relative environmental stability. Hagemeyer's basic assumptions regarding the college's relationship to its environment and regarding the nature of reality and truth, of human nature, of human activity, and of human relationships became the cultural assumptions of the college. The embedding and continual reinforcing of those strong cultural assumptions made the college a reflection of the founder and promoted the college's rise to excellence.

As reflected in current literature, however, leadership must be able to manage culture so that it is adaptable in turbulent times, like those times that marked the latter years of Central Piedmont's maturity. During turbulent times, to adapt is to survive and/or, in the case of the college, to reach new levels of excellence. Albrecht and Albrecht (1987) predict: "For the rest of this century, the management of organizational success is going to be all about culture—understanding it, respecting it, shaping it, and reinforcing it along the lines of success in the environment" (p. vii). When signs of the need for either external adaptation or internal integration arise, leadership must be able to move the culture toward that adaptation or integration.

Bennis (1989) notes that leaders must learn to recognize that in an information-intensive, service-intensive society, people are the primary resource of the organization—assets rather than liabilities—and that organizations must deploy themselves and all of their assets. Naisbitt and Aburdene (1990) similarly point to the paradigm shift from "management in order to control an enterprise to leadership in order to bring out the best in people and to respond quickly to change" (p. 218). They see the recognition of the individual and the "doctrine of individual responsibility" (p.298) underlying the trends of the 1990s.

According to Bennis (1989), a failure to recognize the individual leads to a scenario much like Henry Ford's, whose company was an extension of him as the founder. Bennis characterizes Ford as a man of "extraordinary vision" (p. 178); however, "vision, like the world itself, is dynamic, not static, and must be renewed, adapted, adjusted. And when it becomes too dim, it must be abandoned and replaced" (p. 178). Bennis (1989) describes the replacement of Ford at Ford Motor Company: "Its one-man band [was]. . . replaced by a string quartet—an assembly of leaders working in harmony toward a common vision" (p. 179). This paradigm shift was also manifested at Central Piedmont.

Analyses of data in this case study indicate the founding president had become a prisoner of his leadership style (Kets de Vries, 1989) and, as such, was incapable of adjusting his leadership behaviors away from the entrepreneurial need for control. As Nanus (1989) asserts: "Nothing narrows the vision and impoverishes an organization so much as a leader locked into an image of the future as a perpetuation of the past" (p. 84).

The flexibility, collaboration, integrative thinking, individualized consideration, and insight into the needs, values, and hopes of followers required for the college's adaptation and integration are leadership behaviors of transformation. These behaviors, data analyses indicate, are among the strengths of succeeding president Ruth Shaw. Transformational leadership by its nature places its focus on the recognition of the individual and teamwork. In this case, therefore, a transformational leader, such as the succeeding president, provides the type and strength of leadership behaviors that are relevant to this period of time, framebreaking organizational change and continuing change for the purposes of internal and external cultural adaptation and integration.

A second conclusion is the apparent effectiveness of what Schein (1985a) identifies as primary and secondary culture-embedding and -reinforcing mechanisms in the initial establishment of a culture by the founding president and, when cultural adaptation, integration, and change become necessary, by the succeeding president. Use of these mechanisms is effective regardless of the differences that may exist in presidential leadership styles or in the values, basic assumptions, and/or beliefs held by the individual presidents.

The third conclusion drawn from this case study is that community college leaders can, with confidence, look to the literature of the corporate world for insights regarding leadership, culture, and organizational change and transition. This study would certainly suggest that, as Schein (1985a) posits:

> There is a possibility—underemphasized in leadership research— *that the only thing of real importance that leaders do is to create and manage culture* and that the unique talent of leaders is their ability to work with culture (p. 2).

In the results of this case study, it is inevitably clear that community college leaders must recognize the interrelationships of the entities of leadership, culture, and organizational change and transition. To guarantee their success, leaders must become adept at the management of all facets of culture. The literature provided by writers from the corporate world— Peters, Waterman, Schein, Bass, Bennis, Nanus, Naisbitt, Tichy, Devanna, Ulrich, Bartunek, Lundberg, Kimberly, Albrecht, Ott, Kotter, and Kets de Vries, for example—yields insights for the community college world regarding those interrelationships and cultural management. This literature can equip the community college world's emerging leaders with a sense of direction and with transforming insights to see it through these current turbulent times.

■

Chapter 10

Culture, Leadership, and Organizational Systems

By G. Allan Clark

For an exemplary illustration of how leadership values and organizational systems shape college culture, one can look to De Anza College, a two-year unionized college in California. De Anza has been able to develop a distinctive set of relationships when dealing with its internal and external environments, and these relationships have earned the college a national reputation for excellence.

This chapter presents a qualitative case study of De Anza College. The literature that has emerged from the examination of excellent corporations is used as a sensitizing device to focus the research. Interviews, college records, data from three leadership surveys conducted by the college over a three-year period, a climate survey, and a four-month period of participant observation comprise the primary sources of data presented in this chapter.

When data were analyzed, a number of attributes of corporate organizational excellence applicable to a public two-year unionized college became clear. An important concept identified—and unique from the literature on organizations—is the concept of shared governance. Stemming from an institutional value system of collaboration and modelled and reinforced by the college leaders, open participation in shaping decisions appeared to be the key variable in maintaining inherent conflict at nondebilitating levels.

Strong emphases on obtaining, maintaining, and developing employee competence, slack resources, leadership encouragement of purposeful change, and shared governance coalesced to enable the college to successfully manage its internal and external environments.

The De Anza Experience

The Foothill-De Anza Community College District, originally called the Foothill Community College District, was established in 1957. Located at the southern end of San Francisco Bay, the district serves the communities of Palo Alto, Mountain View, Los Altos, Cupertino, and Sunnyvale, California. The first college, Foothill College, opened in temporary quarters in 1958.

Enrollment in the district, paralleling enrollment trends throughout North America, grew rapidly; a second campus was soon needed. In 1962 voters passed a bond issue, and construction began on the De Anza campus, located in Cupertino, in 1966. De Anza opened for instruction in the fall of 1967.

There are more than 1,200 community, junior, and technical colleges in the United States. In the fall 1987 enrollment survey of the American Association of Community and Junior Colleges, the Foothill-De Anza Community College District was ranked eighth in size for credit enrollment for college districts, and De Anza College was ranked first for single-campus credit enrollment. In the fall of 1990 De Anza college had 27,000 students enrolled.

District and College Governance Structure

Overall leadership of the district is provided by a six-member Board of Trustees. Five of the six trustees are elected by the voters of the service area, and the sixth member is elected by the student governments of Foothill and De Anza colleges. The Board of Trustees engages a district chancellor who serves as the chief executive officer of the district. The board also appoints the presidents of each college. In the case of De Anza College, A. Robert (Bob) DeHart, named as president by the Board of Trustees to oversee the campus construction that began in 1965, has served in this role since.

The Board of Trustees meets biweekly and is described by many district employees as a hands-on board, in that board members are keenly interested in and committed to the college mission but expect administrators to provide leadership and give them the space to do so. The Board of Trustees places emphasis on extensive searches and rigorous selection procedures for all members of the leadership team. This emphasis permeates the entire district, and every reasonable effort is made to recruit, select, and retain the highest possible caliber of staff.

A high degree of employee continuity characterizes the Foothill-De Anza Community College District. Many employees who joined the district in the 1960s were still providing leadership in the fall of 1990. Fifty-seven percent of the key administrators and faculty leaders interviewed in the fall of 1990 had served the district for twelve or more years. Forty percent of those interviewed had been employed by the district for twenty or more years. It was not uncommon to hear employees express the desire that there be a position at the college for one of their family members as, in their opinion, the college district was a fine place to work.

The cornerstone of the Foothill-De Anza Community College District's shared governance approach is a districtwide committee known as the District Budget and Policy Development Group (BPDG). The BPDG is more than a "Chancellor's Cabinet," as it is the vehicle that provides all segments of the college community with the opportunity to offer input on a host of decision processes. Gulassa (1989), president of the Faculty Association in the fall of 1990, notes:

> All members, from the chancellor to students, are seated at the boardroom table at the same time, and all engage in a discussion/ debate that assures a clear understanding of the problems, explores different options, and generally leads to modified consensus. Thus the entire hierarchy simultaneously collaborates in the end product—the decision or board recommendation (p. 3).

An administrative realignment resulting in a structure of three vice presidents—for instruction, student services, and administrative services— took place during the course of this case study. The redesign for De Anza College was based on the premise that the college must fashion a system of formal positions that will allow for better linking between units. At the same time the college became "flatter," with fewer positions between the president and the staff and faculty.

In addition to the formal organizational components, there are other groups that are influential in the governing of De Anza College. The first of these is the Faculty Senate. The senate is "an institutional organization whose primary function is that of being a representative of the faculty [and] to make recommendations pertaining to professional and academic matters to management and the governing board" (Douglas, 1980, p. 4). The president of the Faculty Senate and senior deans of De Anza meet monthly to exchange ideas and plans in a forum cochaired by DeHart and the Faculty Senate president. These meetings facilitate effective coordination of the instructional leadership provided by faculty and members of the management team, consisting of three administrative deans, five division deans, and the vice president of instruction. Other members of the college community attend these meetings when matters of particular concern arise or when their expertise is required to assist with a particular challenge.

The vice president of instruction, the three senior instructional deans, and the ten division deans meet on a weekly basis. All college deans meet for a one-hour session once a week to foster their own professional development.

The vice president of instruction and the three senior instructional deans meet weekly to coordinate all matters relating to instruction. The major responsibility of this group is the leadership for, and active participation in, the search, hiring, and tenure review processes of the instructional faculty. These structural and organizational systems provide the opportunity for extensive communication flow. Galbraith (1972) indicates that predictability of task is one primary aspect of organizational form.

Decision-Making Systems

In an organization, the essential ingredients for the development of shared values and a shared culture are comprehensive formal and informal communication networks (Peters and Waterman, 1982; Waterman, 1987). These networks provide the raw material of decision making: information. The decision-making processes at De Anza College are, in large measure, a reflection of the processes in place at the district level. The values that undergird the BPDG support similar systems at De Anza.

Cohen and March (1986), in their study of decision-making systems in some university organizations, argue that the classic models of decision making do not apply in many educational settings. They suggest educational decision making differs from the classical model in three important ways: preferences are problematic, a known way of dealing with complexity is unclear, or participation is fluid. In the Foothill-De Anza Community College District, as in the case in any environment that is subject to rapid change, the appropriate choice is problematic and consistent with the Cohen and March analysis. However, the district has a better understanding of the sum total of the processes that yield results. In the district, and at De Anza, the organizational goals are very clear; there are loosely coupled linkages that tie together the various units within the organization.

The need to unite various components, often in an environment that is unstable, creates a degree of task uncertainty. For community colleges, vagaries of government funding, shifting community demographics, influx of international students with diverse needs or local students at various competency levels, and shifting demands of the business community all add to the task complexity. In this milieu, many discrete elements of information are required in a college's decision-making process. Because of this complexity, various divisions and sectors of the college are interdependent and interrelated.

Galbraith (1972) suggests that mechanisms to coordinate information flow must be supplemented by an organizational design that does not overwhelm participants with information so that inaction results. If one essential component of organizational growth is a network of communication systems, then the structural design must fit the flow of information in the least destructive manner.

De Anza College has been successful in integrating organizational systems and structures in a manner that not only encourages, but mandates information flow. The confluence of structure and systems is one of the key attributes of the culture of excellence at De Anza College. For example, DeHart's critical success factors, i.e., enrollment patterns, demographic information, and success rates in transfer, provide data to guide the decision-making process.

The Importance of Values

Beyer (1981) states that values are normative systems of preference for certain courses of action or particular outcomes. Pettigrew (1979) posits that organizations can in part be defined by the values that the leader expresses. He goes on to suggest that the founder can put a personal stamp on specific components of an organization in a way that creates a particular culture. The culture is further enhanced by recruiting, hiring, and retaining followers who fit the particular cultural mode.

Pfeffer (1981) argues that one of the important functions of leadership in an organization may be to provide explanations, rationalizations, and legitimizations for a number of activities that are taken in the name of the organization. According to Pfeffer, the construction and maintenance of a system of shared values can lead to a particular organizational culture.

For De Anza College an evolving statement of values is present in the form of the annual address the president makes to the entire college community. As one member of the college said, "I would not miss these speeches, as it is when we learn of the major priorities for the upcoming year." In addition to these annual addresses, a formal statement of values has been collaboratively prepared by the key staff, faculty, and administrative leadership. The value statement, or portions thereof, are often referred to in informal and formal college gatherings (See Figure 10.1).

The Value of Innovation

Daft and Becker (1978) indicate that if there are good horizontal and vertical communication systems within an organization that expose members to new information, and if the organization has what they identify as "enabler" variables, then innovation will be maximized. One of the

---

Figure 10.1
De Anza College Value Statement

De Anza College Values:
- Institutional integrity, meaning the congruence of programs, activities, and behaviors with institutional beliefs
- Community relationships, both internal and external
- Institutional diversity among its people and programs
- The quality of student and staff life
- Learning
- Access and quality in concert
- Collegiality
- Self-assessment and innovation
- Student success
- A "personal best"

---

key enabler variables they identify is a pool of slack resources. DeHart and the three vice presidents, and the Foothill-De Anza Community College District, by deliberate plan provide for resources that can be committed on a "needed-now" basis. For example, the senior members of the management team—president and vice presidents—all have discretionary funds in their budgets.

In interviews many members of the college community identified the college's practice to "not over-regulate its employees" as a major contributor to innovation. In developing the organizational system of the college, DeHart and the leadership team paid close attention to the criticisms of the traditional bureaucratic model of organization suggested by Gouldner (1964). Gouldner argues that while organizational rules explain in concise terms the specific obligations of employees, they also set out the minimum levels of acceptable behavior and may perpetuate mediocre levels of performance. Gouldner also indicates that a hierarchy of authority can enhance coordination, but frequently does so at the expense of communication.

The Value of Quality Faculty and Staff

The second De Anza value identified and corroborated by district reports deals with the quality of faculty and staff. The formal value statement indicates that enhancing "the quality of staff life" contributes to the recruitment and retention of quality staff, improves morale and motivation, and increases teaching and learning opportunities in the classroom. In addition, quality staff and faculty contribute to the institutional identity. These statements also suggest that professional growth opportunities ultimately enhance learning and are beneficial to staff, students, and the institution as a whole. Figure 10.2 summarizes De Anza's strengths as identified by the twenty-one members of the college community who were interviewed in the course of this case study. They strongly indicate that quality people are the major strength of the college.

Figure 10.2
De Anza College Strengths Identified by Interview Respondents

Strength	Number of Responses
1. Our people and how we support each other	11
2. The leadership of the college, particularly of the president	8
3. The ambience of the campus, the college resources, and the "energy" of Silicon Valley	6
4. The commitment of employees to the college, to instruction, and to shared governance	6
5. Lack of constraint by a formal bureaucracy and the emphasis on "empowerment" of all employees	4

Extensive procedures are in place at De Anza College to recruit quality staff from across North America. Advertisements are placed in a comprehensive list of journals, periodicals, and other publications of particular interest to the community college movement. In one case, the district authorized the hiring of a consultant to identify particular institutions and publications that, if they carried advertisements about the college, would alert potential applicants of opportunities in a specialized area of college endeavor.

The recruitment procedures are followed by interview processes that involve the college's senior management. The usual pattern is for the vice president of instruction to sit on the final selection committee for all tenure-track faculty positions and as many part-time or leave-replacement positions as time allows.

Following the selection procedure, there is an extensive orientation of new faculty in early September each year. For those faculty who are on a tenure track, the college has developed extensive evaluation procedures (De Anza College, 1989). *The Foothill-De Anza Community College District Tenure Review Handbook* is provided to all of the tenure-track employees, and a day-long workshop is held to explain the procedures. In the fall of 1990, with the support of the statewide union leadership, the time period for review of the competencies of new faculty prior to being advanced to tenure was extended from two to four years, beginning in the 1991 academic year.

Once faculty and staff are recruited, selected, and placed, they receive support for their continued development within the organization. When faculty reach the top step on the salary grid, they are rewarded for continued innovation and excellence. The Professional Achievement Award program, part of the collective bargaining agreement, recognizes the extra contribution that faculty make to the teaching and learning process. Upon application and approval by the board, faculty receive a monetary award that is applied to their base salary. A similar achievement award is provided for members of the administrative team.

The Value of Mutual Trust

The third value identified is that of trust. Fox (1974) provides a framework useful for analyzing the trust relationships that have developed at De Anza College and in particular for understanding the strategies De Anza leaders use to influence the trust values at the college. Fox suggests that trust can be viewed in reciprocal terms. If there are high levels of trust, and if the trust is reciprocal, an organizational emphasis on open communication and an atmosphere of give-and-take are likely to exist. In a low trust reciprocal relationship, there are carefully delineated roles and expectations within the organization and regular record keeping of the "give" and "takes." The leadership and the employees of the organization often have divergent views concerning organizational goals.

Specific behaviors that enhance trust by the leadership of De Anza College center around the steps that were taken to delegate and "push things down" the hierarchy of the organization. Members of the leadership team publicly recognize the positive contributions other team members, staff, or faculty members make to the college. The college leaders also enhance the trust relationships through their ability to influence perceptions. No matter how difficult the situation, positive thinking is always used to help solve the problem.

Another strategy that bolsters the trust dynamic is the encouragement DeHart provides to the senior management to gain visibility outside the immediate college community. Support for participation in a variety of national conferences and workshops is evident at the college. The recognition that comes from participation in leadership roles outside the immediate community signals to the internal college community that the senior leadership of the college knows what it is doing. In part, this strategy is sympathetic to the value that is placed on quality faculty and staff.

In summary, common appreciation of organizational goals, competent staff who keeps the college on the move, recognition by others outside the college of the competency of college leaders, and collaborative governance have created a synergism that enhances the trust relationship at De Anza. In the analysis by Fox (1974), De Anza College has a trust relationship that flows from a consensual dynamic, and organizational members interpret college events from a unitary frame of reference. The unitary frame of reference emphasizes an articulated vision of the future that becomes shared by all members of the organization.

The Value of Shared Leadership

In the early 1960s, the rapid growth of the community college movement in North America increased the demand for qualified college faculty and staff. Many of the faculty who joined these new community colleges came from university settings and were familiar with collegial forms of decision making. Many expected to be partners with the administrators of the colleges in developing programs responsive to community needs. However, the rapid growth of colleges and the need to make immediate decisions on a broad range of matters precluded extensive consultation with faculty. Vaughan (1986) identifies the early leaders of the community college movement as the "builder presidents." Presidents were often selected by college boards on the basis of their reputation for getting things done (See Chapter 8 for the characteristics of the "builder presidents").

As the college movement matured, it was influenced by some of the social unrest of the late 1960s and early 1970s, the Vietnam War and the tail-end of the Civil Rights Movement. Denison and Gallagher (1986) explain that the expanding community college movement depended heavily on universities, school districts, and vocational trade organizations for their new employees. These groups tended to bring their customary governance and union affiliations with them. Some community colleges, often reflective of local or state traditions, became unionized, while others tended to travel a different road. Participation in the leadership of the unionized colleges took on a different texture than it took in those colleges that remained non-union. In the unionized colleges, traditional forms of collegial decision making and shared leadership were confounded by the existence of a collective agreement structure.

It is impossible to examine specific strategies used by the De Anza leadership to foster values without discussing the district governance pattern. In the Foothill-De Anza Community College District, an experiment with shared governance was begun in the early 1980s. The first contract between the district trustees and the Faculty Association was negotiated in 1977. This was followed by the passage of SB 160, which enabled California community college faculty to organize for collective bargaining. Members of the college community indicated the first three years of collective bargaining were rather stormy. One member, in commenting on the period 1977–1980, said, "Once we got past the 'wars,' a strong, constructive union leadership emerged."

Against this backdrop, and under the leadership of District Chancellor Thomas Fryer, with assistance from the presidents of Foothill and De Anza Colleges, the full support of the Board of Trustees, and active participation by the collective bargaining units, the District Budget and Policy Development Group was formed. Fryer (1989) suggests that not only are mechanisms to foster an alignment of interest needed, but a system of values is required to undergird the excellent college. He argues:

> That employers have a responsibility to the human beings in their employ to attempt to make work meaningful for them in a rich and positive sense. . . . In so far as possible, employers should attempt to help workers make lives while they make a living. Thus, the sense of commitment to institutional purpose that the organization seeks to evoke from the worker is reciprocated by a comparable sense of organizational commitment to the worker. Underlying this commitment, of course, is a profound respect for, and deep sense of the intrinsic value of, every person who is a stakeholder in the organization (p. 226).

The Value of Learning

Since the college opened in 1967, De Anza has placed a high value on learning. In DeHart's early speeches and in published college documents there are many phrases such as "recognition and establishment of teacher-student relationships as the most influential factor in the learning process," "participants in our learning community," and "a diverse student body and staff who encourage various learning and teaching styles."

College leaders enhanced this value through both formal and informal rewards. Formal rewards are available to faculty and administrators through the Professional Achievement Awards program. This program, described earlier, is an extension of the district's commitment to promote the development of individuals' abilities. The Philosophy, Mission, and Priorities Statement of the district identifies the development of human potential, creativity, and excellence in individuals and groups as fundamentals of the value system.

The emphasis on innovation and leadership that permeates all De Anza College values is fully evident in the support given to college members interested in increased access to learning opportunities. The phrase "constant, purposeful innovation" is often heard around the college. There is ample evidence of the benefits of this imperative in the number of new ideas or programs that come before the Deans' Council, the senior budget and decision-making body at De Anza.

The Value of Change with Purpose

This "constant, purposeful innovation" is also seen in one college leader's testimony:

De Anza is a place where the focus and emphasis are on short-term projects—things we want to do now. We have long-term planning, but many of our initiatives are short-term. We decide what needs to be done, and we do it. This is an important part of our culture. We develop a lot of things—some not well connected—some not related to budget—and sometimes not philosophically connected, but we go ahead and experiment. One of the members of the leadership team, in commenting on the president's emphasis on change, suggested that 'He encourages innovations, he encourages the managers to pay attention to the innovations, and he rewards them. He models that in his own relentless, sometimes exhausting, search for new things, new approaches.'

The leadership team of the president and the three vice presidents keeps the need for more broadly based institutional change before the college community. The planning documents prepared for the mid-1980s accreditation process note:

The college must be able to adapt to sudden change, and to avail itself of new opportunities. A time of turbulence is a dangerous time, a period of rapid innovation, a period of fast and radical structural shifts, but it is also one of great opportunity for those who can understand, accept, and exploit the new realities. Never before have we had a stronger need for the strategies that will convert the threat of change into opportunities for productive contributions to society, the economy, and the individual. The leadership of the college uses a broad range of strategies to enhance the value of change—change at a personal and institutional level (De Anza College, 1986, p. 2).

The Value of Community

The term "community" appears regularly in many college publications. The De Anza value statements speak specifically to both internal and external community relationships. Many of DeHart's speeches also use the term with considerable regularity. In the discussion that follows, the term "community" is used in two ways: in a geographic sense and in an internal sense (i.e., sharing, or a community of interest).

College leaders build relationships with the community outside of the college in a variety of ways. A campus theater serves the community of Cupertino and provides a well-equipped facility for conferences, meetings, workshops, seminars, concerts, and a number of joint college/community-sponsored events.

Administrative leadership in the student services division has enabled the De Anza student body to carry forward a number of innovative projects. Since the college's extensive parking facilities are not used to full capacity on weekends, the student government sponsors a monthly flea market. The flea market has grown in size over the years and now produces a flow of dollars for specific college projects.

The Value of Organizational Integrity

The De Anza values statements place integrity first on the list and suggest that "honesty, credibility, clear communication, and 'walking the way we talk' are all aspects of institutional integrity, as well as shared governance, which recognizes the integrity of the individual as part of the larger college whole."

College leaders use a variety of techniques to enhance institutional integrity. In 1989, drawing on research conducted in the Community College Leadership Program at The University of Texas at Austin, the college leadership provided employees an opportunity to assess the climate of the college.

Climate studies emphasize the impact of the social context on the actors. The instrument used at De Anza College to assess climate was similar to the one used in the 1987 Roueche and Baker study of Miami-Dade Community College. The instrument sought to tap climate dimensions of leadership, motivation, communication, decision making, rewards, and job satisfaction. The climate data were collected and organized in a manner that enabled the development of a college climate profile along twenty-six specific attributes. In addition, each major college department could use the data to compare its profile with the aggregated profile for the college community.

College leaders communicated the survey results in an honest and credible manner to assist employees in making changes that would bring the positive attributes of the college into alignment with those of each department (See Chapter Two for an example of survey results).

Major components of institutional integrity are honesty and "walking the way we talk," yet the very nature of a community college creates a competition among student services, instruction, and administrative services for limited funds. During the research conducted for this case study, there were numerous honest exchanges completely devoid of rancor. Interviewees expressed an overarching desire to maintain the integrity of the enterprise.

The Value of Planning

Waterman (1987) identifies planning as one of the two "global" aspects of organizational excellence. Morgan (1989) suggests "intelligent organizations scan their environments and position themselves to deal with the challenges that lie ahead" (p. 73). He argues:

> More and more, the task of strategic management becomes that of reading the environment and of creating initiatives that will resonate with the changes that are occurring. In this way, organizations can develop a capacity to adapt to critical changes, and, through the management of key and environmental relations with government, customers, competitors, and potential collaborators, actually shape the changes that are occurring (p. 73).

The emphasis the leadership places on planning, incorporated in value statements and documents, was identified in many of the interviews for this study as one of the strengths of De Anza College. For example, one respondent suggested that "planning would be the second-greatest strength at De Anza. Bob DeHart is constantly assessing the environment and moving to position the college so that it can respond in effective ways." Another respondent, when commenting on De Anza's strengths, indicated:

> . . . DeHart's ability to set a vision. He has been here since the beginning, and this has given a sense of stability. In addition, DeHart has always emphasized the mission, not in a pro forma way, but in a serious way that meaningfully engages the college community in the dialogue. In addition, DeHart places strong emphasis on the planning process. He has a gift for figuring out what the educational purposes should be and then finding the resources to meaningfully pursue those purposes. DeHart has gotten better and better over the years at setting the broad view and letting other people take control of it.

In his 1990 speech to college employees, DeHart used the metaphor of "tree of excellence." He identified the tap root of his tree of excellence, and the base upon which everything else grows, as the employees. He went on to suggest that the trunk of his excellence tree was De Anza's

commitment to planning—long-term strategic planning and annual oper-
ational planning. He suggested that the desire to continuously innovate
and improve was not enough to achieve excellence; a plan was required
to give the necessary focus.

Some of the members of the college community that were interviewed
spoke highly of the commitment to planning at De Anza and in particular to the leadership DeHart gives in this area. One member observed:
"His vision has set this college on the right road. He has an evolving
vision of De Anza and has set things in motion to help us reach this
changing dream. He is now thinking where De Anza will be in the year
2025." Another member suggested: "DeHart places strong emphasis on
the planning process. He has a gift for figuring out what the educational
purposes should be and then finding the resources to meaningfully pursue them."

In the foreword to *A Proud Past, A Vital Future: Planning for the Eighties
and Beyond* (De Anza College 1986), DeHart states: "Our continuing commitment to good planning promises an even brighter future." The same
document states:

> Planning is the conscious process by which an institution assesses
> its strengths and weaknesses; assesses the likely future condition
> of its environment; identifies the future state for itself; and then
> develops strategies, policies and procedures, and work plans for
> reaching that state.

Case study data suggest that college leaders use the planning function to keep De Anza in the forefront of the community college enterprise in California. The overarching strategy of the leadership is to embed the value of planning. The "looseness" evident in the planning process
may be in fact fostering the loose coupling so critical for innovation to
prosper. As indicated in the earlier discussion of the strategies leaders
use to foster innovation, one of the key strategies is the freedom and encouragement to experiment.

The Value of Communication

De Anza's leadership team uses a variety of specific communication
techniques to embed college values and to support the value of communication itself. Phrases that include "communication must be a continuous program, not a brief campaign," "we should communicate in the most
direct way consistent with good sense," and "the division chair is the
focal point of organizational communication," demonstrate some of the
specific strategies that the leadership wants to embed within the college
ethos. During the course of this case study, members of the leadership

team moved responsibility and authority down the organizational hierarchy. There was a growing appreciation of the pivotal roles of department chairs within the enterprise. The leadership behavior was consistent with the value placed on the pivotal communication role played by the division deans. For example, in the budget development process all information relating to staff, purchases, etc. was shared openly and completely.

The Importance of Structure

Beyer (1981) posits that values can be transformed into a variety of institutional rules that are often imported into an organization and integrated into the structure. Structural form then becomes an expression of values. Harrison (1987) describes a symbiotic relationship among culture, person, and organizational structure. He suggests that if an organization's structure is created in appropriate ways, an individual can learn from structural constraints as well as have an impact on them. Harrison (1987) also notes if an organizational structure that enhances interaction among organization members is established, innovation increases, and member's ability to shape both structure and culture are enhanced. Waterman (1987) also indicates that organizational culture can be enhanced if structural attributes and values are in synchronization.

With the advent of the BPDG in the last decade, the values of mutual trust, shared leadership, and community have combined in a synergistic way to foster the emergence of a particular culture. A number of the interview respondents described the culture at De Anza as: striving, innovative, task-oriented, intense, nurturing, encouraging of team building, encouraging of individual responsibility, cohesive, energetic, dynamic, and achievement-oriented.

The organizational structure sets the parameters for an organization, but what takes place within those boundaries is an expression of the values of the organization. The values at De Anza place an emphasis on horizontal communications and a devolution of responsibility. The values are then translated into a culture that emphasizes vision, creativity, entrepreneurship, and freedom.

An Integration of Theory With Practice

The social and political milieu within which the community colleges in North America function has undergone a rapid change within the last decade: unionization of faculty and staff, rapidly changing student profiles, partnerships with industry to share costs of expensive capital equipment, growing pressure for central government control, and a demand by the public for outcomes-based funding models continue to challenge college boards, students, staff, administrators, and faculty. In meeting these challenges, some colleges have been singularly successful, particularly those that employ a combination of leadership strategies, organizational structures, and appropriate support systems in responding to environmental changes.

The literature on organizations identifies an emphasis on lateral communication systems and a balance between "loose" and "tight" decision-making and accountability systems as key attributes of the excellent organization (Blake, et al., 1964; Daft and Becker, 1978; Galbraith, 1972; Weick, 1976). In addition, a structural design that provides a sympathetic nexus among these attributes is vital to fostering an organizational value system that will nurture nondisruptive innovation and change (Daft, 1988; Hoy and Miskel, 1987; Waterman, 1987). Examination of the literature on unionized organizations provides evidence that an atmosphere of trust, based on a clear articulation of an organization's goals, keeps more traditional union/management conflicts at levels that enhance, rather than hinder, organizational capacity (Angell, 1983; Cresswell, Murphy, and Kerchner, 1980; Fox, 1974; Stephenson, 1986). A trust dynamic and a value system expressed, modeled, and rewarded by the organizational leadership can lead to the development of an organizational culture that can intensify the organization's ability to deal with its environment (Deal and Kennedy, 1982; Denison, 1990; Morgan, 1989; Schein, 1985a).

The case study of De Anza College identifies four interrelated themes as fundamental attributes of excellence at the college: organizational values, shared governance, leadership, and internal information strategies.

Organizational Values

The value statements at De Anza create the foundation upon which the reputation for innovation and excellence rests. Data from this case study support the author's conclusion that values, and their expression and embedding by organizational leadership, will determine the structure, quality of staff, decision systems, and ultimately, the culture.

A broad range of literature demonstrates the requisite importance of value statements that project a possible, attainable, and positive organizational future (Bennis and Nanus, 1985; Deal and Kennedy, 1982; Denison, 1990; Schein, 1985a). The basic values of an organization can become expressions, over time, of an organization's ideology or philosophy. As members of the De Anza community learn the culture of the organization, they are engaged in a process of internalizing the expressed values of what "ought" to be. At De Anza, the values supporting cultural learning are reflections of both the Board of Trustees and of President DeHart. The values have permeated the entire organization and have become the basic ideology and philosophy of the organization. In this way, the values serve as a guide to all members of De Anza as they deal with a changing environment.

The social and political milieu of the college district is in flux. In the heart of the high tech area of California, and with an economy dependent on rapidly changing technologies, De Anza must deal on a daily basis with uncertainty. Management of internal events—staff changes, physical plant changes, new learning technologies—as well as the external environmental factors are facilitated by the strong positive value frame at De Anza. A major financial crisis and the sudden illness of DeHart presented two major challenges to the district and college. The values, so strongly embedded into the fabric of the organization, have enabled De Anza to cope with these exigencies in an unrestrained manner.

A member of the college community said, "My values are parallel to the values that this college stands for." When there is empathy between the espoused values and the values in practice, the potential for an organization to develop a skill and capacity for its own development is increased (Argyris and Schon, 1974). For example, while there was emphasis on quality staff, there were also policies and procedures in place to realize that value, and these were evident in the extensive resources devoted to faculty selection, orientation, and retention.

The culture of De Anza is an expression of values that support innovation, assumption of responsibility by employees, freedom to act on that responsibility, and the concept that "excellence is a journey, not a destination." It is upon clearly articulated values, and the leadership behaviors that animate them, that the culture of De Anza rests.

Shared Governance

The values that support the culture that has emerged at De Anza, combined with an emphasis on trust and the leadership of the district chancellor, served as a catalyst in the creation of the system of shared governance in the Foothill-De Anza Community College District. The values expressed at De Anza College since its founding supported the district initiative taken in the early 1980s to reduce, to non-debilitating levels, the conflict with the collective bargaining unit representing the faculty. Under the leadership of Chancellor Fryer, both colleges accepted the challenge of participatory decision making.

Many colleges have not reached their potential because, in part, they never developed effective ways for faculty and administrators to work together to set institutional priorities (Keller, 1989; Leatherman, 1991). The formation in the early 1980s of an effective and appropriate decision-making structure—the Budget and Policy Development Group—has enabled the Foothill-De Anza Community College District to deal with pressing college issues that emerged during the last decade.

The decision structure of the BPDG has served the district and De Anza well. Its approach to shared governance has been studied and adopted by other districts, not only in California, but in other North American college systems as well. This contribution to the community college movement continues to enhance the district's reputation for innovation and excellence.

Beyer (1981) notes "decisions made in organizations can be affected in many ways by the ideologies and values of the decision makers" (p. 187). In the district, and at De Anza, shared leadership values among the boards of trustees, chancellor, college presidents, and collective bargaining representatives meshed with a trust dynamic to produce a decision structure that was relevant to the tasks at hand. DeHart, in the emergent planning cycle leading to the next accreditation, strongly encouraged the development of an approach at De Anza that would directly involve stakeholders in decisions relevant to their area. Aware of the likely shift in state funding patterns that would place emphasis on outcome measures, DeHart's "future" orientation enabled key college leaders to clarify and make routine collaborative strategies to minimize the disruptive aspects of this change.

Leadership

This case study supports the literature indicating that values, trust, and appropriate decision models are necessary requirements for organizational excellence (Bennis and Nanus, 1985; Beyer, 1981; Fiedler and Chemers, 1974; Fox, 1974; Yukl, 1989). Data from this case study strongly indicate the essential role leadership plays in orchestrating a synergism among the employees, thus enabling maximum organizational benefit from the many and variant skills employees bring to an organization. The traditional leadership literature suggests two basic dimensions of leadership behaviors: concern for task, and concern for the individual. Situational variables such as task structure, leader-member relations, and position power often mediate leadership behaviors (Yukl, 1989). DeHart as president certainly is a task-driven leader, but it is also clear that he has great respect and concern for each member of the college team.

Recent literature on community college leadership has emphasized the concept of transformational leadership. Roueche, Baker, and Rose (1989) developed a definition of leadership specifically related to the community college setting: "Leadership is the ability to influence, shape, and embed values, attitudes, beliefs, and behaviors consistent with increased commitment to the unique mission of the community college" (p. 34).

An extensive review of literature on leadership and organizational culture (Trice and Beyer, 1992) has suggested two different cultural consequences of leadership behaviors: cultural change, or cultural maintenance. They suggest the cultural leader emphasizes influencing the understanding and networks of meanings that members of an organization hold. They also hypothesize that the variant leadership processes within the basic elements of leadership will have different consequences for the culture of the organization.

Both the Roueche, Baker, and Rose (1989) study and the Trice and Beyer (1992) framework provide insight into how DeHart shapes the values of De Anza College. He has been able, over the last twenty-five years, to shift his leadership behaviors from those that create and change culture to those that maintain culture. Analysis of the value themes in his addresses to the college community and discussion with members of the college community provide potent evidence of alternating leadership strategies. For example, the vision articulated by DeHart and the various versions of the college mission statement reflected at times a conservative ideology and at other times a more radical approach to community college education. De Anza's reputation for excellence and evidence supporting it would indicate that the leadership also demonstrated repeated success in managing crisis, a culture change consequence in the Trice and Beyer typology.

The majority of structural changes at De Anza have been incremental, with emphasis on minor changes and refurbishing present patterns. DeHart's approach to structural change was described by one member of the leadership team as "tinkering." These leadership processes are consistent with cultural maintenance initiatives.

Internal Information Strategies

The fourth major attribute of excellence identified in this study is related to the internal information strategies. The strategies are discussed within two contexts, ongoing planning and financial control. The separation is necessary to explore the subtle information processes that either enhance or limit innovation and the organization's skill to enact its environment.

De Anza College has sophisticated systems for monitoring a variety of factors that are influenced by both internal and external environments. The Institutional Research Department regularly maintains and monitors a set of data defined as "critical success factors." These data, distributed to key college groups—Faculty Senate, Deans' Council, Division Deans' Group, staff associations—keep all stakeholders apprised of environmental factors that could influence the college negatively or positively.

The distribution of data on the success factors, and active discussion of the implications of these data, emphasize using information to guide decisions. Frequently when a new concern arises, the response is "What does the research indicate others are doing?" There is emphasis on exploring other colleges' responses to problems, and then, in a "value-added" sense, De Anza takes the idea and modifies it to fit its milieu. De Anza respects the expertise of others and is adept at modifying that experience to more effectively interact with its own unique environment.

■

Chapter 11

The Future of the
Community College in Evolution:
Approaches to Analysis of Organizational
Culture and Functioning

By George A. Baker, III

est-selling books on management, such as *In Search of Excellence* (Peters and Waterman, 1982), *Megatrends* (Naisbitt, 1982), and *The One-Minute Manager* (Blanchard and Johnson, 1982), have reiterated that groups in various work settings are the backbone of organizations. This concept has been illustrated by the chapter authors throughout this book. As vehicles for planning, organizing, accomplishing work, and enhancing the satisfaction of the workers, healthy and interacting work teams are important in improving both the quality and productivity of an organization (Mink, Mink, and Owen, 1987). In *Managing for Excellence*, Bradford and Cohen (1984) report that high-performing departments in the work setting are characterized by cohesive, synergistic teams and collective group action. The conclusion that in general groups "can become the basic building block upon which a high-involvement organization is constructed" (Lawler, 1986, p. 118) has been strongly supported by research over the years. Chapter Two demonstrates that the climate of community colleges can be determined and measured. Further, that organizational climate "as a set of attributes of a particular organization are identifiable in the collective attitudes, perceptions, and expectations of its members" (Davis and Newstrom, 1985, p. 23). Unfortunately, however, many traditional managers, functioning with transactional paradigms, have little training or knowledge of group dynamics and are pessimistic about its value.

This concluding chapter aims to accomplish the following objectives: to identify and discuss the components of Lacoursiere's five-stage organizational development model, so that it can be used by institutions that seek educational excellence; to use Lacoursiere's model and the Hersey-Blanchard

Model of Situational Leadership Styles to highlight the importance of integrating the appropriate situational leadership style with the organization's developmental stage; and to present the three viewpoints of organizational evolution—ecological, contingency, and strategic—as futuristic views of evolving community colleges. The effective community colleges of the future will be capable of dealing with access, cultural diversity, and excellence as they evolve within multicultural and multinational environments.

Organizational Life Cycle and Situational Leadership

In spite of the fact that every organization is a unique, dynamic, complex, ever-changing living system different from the sum of its individual members, all organizations undergo similar developmental stages as they grow from a collection of individuals to a smoothly functioning and effective team or unit. By understanding the dynamics, systemic process, and patterns prevalent in an organization, leaders or members develop the ability to diagnose and describe what is going on, to anticipate what might be forthcoming, and to act in ways that will facilitate the development and productivity of the organization. A skillful leader or member will become proficient in listening to and observing the organization in action and will be able to identify a number of variables that influence the interaction patterns, motivation, development, decision making, cohesiveness, and productivity in the organization.

To improve their observation skills, leaders and members alike need to develop the ability to differentiate between the group's task (i.e., its content, or what the group does or talks about) and its processes (i.e., its communication and interpersonal activities, or how it is functioning) (Schein, 1969). Research studies, however, show that most attention is given to an organization's content or task activity. In contrast, little or no attention is devoted to organizational processes: for example, how the group handles its communication, what leadership functions are being performed, how people feel about meetings, how decisions are made, what norms or rules are influencing how the group operates, and how interpersonal conflict is managed. In order to understand how to improve the organization's effectiveness, effective leaders focus on the interpersonal behaviors or actions of members within the organization. When used correctly, careful observation becomes the cornerstone for understanding the influences that interaction patterns have on the morale and productivity of the organization, for helping group leaders and members act in ways that will meet organizational needs, and for informing outsiders about the developmental stage of the organization at any moment in time.

Lacoursiere's Five Stages of Organizational Development

One of the most recent and thorough efforts that documents how groups go through a series of predictable developmental stages during their life cycles was completed by Lacoursiere (1980). The researcher reviewed over 200 articles and studies of group dynamics and developed a five-stage model that synthesizes most of what is known about group development and the life cycle. Lacoursiere's five-stage developmental model, shown at Figure 11.1, consists of orientation, dissatisfaction, resolution, production, and termination. Using this model as a framework for observing and understanding organizational processes, an observer can isolate what changes are occurring as the organization develops and ultimately can predict what changes in the organization's needs must be addressed. When this model is coupled with the climate measurement processes described in Chapter Two, one can actually calculate the progression of an organization's cultural development.

While these stages are described as separate and distinct, it is important to remember that there is a considerable degree of overlap, and, in fact, some elements of most stages can be found in every other stage. However, those behaviors that seem to predominate provide the data for determining the developmental stage of the organization at any moment in time. In the following paragraphs, a brief description of the characteristics of members in an organization and the group's work at each developmental stage is presented.

Figure 11.1
Lacoursiere's Five-Stage Developmental Model

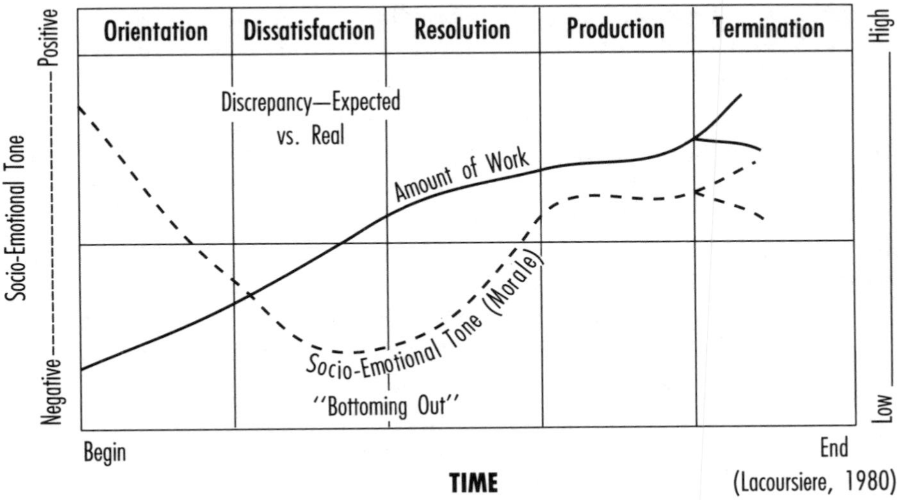

(Lacoursiere, 1980)

Orientation Stage (Low Development Level). The length of this stage depends on how clearly the organizational task is defined and how easily it is achieved. With simple and easily defined tasks, the orientation stage is relatively short and distinct, requiring perhaps only 5 to 10 percent of the organizational life cycle. On the other hand, in organizations with complex goals and tasks, this stage may extend over 30 to 60 percent of the life cycle.

During this stage, team members are mildly to moderately eager, have generally positive expectations about outcomes of the experience, are independent of authority, and show some anxiety about other team members, such as who they are and what they are like. Furthermore, they show some concern and anxiety about why they are there, what they will get, what the stated purpose of the organization means for them, what they will do, what the leader will do, and where they fit. During this stage, the organization's work can be characterized by low to moderate task accomplishment; most of the organization's energy is focused on defining the goals and tasks by delineating how to approach them and what skills are needed.

Dissatisfaction Stage (Low to Moderate Development Level). This stage is characterized by a dip in morale and intensity that is correlated to the degree of discrepancy team members percieve between their initial expectations and the reality of the situation. They become dissatisfied with dependence on authority while experiencing feelings of frustration or anger about goals and tasks. Some may even have negative reactions to the formal leader or other members of the organization and may experience feelings of incompetence or confusion. Although group work on tasks may be disrupted by negative feelings, the work is found to reflect slowly increasing task accomplishment and skill development. Some evidence of the dissatisfaction stage was demonstrated in the analysis of the medium-sized, single-campus college in Chapter Two.

This stage often starts later in organizations with complex goals and tasks. Generally, this stage constitutes a relatively small fraction of the organization's life cycle; however, some groups may become stuck in this stage and continue to be demoralized and relatively unproductive. Resolution of this stage depends partly on redefining goals and tasks so that they are achievable.

Resolution Stage (Moderate to High Development Level). The length of this stage depends on the ease of resolving feelings of dissatisfaction, the ease of learning new skills, the quality of interpersonal relationships, and the ability of members to develop norms and processes that enhance their ability to work together and to value differences. If these conditions are unfavorable, the organization may dissolve or deteriorate while remaining in the dissatisfaction stage. Since feelings of cohesion and confidence are new and somewhat fragile, the organization may tend to avoid conflict or differences for fear of losing the positive climate. This could retard the organization's development and lead to less effective decisions. Some evidence of the resolution stage was demonstrated in the analysis of the medium-sized technical college in Chapter Two.

When observing an organization in this developmental stage, members are found to become less dissatisfied as ways of working together become clear. They start to resolve differences between initial expectations and realities in relation to goals, tasks, and skills. By decreasing their animosities toward other members or leaders, they develop feelings of mutual respect, harmony, and trust, all of which are characteristic of group cohesion. As they accomplish tasks, a feeling of pleasure overcomes earlier negative feelings, and they begin to feel more self-esteem in relation to organizational membership and task accomplishment. Group work is found to slowly increase as skills and understanding develop, and it is enhanced by positive feelings among members of the organization.

Production Stage (High Development Level). This developmental stage continues with only moderate fluctuations in feelings of satisfaction until the final stage of termination is reached. Work levels remain high, and the socio-emotional perspective remains positive. The time it takes an organization to arrive at this stage depends on the successful resolution of dissatisfaction, the complexity and clarity of the task, the ease of acquiring the essential skills, and the discrepancy between the original expectations and later realities. Although this is called the production stage, it does not mean that no work on the task goes on at the other stages. Some work is being accomplished from the beginning, but at a lower level of effectiveness and with less satisfaction than is characteristic of this stage. This phenomenon was demonstrated in the analysis of the large multi-college campus in Chapter Two. While some aspects of the climate were considered "consultative," "decision-making" aspects were barely acceptable to the composite group.

During this stage members of the organization are eager to be part of the team, feel confident about outcomes, and work well together and agree on the nature of their relationships with others. Furthermore, they are autonomous (not dependent on a designated leader), can communicate openly and freely without fear of rejection or conflict, and can recognize, support, and challenge each other's competence and accomplishments. Their energy is focused on task accomplishment rather than on resistance and dissatisfaction. They feel positive about membership in the organization (because of high task accomplishment) and about their ability to relate to one another and the organization, in terms of complementary task functions as well as interpersonal support. Group work on tasks is enhanced by positive feelings of a job well done, as well as by team cohesion. Group work is easier, more efficient, and satisfying, with a continuing increase in skills, knowledge, and confidence.

Termination Stage. With ongoing intact work groups, this stage is not reached unless there is some drastic reorganization. However, in ad hoc groups and temporary task forces it does occur, and leaders need to be aware of some of the characteristics of this stage. If this stage occurs with the ending of the work assignment, its length varies depending on the length of the experience, the personal meaningfulness of the task, and the closeness of interpersonal tasks. While within the college, task forces and often academic programs are born, blossom, and die, the goal is for the overall organization to continue to serve its clients and community.

While at this stage, group members begin to be concerned about impending dissolution. Although they often may have strong positive feelings about accomplishment, they experience a sense of loss or sadness about ending the task or separating from group members and the leader. Group work on tasks generally decreases, but in some cases there may be increased work activity to meet deadlines, to achieve closure, and/or to overcome loss.

So far, Lacrousiere's five developmental stages have been described in terms of their sequence and the specific variables that characterize group members and group work at each stage. In the next section, the discussion will focus on the precept that flexible leadership style can be effective only if appropriately applied at a specific time and stage in the organization's life cycle. Over the years, research has shown that leaders have to perform both task and maintenance functions in order for an organization to develop into a healthy and productive system. However, what has not been clear from the research is in what combinations and when in the life cycle these behaviors are most appropriate. Integrating the Hersey-Blanchard Model of Situational Leadership with Lacoursiere's five stages of organizational development provides a framework for answering these questions.

Hersey-Blanchard Model of Situational Leadership Styles

In general, leadership behavior that is supportive, democratic, decentralized, and participative seems to be related to poorer functioning in the early stages of the group's development, but when this behavior is maintained through the life of the organization more productivity, satisfaction, and creativity result (Shaw, 1981; Lacoursiere, 1980). Conversely, leadership behavior that is active, aggressive, directive, structured, and task-oriented seems to have favorable results in the early developmental stages of an organization. Yet when this behavior is maintained through-out an organization's life cycle, it seems to have a negative impact on cohesiveness and quality of work. Based on these findings, directive and task-oriented leader behavior is appropriate in the early stages of development, but as the group develops, the focus should shift to supportive and participative behavior.

The Hersey-Blanchard Model of Situational Leadership II (Blanchard, 1985) has been accepted over the past several years as a practical, easy-to-understand approach for analysis of processes for managing and motivating people. For leaders who are trying to facilitate group growth and development, the situational leadership model has tremendous implications.

In this model, supportive behavior (which is related to maintenance functions) and directive behavior (which is related to task functions) are patterns of leader behavior that can be plotted on two separate and distinct axes. Therefore, a framework for defining leadership style in terms of various combinations of directive and supportive behavior can be created.

According to the Hersey-Blanchard Model, each of the four leadership styles (viz., directing, coaching, supporting, and delegating) represents different combinations of directive and supportive leader behavior. One may distinguish between these combinations by considering the amount of direction the leader provides, the amount of leadership support and encouragement that is available, and the amount of follower involvement in decision making.

Supportive behavior is defined as the extent to which a leader engages in two-way communication, listens, provides support and encouragement, facilitates interaction, and involves subordinates in decision making. On the other hand, directive behavior is defined as the extent to which a leader engages in one-way communication; spells out member roles; tells subordinates what to do, when to do it, and how to do it; and closely supervises work activities. Biggerstaff in Chapter Three and Roe in Chapter Five provide a foundation for this concept. Nelson in Chapter Seven, Barber in Chapter Nine, and Clark in Chapter Ten provide ample examples of supportive behavior.

Situational leadership is based on the notion that there is no single best leadership style, so leaders who are able to positively impact performance and satisfaction are those who are able to adapt their style to fit the situation. In the first leadership style, which is referred to as directing, leaders are high on direction and low on support. They spell out roles and goals, provide specific instruction, and closely supervise task accomplishment. When using the second style, coaching, leaders are high on both direction and support. In addition to clarifying purpose and direction and continuing to direct task accomplishment, these leaders attempt to hear the feelings of subordinates about decisions as well as their ideas and suggestions. The third style, supporting, is characterized by high supportive and low directive behavior. Unlike the previous two styles, leaders who use the supporting leadership style make decisions together with followers and actively listen, support, and facilitate the followers' efforts at task accomplishment. Finally, in the fourth style, delegating, leaders provide low support and direction. However, that does not mean there is no direction or support; workers provide those needed functions for themselves and each other. At the same time, decision making and responsibility for task accomplishment are turned over to subordinates.

Directing Is for the Orientation Stage. The integration of situational leadership with group development suggests that directing is for the orientation stage. That is, the focus should be on task-related behaviors and not so much on supportive behavior. In general, at the beginning of any small group, people are relatively eager to be there and have high expectations. There is some anxiety about the nature of the situation, and they are looking for something they do not have. People are usually feeling very dependent and look to the leader to satisfy their needs. Morale starts out at a fairly high level, but decreases fairly rapidly during this stage. The work accomplished begins at a low level and gradually increases as understanding and competencies develop.

The most appropriate leader behavior at this stage is to help the group with the task by clarifying what the task is, setting realistic and attainable goals, and planning for the acquisition of the necessary skills. During this stage there is some need for supportive behavior, especially that related to acceptance by the leader and other members. However, the need for supportive behavior is much more moderate than the need for task-related behavior. Being overly personal or supportive at this stage can lead to unrealistic expectations and, therefore, greater disappointment during the next stage. Barber in Chapter Eight demonstrates how a founding president established the college culture by directing the staff through the orientation stage.

Coaching Is for the Dissatisfaction Stage. This stage is characterized by a decline in morale, with the major morale issues being frustration, discouragement, and sometimes anger about task success and competition among members of the organization and between the formal leader and other members of the organization. There is a testing of both the task and process goals and confusion about roles. The dissatisfaction comes from the discrepancies between the initial hopes and expectations and the realities of the situation.

For this developmental stage, appropriate leader behavior calls for a balance between directive and supportive behaviors and high levels of both. Task behaviors may include the redefinition of goals and expectations to make them more realistic and attainable, and continued training and coaching in skills and knowledge about task and group process. Supportive behaviors would include more active listening and encouraging input from subordinates, acknowledging difficulties, and focusing on building supportive subordinate relationships and group cohesion. The leader needs to be concerned with helping members develop not only task-related skills and knowledge, but also interpersonal and group maintenance skills.

Supporting Is for the Resolution Stage. In this stage, morale, harmony, and task competence are increasing. There is less resistance, more comfort with the reality of the situation, a progressive internalization of goals and skills, and more inclusion and integration within the organization so that fewer fears of rejection and incompetence are felt.

As the group moves from dissatisfaction, the leader's behavior places less emphasis on task and goal clarification and more emphasis on supporting and acknowledging the efforts of subordinates to assume both the task and group maintenance functions that the leader previously provided. There is less need for directive leadership behavior, a behavior that slowly decreases as subordinates assume more and more confidence, cohesiveness, and maintenance functions.

Delegating Is for the Production Stage. Skills in both task and maintenance functions continue to increase during this stage. Task skills are mastered and goals are internalized. As positive feelings match and exceed initial desires, there is a high level of work on task and more efficient use of time. This ultimately results in developing positive feelings about the organization and feelings of self-esteem and confidence. Subordinates work well together, differ without competition, and function autonomously without dependence on the leader. This stage can be the most difficult stage for the leader, since his or her special status in the group is eliminated. In general, there is less need for either directive or supportive leadership behaviors during delegation.

To summarize this first section of the chapter, the discussion began with a brief description of the five developmental stages—orientation, dissatisfaction, resolution, production, and termination—in the life cycle of an organization as defined by Lacoursiere. The Hersey-Blanchard Model of Situational Leadership Styles was described, which includes delegating, supporting, coaching, and directing. Subsequently, the point was made that the integration of the appropriate situational leadership style with the organization's developmental stage yields a useful framework for identifying leader behaviors that will most likely meet the needs of the organization and help the organization move through its developmental stages.

The next section introduces the Community College Effectiveness Model. Effectiveness is defined, and a discussion of the need for and the developmental stage used in producing such an assessment instrument (which was used in model studies of excellent institutions and leaders) is presented. Finally, the components of the Community College Effectiveness Model are identified and briefly discussed so as to give leaders in institutions of higher education an idea of what they should look for when attempting to initiate a movement toward educational excellence.

Community College Effectiveness Model

Institutional effectiveness is a leadership challenge. It essentially involves a systematic comparison of institutional performance to institutional purpose. An assessment of effectiveness can be accomplished only if the chief executive officer of the institution provides the active leadership necessary to ensure that a clearly defined statement of purpose for the institution exists. Furthermore, the leader has to ensure that the entire institution and each of its sub-units have clearly articulated goals, means for evaluating achievement of those goals, and processes for using the results of evaluation to better meet the needs of students, the college community, and the region served.

The major challenge of leadership is to determine what is to be evaluated, how evaluation will be accomplished, and what will be done with the results. In making these decisions, institutions and their leaders must strive not only to use explicit language, but also to specify appropriate time frames and expected standards, and design a system for collecting and analyzing results. It is the systematic collection and analysis of data that constitutes the essence of this process.

Assessment Procedures

From the time of the industrial revolution, individuals and organizations have studied so-called scientific management as a means of building more effective organizations. We have progressed from Frederick Winslow Taylor's time/motion studies to Allen A. Kennedy's corporate cultures in an attempt to design and achieve excellence in public and private institutions. Between the two, we have progressed through sensitivity training, T-Group sessions, and human resource concepts to the organizational culture model of organizational effectiveness. Today's approach calls for assessments of values, beliefs, organizational and individual goals, and team structures, and a clear understanding of the organization's culture and how to influence the morale and performance of those who must be empowered to accomplish the organization's goals.

The Community College Effectiveness Model is an attempt to convey a universal framework for macro analysis that allows for the development of processes appropriate to the institution's uniqueness. What are presented and ultimately controlled through the model are the essential elements of all organizations of higher education.

The institutional effectiveness movement was born out of a frustration of national leaders; federal, state, and local agencies; and various accrediting agencies in their inability to discover standards for which public and private educational entities could be held accountable. The accrediting agencies, such as the Southern Association of Colleges and Schools, have expressed a desire to move the process from the measurement of resources to the inclusion of measures of effectiveness of outcomes. The concept also focuses on the extent to which the institutions use assessment information to re-evaluate goals, to make essential improvements, and to plan for the future.

A recent interest in educational excellence in higher education has focused the attention of researchers and practitioners alike to the fact that institutional assessment at the university and college levels is almost totally unstructured. A systematic set of assessments does not exist, yet thousands of institutions are required to invent appropriate measurement processes. The best guidance these institutions now receive is the expectation that they will develop processes appropriate to their purposes, resources, and environments. This problem militates against a set of universally appropriate procedures and ultimately against standards by which institutions can measure progress toward institutional effectiveness.

In their search for excellence in community colleges, Roueche and Baker (1986) reasoned that one means of providing a systematic set of assessments would be to identify institutions and leaders with excellent reputations, discover what they actually do, and then use organizational theory and behavioral concepts to develop a set of university- and college-appropriate measures that would provide the framework from which processes-to-outcome measurement can be developed.

To actualize this goal, Roueche and Baker initiated a study that discovered, analyzed, and evaluated exceptional community colleges. The purpose of their project was to research, develop, field test, and validate a model of institutional effectiveness to be employed by two- and four-year colleges in order to make effective improvements. The authors aimed to develop a model that could quantitatively describe the extent to which colleges were meeting their missions and the needs of their students and constituencies. Roueche and Baker reasoned that other institutions could

use these exceptional institutions as models to initiate a movement toward educational excellence.

Roueche and Baker decided that, since community colleges are teaching institutions, the criteria by which colleges would be selected for the
study would have to focus on the effectiveness of their instruction. Therefore, a study that attempted to analyze, evaluate, and determine effective climate, exceptional leadership, and teaching behaviors in community colleges had to focus on institutions that were recognized for their
efforts in promoting and enhancing teaching quality.

To strengthen their study further, a panel of fourteen national experts who had considerable experience in analyzing and evaluating teacher
performance, leadership, and culture conducive to student learning in
community colleges were asked to select the top five community colleges
that: were recognized nationally for their ability to maximize student success; were able to develop and pursue policies and standards that combine open-door admissions with quality academic programs; were led by
presidents who were perceived to be pursuing excellence; and selected,
evaluated, rewarded, and developed exceptional teachers in all aspects
of the comprehensive mission of the community college.

Of the thirty-three community colleges that were nominated, Miami-
Dade Community College, Florida, received twelve first-place ballots and
ranked near the top of the other two experts' ballots. Given this strong
ranking, Roueche and Baker decided to conduct an in-depth analysis of
Miami-Dade Community College.

What ensues is a brief description of the components of the Community College Effectiveness Model eventually developed by Baker, based
on the foundation established in *Access and Excellence*. The Community
College Effectiveness Model is presented in Figure 11.2.

Section One: The Personal Assessment of the College Environment (PACE)

This section of the Community College Effectiveness Model provides
the most abstract and global view of the organization. Various groups
such as faculty, staff, and administration are given the opportunity to
assess the quality of perceived leader influence on follower behavior, communication, collaboration, organizational structure, work design, and the
extent to which the college is perceived to be focused on student success.
Therefore, PACE will provide answers to the question: "What is it like
to work here?" PACE attempts to measure a complex mixture of feelings, beliefs, perceptions, expectations, norms, values, policies, and procedures that in the aggregate assess the culture of the organization. As an
assessment process, a climate study has the following characteristics:

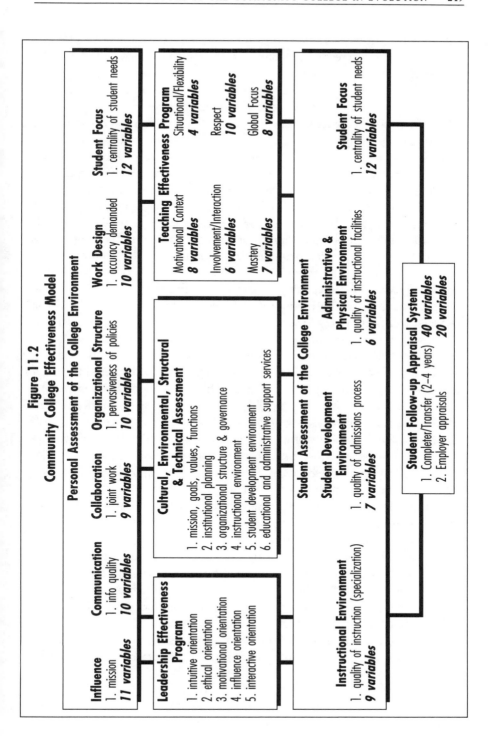

Figure 11.2
Community College Effectiveness Model

differentiates one organization from another; is perceived and experienced either directly or indirectly by the institution's members; is related to, but distinct from, other aspects such as size, formal structure, or the design of specific jobs; influences each individual's motivation and performance on the job; and can be changed through direct and indirect management and leadership.

Furthermore, climate studies can provide information on the following institutional effectiveness concepts: how well the technology, strategies, planning, organization, work design, management procedures, and policies and procedures are integrated in the eyes of the various members of the organization; how the various members of the organization see and relate to their leaders and supervisors; and how individuals' perceptions relate to their bottom-line performance, such as their work with students, efficient use of the organization's resources, and perceptions of the quality of the service provided to students and the community.

Section Two: The Leadership Effectiveness Program

Section Two of the Community College Effectiveness Model is the Leadership Effectiveness Program (LEP). Here the idea of organizational climate is seen as being highly correlated to the idea of leadership effectiveness. LEP measures the use of certain leadership behaviors that are intended to influence the performance and morale of members of the organization. Since any effort to influence the behavior of another person is viewed as an act of leadership, leadership is seen as an influence process. Leaders are individuals who are interested in developing staff or followers and building motivating climates that result in high levels of productivity, as well as extrinsic and intrinsic satisfaction. Leadership style, therefore, consists of the patterns of behaviors that leaders use when they are attempting to influence others' behavior.

Research supports the idea that leadership styles tend to vary considerably from one situation to another. Insights into one's situational leadership style may emerge from assessing the leader's own self-view and the view of the followers; LEP allows for both. The instruments can be administered and analyzed in team-building sessions designed to improve leaders' effectiveness. As followers are empowered through experience, they can perceive the culture of the organization as much more satisfying. Thus, LEP consists of two instruments: a follower form and a self-evaluation form, each of which contains thirty-four items about leadership skills. A workbook for use with the system is among the products being developed.

Section Three: CESTA, TEP, and SACE

The third section of the Community College Effectiveness Model consists of three sets of instruments and analytical procedures: the Cultural,

Environmental, Structural, and Technical Assessment (CESTA); the Teaching Effectiveness Program (TEP); and the Student Assessment of the College Environment (SACE). These instruments are designed to be administered to various members of the college community: the CESTA to faculty, staff, and administrators; the TEP to full- and part-time faculty; and the SACE to full- and part-time students.

The Cultural, Environmental, Structural, and Technical Assessment (CESTA). This instrument measures values, beliefs, and perceptions related to the institution's mission. These elements provide the framework for the governance and decision-making structures that evolve at an institution. Values and beliefs provide a basis for understanding human behavior but must also be brought into congruence with an institution's stated purposes or mission if the organization is to be effective. Moral values will determine what decisions are made and how they are made. Values and beliefs ultimately are converted to decisions, and decisions are converted to behaviors that directly affect students and their motivation to achieve their educational goals.

While values and beliefs provide a framework for human behavior and responses to influence, organizations must eventually develop planning processes to orchestrate the behavior of individuals and groups and align their activities with organizational purpose. Society expects colleges to serve the specific purposes expressed in their stated missions. The mission, therefore, must contain support criteria for assessing the long- and short-term effectiveness of the college. Effective leaders are able to craft the written and stated mission of the college in terms of these conditions; when the conditions are met, the survival and health of the college is ensured. Although mission statements are broad, abstract, and value-laden, they must express a vision of the future so that followers will be able to align with and accomplish the tasks necessary for fulfilling it.

Organizational structure and its attendant processes are also an extremely important influence on the behavior of individuals in organizations. Structure is defined as those features of the organization that serve to control or distinguish its parts. The uniqueness of the setting is critical to the development of effective organizational structures because college professionals (especially faculty and counselors) are afforded the freedom to work independently and often in isolation from one another. Yet the mission of the college is accomplished through the holistic development of the student. Consequently, the organizational structure system must result in the reasonable control of individuals working in teams to accomplish the goals of student development.

The organizational structure and processes not only must shape the jobs of individuals, but also must result in the effective organization of departments, divisions, or units into groups of jobs. The college or university is made up of several academic and administrative support units, as well as student services. Each of these units contains individuals performing different jobs that combine to produce a larger outcome of student success. This larger outcome becomes synergistic only when the college's mission and beliefs produce goals that require an integrated effort. Advisement is a concept that fits this test. The student does not typically have an "adviser," but a system of advisers; namely, faculty and student development experts who provide a variety of academic assessment and career advice.

It is envisioned that the assessment of the organizational structure, processes, and procedures, including resource development, instruction, curriculum development, student development, performance appraisal, support services, administrative services, and the physical environment, would lead to goal-setting, job description, and team-building activities designed to align effort and motivation toward student success. In turn, processes to aid in organizational structure for academic, student, and administrative services would be developed. All of these activities ultimately lead to institutional effectiveness.

Moreover, the ultimate measure of leadership effectiveness is the quality of decisions that affect the success of students and the accomplishment of the organizational mission. The concepts of governance and leadership, however, are not discrete; they tend to overlap and are often used interchangeably. These concepts actually encompass both structure and process. Although governance is related to decision making, leadership relates to influencing the execution of the decision. If the college is viewed as a government, governance becomes the process with which students, faculty, staff, administrators, and board members, associated together, establish and carry out the rules and regulations designed to control individual and collective behavior. These processes are intended to reduce conflict, facilitate collaboration, and preserve essential individual freedom to act in the best interests of the students and the followers.

Since a collegial model is based on group process, a method must be developed to allow for periodic examination of goals, tasks, and perceived shared decision making. The CESTA addresses the specific decisions regarding academics, student development, administration, and personnel. Staff, faculty, and administrators determine at what level in the governance structure the decision is perceived to be made. The institutional report generated from the CESTA analysis suggests how the governance process could be improved and how individuals could be allowed to participate to a greater extent in the governance process itself.

The Teaching Effectiveness Program (TEP). The pursuit of institutional effectiveness and quality education has several integral components, with the primary element being the individual instructor. Within colleges and universities, the primary goal is student learning, and the key to quality teaching is an effective and situational instructor. To be effective with the typical college student, the instructor must possess characteristics and behaviors that inspire learning. Experts argue that most individual characteristics are innate, but many behaviors can be learned. For each individual instructor, the inner experience of teaching is different. For one individual, teaching is a misery; for another, teaching is a joy; the behaviors or strategies differ for both individuals. One fills up work time thinking about other things, while the other is engrossed in teaching and thinks often about improving skills and performance. These two extremes in the college culture illustrate the fundamental dilemma in the management and leadership of colleges and universities. These organizations provide service to humans, but the quality and effectiveness of those services varies tremendously due to the competence and motivation of the faculty.

It should be noted that the history of faculty development in higher education is in its early stages. Faculty development in the past thirty years has been haphazard and perfunctory. With its demand for accountability and measurement, the institutional effectiveness movement has found this concept thirty years behind maturity and institutional mastering.

The instruments and decision process associated with TEP can result in a program of faculty development that centers on the following essentials: clearly defined purposes; universal standards; multiple sources of input on development; competencies of highly effective teachers; and a need for flexible and individualized development plans. TEP consists of a set of competencies related to motivation, involvement and interaction with students, situational responses and flexibility, respect for students, mastery of subject, and a global focus on teaching discovered as a result of analyzing studies of effective college teachers. The program provides for a multiple set of sources of input, such as student ratings, peer and supervisor assessment, and self-appraisals, for the faculty member to facilitate the development of a personal growth plan.

TEP, now in the pilot testing phase, will consist of instruments for several sources of inputs into the self-appraisal process. These sources of inputs will also be aggregated by computer at the program, department, division, and institutional levels in order to provide information for the college's effectiveness plan.

Student Assessment of the College Environment (SACE). If human service organizations exist to serve humans and to change them in some measurable and pervasive way, the most important perceptions of institutional effectiveness certainly should be provided by students who matriculate at the college. The process of matriculating forms a psychological con-tract between the college and the student. The basic unwritten mutual expectation is that in exchange for the expenditure of energy, effort, and perseverance, the college will provide a set of educational and instruc-tional services that will add value to the individual. This added value should provide the student with skills necessary to live a better life and participate in society.

In the execution of the psychological contract, the student is assessed on many occasions. However, the student is afforded few opportunities to assess the college. The opportunity to complete the SACE instrument allows the student to assess the instructional, student development, ad-ministrative, and physical environments at the time when the student has traditionally only assessed the instructor, at the end of an academic period. The student would be able to assess the quality of instruction in specialization courses, as well as in general educational courses. These assessments would be general impressions, but collectively would provide a picture of the college's culture as perceived by the student. In addition, aspects of teaching in general would be collected. Concepts would allow for measures of faculty attitude toward students, the intellectual orienta-tion of faculty, their availability, and the extent to which the student's expectations are met.

The student would also assess the student development dimensions of the college to include perceptions of assessment, admissions, orienta-tion, advisement, counseling, financial aid, and job placement services. Finally, the student would assess the administrative and support environ-ment, to include library and remedial services, recreational facilities, phys-ical appearance of the campus, and such aspects as cultural diversity and harmony.

SACE consists of instrumentation and software to display the data in ways that would lead to institutional decision making and the improve-ment of individuals, teams, and units toward the goal of service to the student and to his or her community.

Section Four: The Student Follow-up Appraisal and the Employer Survey

The overall measurement of institutional effectiveness is not com-plete unless the success of a college's students is measured once the stu-dents have left the campus and have had an opportunity to apply what they have learned. From a cultural perspective it is also important to ask "those who were there" to recall and report their perceptions after they have entered a new culture.

The Student Follow-up Appraisal System (SFAS) is designed to appraise the performance of an institution as related to its students' ability to achieve additional educational or employment goals, as well as to assess the general competencies actually used on a job. A follow-up study focusing on students who have left the college or university would be conducted after a period of time, generally two to three years, to assess students' subsequent success in the workplace or in institutions of higher education. Former students would therefore have the opportunity to provide input on the effectiveness of the education and training that they received at the institution being evaluated.

Employer Survey. In addition, employers would have a chance to assess the quality of some of their employees' preparation and performance via the Employer Survey. Thus the SFAS instrumentation provides an evaluation of institutional effectiveness in the community as perceived by employees and employers. The system consists of instruments, a computer program for decision support, and strategies for improving institutional, program, and individual effectiveness.

To summarize, the discussion in this part of the chapter focused on a brief description of the Community College Effectiveness Model, which is under development at the University of Texas at Austin and is designed to discover, analyze, and evaluate exceptional community colleges. The initial intent of the study was to document how climate, leadership, systems for success, and teaching for success can be synthesized. Using Miami-Dade as a model of an exceptional community college, Roueche and Baker discovered strong evidence that supports the existence of a culture for excellence. In this exemplary college, leaders were paying attention to student success, were attempting to become role models for excellence, and were reacting well to critical incidents through a conscious attempt to minimize crises and surprises. In addition, the researchers discovered that the college had integrated systems that were helping personnel make decisions with and for the students to promote student success. College personnel were using current information effectively to chart a path toward the future. The studies of leaders and the case studies presented in this book re-enforce that conclusion.

In their attempt to improve performance, college presidents employ considerable coaching and teaching in their relationships with college personnel; college leaders were found to be actively improving rewards for, and positive expectations of, all college personnel. In terms of teaching excellence, the colleges have been found to have many exemplary professors and are dedicated to improving the quality of teaching in general and increasing the number of professors who demonstrate excellence.

The relationship between cultural leadership and the Community College Effectiveness Model is clear: effective leaders must find ways to assess their climate. The Community College Effectiveness Model provides a means to gain perceptions from all constituents related to the college. In addition, this process provides insights and a way to utilize the information to make changes, which should provide impetus toward a productive culture.

In the next part, three futuristic views of community college organizations evolving in multicultural and multinational environments are presented. These views of organizational evolution are adapted from Hampton, Summer, and Webber's (1987) book on this topic. This futuristic approach views the total organization, immersed in its environment, evolving from one form to another over very long periods of time. In presenting ecological, contingency, and strategic theories of organizational functioning, this last section attempts to respond to the question "Why do some community colleges survive and grow while others decline, stagnate, or die?"

Viewpoints of Organizational Evolution

The ecological, contingency, and strategic frameworks provide a view of organizations evolving from one developmental stage to another and from one cultural framework to another over time while attempting to respond to the two vital challenges of innovation and change.

Ecological Viewpoint and Evolutionary Determinism

Using evolutionary laws, the ecological framework compares social organizations to biological organisms. Aldrich (1979) explained the population ecology theory of organizational evolution, a theory whose essence is derived from Darwin's *The Origin of Species* and from Herbert Spencer's application of Darwin's concepts to the evolution of social organizations. According to Aldrich (1979), the world is made up of populations (or species) of social organizations that are constantly engaged in a process of variation. As a result, the organizations that evolve differ from one another in terms of their internal organizational structures, rewards, or control systems and their external outputs to society or goals.

According to the population ecology viewpoint of evolution, organizations are seen as having very limited free will to govern their own destiny. In addition to assuming that environments are constantly changing and as a result organizations vary, the ecological viewpoint presumes that there are not enough resources in society to support just any random organization. To strike a balance between the available resources and number or type of organizations that can grow and develop to maturity in a given environment, society (rather than the organization itself) is found to be constantly engaged in a process of natural selection. The only organizations that the society selects for survival are those that are able to develop unique characteristics to help society members fit better to their ever-changing external and/or internal conditions. On the other hand, those organizations that are incapable of implementing organizational change to accommodate environmental pressures (whether internal or external) will eventually stagnate and die.

In addition to selection, the ecological viewpoint holds that society plays an instrumental role in the permanent retention of social organizations. Initially, the society selects a unique organization through ongoing searches and experimentation. Once selected, the society proceeds to make sure that this unique organization is retained by rendering more permanent the organization's particular services and its internal structures, technologies, or control systems.

Given that organizations vary in terms of their goals and their internal activity systems, and given that society does not have enough resources to support just any random organization, the ecological viewpoint is based on the premise that society selects for survival only those organizations that have a relatively superior fit of goals and activity systems to their environment. Although an organization is seen as having some control over its own destiny, the environment itself is what determines the survival of the fittest one. Therefore, the environment, or what is "out there," can cause some organizations to fit and others not to fit; some to grow and others to die. Since certain environmental characteristics make it either easy or difficult for organizations to secure resources and support, the following paragraphs will discuss the four resources that Aldrich (1979) isolated and identified as being important in understanding the ecological viewpoint of organizational evolution.

Carrying Capacity. Even though a given environment may have many or few resources, Aldrich (1979) believes that the quality of available resources limits the size of the organizational population that can exist. With a relatively fixed number of environmental resources, new organizations can be started fairly easily; a population of organizations arises, each with its share of the available resources. This population approaches a steady state only when the environmental carrying capacity is reached. However, when the steady state is about to be reached, the environment again emerges as the trigger agent. This is to say that organizations, like living organisms, cannot exist in a steady state; they must always be in motion.

Based on the carrying capacity precept, the ecological viewpoint presumes that the number of social organizations will decrease whenever the available resources are depleted. On the other hand, available resources may remain the same but competitors with innovative approaches may arise, thus attracting more of the available resources away from the original organization. Therefore, no peaceful coexistence will predominate in the environment and no equilibrium will be reached as long as resources are scarce and the population of organizations must depend on the same pool of resources for survival and growth. Eventually, some organizations will be eliminated, changed, or forced to adopt the form of the "fittest" competitor to survive and grow.

Stability. Within the context of the ecological viewpoint, environments are seen as stable whenever their human resources and technologies remain the same. Here, unstable environments (which witness constant changes at a fast rate) are seen as advantageous to the newly formed organizations but make it difficult for older, well-developed organizations. Conversely, stable environments make it difficult for new organizations to grow but are an asset to the already developed organizations. In a stable environment, organizations can afford the time to learn standardized, efficient, and highly interrelated ways to optimally fit with the environment. This learning curve effect explains the reasons behind the difficulties facing the newer organizations when competing with older organizations for resources.

Domain Consensus. The survival of an organization is also influenced by whether other organizations recognize its claim to its domain (resulting in "domain consensus"), for example when a proprietary school is established within the service area of a public two-year college. If the public college accepts the presence of the intruder, the environment will be more receptive to co-existence. However, if there is great controversy, the "domain conflict" that arises among the different organizations makes it more difficult to collectively serve the constituents.

Resource Concentration. Finally, organizational form is found to be determined by whether or not vital resources are concentrated in one location or dispersed more evenly or sparsely. Previous success stories have shown that for organizations to grow and develop, they must be located close to where the needed resources are concentrated, thus rendering them easier to attract and retain. On the other hand, if resources are dispersed widely, different and more decentralized organizational structures will have to be adopted. In essence then, the principle of concentration enters into the process of selection, since society will select those organizations that can fit themselves to either concentrated or dispersed resources. It will be interesting to observe how two- and four-year colleges react to a future of scarce resources.

Contingency Viewpoint

This view acknowledges that the destiny of an organization is determined by scarce resources and society's selection process. It is also assumed that organizational leaders command a certain amount of freedom to influence their culture so that they can alter organizational forms in ways that adapt organizations to the environment. However, the contingency viewpoint recognizes that even though this freedom is achieved, it is limited to dealing with only one characteristic of the environment, thus leaving many other aspects of the environment free to impact the overall culture to be created.

The contingency viewpoint is based on the assumption that the degree of environmental instability and complexity causes the development of internal organizational structures to differ from one other. Consequently, a fast-changing environment will result in fast-changing organizational programs and products that necessitate the development of an organic and dynamic system. On the other hand, a relatively stable environment makes it necessary to develop a formal and structured organizational system. Whenever this "fit" between organizational structure/process and external environmental conditions is violated by a given organization, the latter is likely to stagnate or die.

When compared to the ecological viewpoint, the contingency views are similar in one important respect: both theories recognize that organizational form and culture must fit the environment. Unlike the ecological viewpoint, however, the contingency theory is different in four respects: determinism vs. free will; form of organization; concept of environment; and time span.

First, the contingency theory holds that organizations can change their form and that organizational leaders have the power to create the culture they envision. As a result, leaders are seen as being able to calculate the degree of environmental turbulence and match their organization's information and decision systems to it. Second, the contingency viewpoint clearly specifies what to look for inside the organization. Specifically, it initially identifies the complexity of organizational specializations and the uncertainty in the decision-making process, and then designs information systems to fit these criteria. Third, the contingency theory clearly specifies what to look for in the external environment, namely, its degree of uncertainty and complexity. Finally, the contingency viewpoint specifies the time period over which the organization is to be viewed. In more specific terms, the theory suggests that organizational leaders identify the existing degree of environmental uncertainty and then match the organization's current resources to this turbulence.

Strategic Viewpoint

"A strategy is a comprehensive, gestalt, holistic 'picture' or 'vision' showing how all elements in a task alignment might, in the future, fit with the needs and demands of constituencies in the environment" (Hampton, Summer, and Webber, 1987, p. 767).

The concepts of organization, environment, and strategic choice are central to the strategic viewpoint. In the following paragraphs, a brief discussion of these three concepts is presented. This is followed by a description of how organizational leaders attempt to achieve a proper fit with society through strategy and policy formulation and relate strategy and policy using elaboration, reformulation, institutionalization, and interdependence. Finally, the strategic viewpoint is compared to the ecological and contingency theories, and points of agreement and disagreement among these theories are identified and presented.

As organizations move through their life cycles, almost all of them proceed from inception and birth to growth and development and then to a period of conflict. Thereafter, they may move either toward realignment and growth or toward stagnation and decline (Hampton, Summer, and Webber, 1987). Being able to continuously align (coordinate or synchronize) organizational form with society is the most instrumental force that propels an organization's movement from one stage to another.

Every organization is nurtured within an "environment/society" that is composed of an amalgamation of special task constituencies (consisting of customers, clients, or resource suppliers) and cultural constituencies (consisting of groups positively or negatively affected by the task alignment) that are unique to only that particular organization.

Task alignment is the most immediate challenge the organization faces in stage one (birth/inception) and stage two (growth/development), since it has to align organizational form with task constituencies. In essence, the organization must coordinate—by logical and conceptual methods—networks of external outputs, internal resource competencies, and constituencies in the task environment. Unlike the first two stages, the problem in stage three (conflict) is cultural alignment. Accompanying the increases in complexity and size of task alignment, there is the creation of another network of constituencies—that are affected by but not directly connected with the main task—which comprise a larger and wider cultural environment. To move to stage four (realignment/growth), and to avoid stage five (stagnation/decline/death), the mature organization will have to not only match its form to task constituencies, but also modify its form to match its new cultural constituencies.

Based on the precept of outside constituencies, the elements in the task alignment are competencies that the organization must be capable of in order to serve society rather than to exploit it for the organization's advantage. As a result, resources and/or rewards are given to those species of organizations that have a comparative and distinctive advantage over others. Furthermore, it is important to note that organizations with the most distinctive competencies are the ones that receive resources from their outside constituents.

Finally, the strategic viewpoint assumes that the real objective alignment of an organization is strongly influenced by the "strategists," "top managers," "key influentials," or "dominant coalition" in the "strategic apex" of a given organization. The behavior of this strategic group is critical to organizational evolution because this group influences alignment, and in turn the degree of alignment can result in organizational growth or decline. To influence alignment, strategists exercise strategic choice (Child, 1972) over a very broad spectrum of alignment competencies. They also influence the organizational culture, which in turn supports or detracts from the organization's alignment processes. Within this context, strategists choose among a wide range of options by employing one of two types of decision making: strategy formulation and policy formulation.

Formulating Strategies and Policies. When organizational leaders formulate a strategy, they base their decision on the organization's total systems of competencies and total system of external supporters. These two systems are related through inductive and conceptual analytical processes, a kind of reasoning that economists have long recognized as "entrepreneurial vision" (Schumpeter, 1950; Penrose, 1968).

For the organizational observer or leader, it is important to understand the limitations and deficiencies of using only strategy formulation. First, the strategic situation with all its environment constituencies and all its task alignment elements is extremely complex since there are so many variables with their own unique levels of accuracy. Second, to add to this complexity, these variables are constantly, unpredictably changing, and no amount of sophisticated forecasting can see the future as it will truly be. Third, the larger the organization is, the longer time it requires to implement a change, because its entire culture (with its complex technology, economics, and human behavior) must learn new alignments gradually. These deficiencies, taken together, cause organizational leaders to use the two types of decision-making processes simultaneously (strategy and policy) rather than only one.

A policy is a piece or increment of a strategy. Like strategy formulation, policy formulation is a conscious and cognitive act. However, it differs from strategy formulation in four respects: what is being formulated; the degree of detailed scientific methods that are used with conceptual reasoning; the time frame of environmental and organizational forecasting; and its continuous and sequential decisions, referred to as "policy episodes."

Since policy formulation focuses on only one element of organizational form, rather than the whole task alignment—as in the case of strategy formulation—there is less complexity and therefore less discrepancy between vison and reality. However, more scientific and detailed policy analysis can take place so that if everything cannot be done at once, an alternative is to develop one policy at a time. In addition, a policy has a shorter time frame, involving shorter-range forecasting, therefore making it more likely to reflect reality rather than simply a perceived vision. Finally, policy formulation is viewed as a series of sequential policy episodes (each with shorter time spans than strategy), which occur in an unending stream.

Strategic choice, therefore, consists of policy formulation and strategy formulation, both of which are performed simultaneously over time and are related to each other in four special ways: elaboration, reformulation, institutionalization, and interdependence.

As a decision-making process, elaboration converts one or more elements in an original strategy to specific detailed actions by using factual details. These details include a variety of organizational and environmental data that can be technical, economic, motivational, or political. Collections of such data are more predictable for three reasons: rather than focusing on the whole strategy, attention is directed to a limited problem; since planning takes place closer to the time of action, data are forecasted less far into the future; and to support conceptual thinking, more scientific techniques can be used.

In the case of reformulation, however, the focus is on a certain element of the policy in the strategy that is not aligned with reality. In solving this particular policy problem, strategists discover that they have to reformulate/change their vision of the whole strategy. On the other hand, whenever elaboration or reformulation is performed by organizational leaders over a long period of time, people who are associated with the organization learn new technolgies, attitudes, beliefs, and skills—a phenomenon that is referred to as institutionalization, or strategic learning. External constituencies, as well as internal leaders and employees, learn to live and cope with different services, structures, or reward systems. A gradual assimilation and institutionalization of the complex alignment with constituencies can be attained through strategic learning. Finally, within the context of interdependence, strategists are constantly engaged in the two processes of "muddling with a purpose" (Wrapp, 1967) and "logical incrementalism" (Quinn, 1980). According to Wrapp (1967), organizational leaders more or less "muddle" through a maze of policy episodes when they attempt to elaborate conceived strategies. Quinn (1980), on the other hand, assumes that, although effective strategists do attack bits and pieces of strategies (in policy episodes), they do not lose themselves in the process, but see the whole picture by maintaining an overall sense of the logic (strategy) and purpose of the policy. Although strategists may sometimes be successful and may elaborate, they may be at other times unsuccessful and must reformulate. The behaviors of the strategic group, however, are not haphazard actions; they are accompanied by an overview or comprehensive logic that is learned and constantly adjusted along the way. These learnings become integrally interwoven into the culture of the organization.

The Strategic Viewpoint vs. Ecological and Contingency Viewpoints. In one respect, the strategic viewpoint agrees with ecological and contingency perspectives; they all share the precept that only organizations whose form or nature fits the environemnt will survive and grow. The strategic viewpoint is also in agreement with contingency theory by assuming that organizational leaders are empowered with the free will to design new cultural forms. Strategic theory, however, differs sharply from the other two viewpoints in four respects: organizational form; environment; time span; and free will.

When defining organizational form, both external outputs (goals) and internal resource competencies are taken into account. Unlike the contingency theory—which takes product outputs for granted and only deals with degree of turbulence or complexity—the strategic viewpoint assumes that product goals are central variables that need to be "created" or "designed." Furthermore, in addition to focusing on the internal communication and decision system, strategic theory includes organizational culture transformation processes: organizational structure, workflow processes, and reward systems.

While only environmental complexity/turbulence is assessed by contingency theory, strategic theory envisions the environment as being composed of a very broad range of constituencies, each of which demands some task or cultural output from the organization. Like ecological theory, strategic theory covers long time spans. Both viewpoints deal with very long-term life cycle changes in organizations.

The strategic theory views organizational leaders as exercising free will through the decision-making processes of strategy formulation and policy formulation. Strategists do not compute only environmental turbulence and then fit only the internal decison-making system to that. Rather, strategists have a broad range of internal elements of form and an infinite discretion to "visualize," "conceptualize," and "design" product or service outputs. In addition, the organization can "create" its own environment or migrate to new environments by including product and service goals as elements of organizational form.

Summary of the Chapter

The first part of this chapter briefly discussed Lacoursiere's five organizational development stages of orientation, dissatisfaction, resolution, production, and termination. Subsequently, the Hersey-Blanchard Model of Situational Leadership Styles of delegating, supporting, coaching, and directing were then highlighted. It was also emphasized that the integration of appropriate situational leadership style with the organization's developmental stage provides a useful framework for determining leader behaviors that will help the organization meet its needs and move through its developmental stages.

In the second part, the Community College Effectiveness Model was presented by initially defining institutional effectiveness, followed by a discussion of the need for a college effectiveness instrument and a synopsis of the developmental stages used in producing such an assessment instrument by studying excellent institutions and leaders. The components of the Community College Effectiveness Model were identified and briefly discussed so as to give institutions of higher education a perspective of what they ought to look for when moving toward quality and educational excellence in their organizations.

Finally, three futuristic viewpoints of organizational evolution theory were presented. The framework of ecological theory projects organizations as being under the direct influence or control of their environment. Contingency theory is based on the assumption that environmental instability and complexity cause the development of different internal and cultural organizational structures. Finally, the strategic view recognizes leaders as having considerable flexibility in helping the organization and its culture to fit, or align, with society by continously and simultaneously engaging in strategy and policy formulation.

The continued growth and health of North American community colleges will depend on the leaders' ability to assess their organizational cultures for both functional and dysfunctional qualities. As turbulence increases and these leaders are required to respond to increasing control and accountablity measures, they must be ready to deal with and solve problems related to external pressure through internal integration.

References

AACJC Commission on the Future of Community Colleges. *Building Communities: A Vision for a New Century.* Washington, D.C.: American Association of Community and Junior Colleges, 1988.

Adams, J.S. "Toward an Understanding of Inequity." *Journal of Abnormal and Social Psychology,* 1963, 67, 422–436.

Adams, J.S. "Inequity in Social Exchange." In L. Berkowitz (Ed.), *Advances in Experimental Social Psychology,* Vol. 2. New York: Academic Press, 1965.

Adams, J.S., and Friedman, S. "Equity Theory Revisited: Comments and Annotated Bibliography." In L. Berkowitz (Ed.), *Advances in Experimental Social Psychology,* Vol. 13. New York: Academic Press, 1976.

Albrecht, K., and Albrecht, S. *The Creative Corporation.* Homewood, Ill.: Dow Jones-Irwin, 1987.

Aldrich, H.E. *Organizations and Environments.* Englewood Cliffs, N.J.: Prentice-Hall, 1979.

Allen, R.F., and Pilnick, S. "Confronting the Shadow Organization: How to Detect and Defeat Negative Norms." *Organizational Dynamics,* 1973, 1 (4), 2–18.

Amabile, T.M., and Gryskiewicz, S.S. "Creative Human Resources in the R&D Laboratory: How Environment and Responsibility Impact Innovation." In R.L. Kuhn (Ed.), *Handbook for Creative and Innovative Managers.* New York: McGraw-Hill, 1987.

Angell, G.W. *Faculty and Teacher Bargaining: The Impact of Unions on Education.* Lexington, Mass.: D.C. Heath and Company, 1983.

Ansari, M. "Organizational Climate: Homogeneity Within and Heterogeneity Between Organizations." *Social and Economic Studies,* 1980, 111 (1): 89–96.

Argyris, C. *Interpersonal Competence and Organizational Effectiveness.* Homewood, Ill.: Dorsey Press, 1962.

Argyris, C. *Integrating the Individual and the Organization.* New York: Wiley, 1964.

Argyris, C. *Increasing Leadership Effectiveness.* New York: Wiley-Interscience, 1976.

Argyris, C. "How Learning and Reasoning Processes Affect Organizational Change." In P.S. Goodman and associates (Eds.), *Change in*

Organizations: New Perspectives on Theory, Research, and Practice. San Francisco: Jossey-Bass, 1982.

Argyris, C., and Schon, D.A. *Theory in Practice: Increasing Professional Effectiveness.* San Francisco: Jossey-Bass, 1974.

Ashforth, B.E. "Climate Formations: Issues and Extensions." *The Academy of Management Review,* 1985, *10,* 837–847.

Astin, A.W., and Scherrei, R.A. *Maximizing Leadership Effectiveness.* San Francisco: Jossey-Bass, 1980.

Athanasiades, J. "The Disruption of Upward Communication in Hierarchical Organizations." *Academy of Management Review,* 1973, *17,* 207–226.

Baker, G.A., III, Roueche, J.E., and Gillett-Karam, R. *Teaching as Leading.* Washington, D.C.: Community College Press, 1990.

Barber, P.A. "Relationship of Founding and Succeeding Presidential Leadership Behaviors to Organizational Change." Unpublished doctoral dissertation, Department of Educational Administration, University of Texas at Austin, 1990.

Barnard, C.I. *The Functions of the Executive.* Cambridge, Mass.: Harvard University Press, 1968.

Bartunek, J.M. "The Dynamics of Personal and Organizational Reframing." In R.E. Quinn and K.S. Cameron (Eds.), *Paradox and Transformation: Toward a Theory of Change in Organization and Management.* Cambridge, Mass.: Ballinger, 1988.

Bass, B.M. *Leadership and Performance Beyond Expectations.* New York: Free Press, 1985a.

Bass, B.M. "Leadership: Good, Better, Best." *Organizational Dynamics,* 1985b, Winter, 26–40.

Becker, C.E. "Deciding When It's Time for a Change in Organizational Climate." *Personnel,* 1975, *52,* 25–31.

Behling, O., and Starke, F.A. "The Postulates of Expectancy Theory." *Academy of Management Journal,* 1973, *16* (3), 373–388.

Bennis, W.G. "The Art Form of Leadership." In S. Srivastva and associates, *The Executive Mind: New Insights on Managerial Thought and Action.* San Francisco: Jossey-Bass, 1983.

Bennis, W.G. *On Becoming a Leader.* New York: Addison-Wesley, 1989.

Bennis, W.G., and Nanus, B. *Leaders: The Strategies for Taking Charge.* New York: Harper and Row, 1985.

Berger, C.R., and Roloff, M.E. "Thinking About Friends and Lovers: Social Cognition and Relational Trajectories." In M.E. Roloff and C.R. Berger (Eds.), *Social Cognition and Communication.* Beverly Hills: Sage, 1982.

Beyer, J.M. "Ideologies, Values, and Decision Making in Organizations." In P.C. Nystom and W.A. Starbuck (Eds.), *Handbook of Organizational Design.* New York: Oxford University Press, 1981.

Biggerstaff, C.A. "Creating, Managing, and Transforming Organizational Culture in the Community College: Perspectives of Reputationally Effective Presidents." Unpublished doctoral dissertation, Department of Educational Administration, University of Texas at Austin, 1990.

Blake, R.R., Shepard, H.A., and Mouton, J.S. *Managing Intergroup Conflict in Industry*. Houston, Texas: Gulf Publishing Company, 1964.

Blanchard, K. *Situational Leadership II*. San Diego: Blanchard Training and Development, 1985.

Blanchard, K., and Johnson, S. *The One-Minute Manager*. New York: William Morrow and Company, 1982.

Block, P. *The Empowered Manager*. San Francisco: Jossey-Bass, 1987.

Bowers, D.G. "Organizational Development Techniques and Their Results in 23 Organizations: The Michigan ICL Study." *Journal of Applied Behavioral Science*, 1973, 9, 21–42.

Bradford, D.L., and Cohen, A. *Managing for Excellence*. New York: Wiley, 1984.

Brown, D.G. *Leadership Vitality: A Workbook for Academic Administration*. Washington, D.C.: American Council on Education, 1979.

Bucholtz, S., and Roth, T. *Creating the High-Performance Team*. New York: Wiley, 1987.

Burns, J.M. *Leadership*. New York: Harper and Row, 1978.

Bush, R.W., and Ames, W.C. "Leadership and Technological Innovation." In R.L. Alfred, P.A. Elsner, R.J. LeCroy, and N. Armes (Eds.), *Emerging Roles for Community College Leaders*, New Directions for Community Colleges, No. 46. San Francisco: Jossey-Bass, 1984.

Calder, B.J. "An Attribution Theory of Leadership." In B.M. Staw and G.R. Salanick (Eds.), *New Directions in Organizational Behavior*. Chicago: St. Clair Press, 1977.

Cameron, K.S., and Ulrich, D.O. "Transformational Leadership in Colleges and Universities." In J.C. Smart (Ed.), *Higher Education: Handbook of Theory and Research*. Vol. 2. New York: Agathon Press, 1986.

Campbell, J.P., Dunnette, M.D., Lawler, E.E., and Weick, K.E., Jr. *Managerial Behavior, Performance, and Effectiveness*. New York: McGraw-Hill, 1970.

Carnegie Council on Policy Studies in Higher Education. *Three Thousand Futures*. San Francisco: Jossey-Bass, 1982.

Carnegie Foundation for the Advancement of Teaching. *National Survey of Faculty*. Lawrenceville, N.J.: Princeton University Press, 1984.

Central Piedmont Community College. Board of Trustees minutes. Charlotte, N.C., April 30, 1965.

Central Piedmont Community College. Board of Trustees minutes. Charlotte, N.C., March 18, 1968.

Central Piedmont Community College. College Cabinet summary. Charlotte, N.C., September 6, 1989a.

Central Piedmont Community College. College Cabinet summary. Charlotte, N.C., October 11, 1989b.

Chafee, E.E., and Tierney, W.G. *Collegiate Culture and Leadership Strategies.* New York: American Council on Education/Macmillan, 1988.

Child, J. "Organizational Structure, Environment, and Performance: The Role of Strategic Choice." *Sociology,* 1972, 6 (1), 1–22.

Clark, B.R. "The Organizational Saga in Higher Education." *Administrative Science Quarterly,* 1972, *17,* 178–184.

Clark, G.A. "Organizational Structure, Leadership Strategies, and Organizational Systems in a Unionized Community College: A Case Study." Unpublished doctoral dissertation, Department of Educational Administration, University of Texas at Austin, 1990.

Cohen, A.M., and Brawer, F.B. *The American Community College.* San Francisco: Jossey-Bass, 1984.

Cohen, A.M., and Roueche, J.E. *Institutional Administrator or Educational Leader? The Junior College President.* Washington, D.C.: Community College Press, 1969.

Cohen, E., and Friedlander, J. *Approaches to Predicting Student Success Study: Findings and Recommendations.* October 1989 (Available from E. Cohen and J. Friedlander, Santa Barbara City College, 721 Cliff Drive, Santa Barbara, Calif. 93108-2394).

Cohen, M.D., and March, J.G. *Leadership and Ambiguity.* 2nd Edition. Boston: Harvard Business School Press, 1986.

Collier, P., and Horowitz, D. *The Fords: An American Epic.* New York: Summit Books, 1987.

Cresswell, A.M., Murphy, M.J., and Kerchner, C.T. *Teachers, Unions, and Collective Bargaining in Public Education.* Berkeley, Calif.: McCutchan Publishing, 1980.

Cross, K.P. "On Leadership and the Future of the Community College." Paper presented at the annual conference of the Association of California Community College Administrators, San Diego, March 1983.

Cross, K.P. "Determining Missions and Priorities for the Fifth Generation." In W.L. Deegan and D. Tillery (Eds.), *Renewing the American Community College: Priorities and Strategies for Effective Leadership.* San Francisco: Jossey-Bass, 1988.

Cross, K.P., and Fideler, E.F. "Community College Missions: Priorities in the Mid-1980s." *Journal of Higher Education,* 1989, *60,* 209–216.

Daft, R.L. *Management.* New York: Holt, Rinehart, and Winston, 1988.

Daft, R.L., and Becker, S.W. *The Innovative Organization: Innovation Adoption in School Organizations.* New York: Elsevier, 1978.

Dalkey, N.C. "The Delphi Method: An Experimental Study of Group Opinion." Rand Corporation Memorandum RM 5888-PR, June 1969.

Dandridge, T.C. "Symbols' Function and Use." In L.R. Pondy, P.J. Frost, G. Morgan, and T.C. Dandridge (Eds.), *Organizational Symbolism*. Greenwich, Conn.: JAI Press, 1983.

Davis, K., and Newstrom, J.W. *Human Behavior at Work: Organizational Behavior*. 7th Edition. New York: McGraw-Hill, 1985.

Davis, S.M. *Managing Corporate Culture*. Cambridge, Mass.: Ballinger, 1984.

De Anza College. *Foothill-De Anza Community College District Tenure Review Handbook*. Cupertino, Calif.: De Anza College, 1989.

De Anza College. *A Proud Past—A Vital Future: Planning for the '80s and Beyond*. Cupertino, Calif.: De Anza College, 1986.

Deal, T.E., and Kennedy, A.A. *Corporate Cultures: The Rites and Rituals of Corporate Life*. Reading, Mass.: Addison-Wesley, 1982.

Deegan, W.L. "Entrepreneurial Management." In T. O'Banion (Ed.), *Innovation in the Community College*. New York: American Council on Education/Macmillan/American Association of Community and Junior Colleges, 1989.

Delbecq, A.L., Van de Ven, A.H., and Gustafson, D.H. *Group Techniques for Program Planning*. Glenview, Ill.: Scott, Foresman, 1975.

Denison, D.R. *Corporate Culture and Organizational Effectiveness*. New York: Wiley, 1990.

Denison, J.D., and Gallagher, P. *Canada's Community Colleges: A Critical Analysis*. Vancouver, B.C.: University of British Columbia Press, 1986.

Donaldson, G., and Lorsch, J.W. *Decision Making at the Top*. New York: Basic Books, 1983.

Douglas, M. *A Study of the Role and Responsibilities of the Academic Senate and the California Teachers Association Bargaining Unit in Educational Matters*. Malibu, Calif.: Pepperdine University, 1980. (ED 186 066)

Dressel, P.L. *Administrative Leadership*. San Francisco: Jossey-Bass, 1981.

Drexier, J.A. "Organizational Climate: Its Homogeneity Within Organizations." *Journal of Applied Psychology*, 1977, 82 (1), 38–42.

Drucker, P.F. *The Effective Executive*. New York: Harper and Row, 1967.

Dyer, W.G., Jr. "Organizational Evolution." Unpublished paper, Sloan School of Management, Massachusetts Institute of Technology, 1983.

Easton, J.Q., Forrest, E.P., Goldman, R.E., and Ludwig, L.M. *National Study of Effective Community College Teachers*. Unpublished manuscript, City Colleges of Chicago, 1984. (ED 245 740)

Eaton, J.S. "Overview: Colleges of Choice." In J.S. Eaton (Ed.), *Colleges of Choice: The Enabling Impact of the Community College*. New York: American Council on Education/Macmillan, 1988.

Fiedler, F.E. "The Leadership Game: Matching the Man to the Situation." *Organizational Dynamics*, 1976, *4* (3), 6–16.

Fiedler, F.E., and Chemers, M.M. *Leadership and Effective Management.* Glenview, Ill.: Scott, Foresman, 1974.

Field, G.R., and Abelson, M.A. "Climate: A Reconceptualization of Proposed Model." *Human Relations*, 1982, *35* (3), 181–201.B

Filley, A.C. *Interpersonal Conflict Resolution.* Dallas: Scott, Foresman, 1975.

Firestone, W.A., and Corbett, H.D. "Planned Organizational Change." In N.J. Boyan (Ed.), *Handbook of Research on Educational Administration.* New York: Longman, 1988.

Fishbein, M., and Ajzen, I. *Belief, Attitude, Intention, and Behavior: An Introduction to Theory and Research.* Reading, Mass.: Addison-Wesley, 1975.

Fisher, J.L. *Power of the Presidency.* New York: American Council on Education/Macmillan, 1984.

Fisher, J.L., Tack, M.W., and Wheeler, K.J. *The Effective College President.* New York: American Council on Education/Macmillan, 1988.

Flanagan, J.C. "The Critical Incident Technique." *Psychological Bulletin*, 1954, *51* (4), 327–358.

Ford, H., and Crowther, S. *My Life and Work.* New York: Doubleday, 1922.

Fox, A. *Beyond Contract: Work, Power, and Trust Relations.* London: Faber, 1974.

Friedlander, F., and Greenberg, S. "Effect of Job Attitudes, Training, and Organizational Climate on Performance of the Hardcore Unemployed." *Journal of Applied Psychology*, 1971, *55*, 287–295.

Fryer, T.W., Jr. "Governance in the High-Achieving Community College." In T. O'Banion (Ed.), *Innovation in the Community College.* New York: American Council on Education/Macmillan/American Association of Community and Junior Colleges, 1989.

Galbraith, J.R. "Organization Design: An Information Processing View." In J. Lorsch and P. Lawrence (Eds.), *Organization Planning: Cases and Concepts.* Homewood, Ill.: Irwin, 1972.

Gardner, J.W. "Leaders and Followers." *Liberal Education*, 1987, *73* (2), 4–8.

Glaser, B.G., and Strauss, A.L. *The Discovery of Grounded Theory: Strategies for Qualitative Research.* Chicago: Aldine, 1967.

Glauser, M.J. "Upward Information Flow in Organizations: Review and Conceptual Analysis." *Human Relations*, 1984, *37* (8), 613–643.

Gleazer, E.J. *The Community College: Values, Vision, and Vitality.* Washington, D.C.: American Association of Community and Junior Colleges, 1980.

Goodstein, L.D. "Managers, Values, and Organizational Development." *Group and Organizational Studies*, 1983, *8*, 203–220.

Gouldner, A. *Patterns of Industrial Bureaucracy.* New York: Harper and Row, 1964.

Graves, D. *Corporate Culture—Diagnosis and Change: Auditing and Changing the Culture of Organizations.* New York: St. Martin's Press, 1986.

Gregory, K. "Native-View Paradigms: Multiple Cultures and Culture Conflicts in Organizations." *Administrative Science Quarterly,* 1983, *28,* 359–376.

Gulassa, C. *Collaborative Governance in the Foothill-De Anza Community College District.* Management Report 1988–89/3. Sacramento, Calif.: Association of California Community College Administrators, 1989.

Guy, M.E. *From Organizational Decline to Organizational Renewal: The Phoenix Syndrome.* New York: Quorum Books, 1989.

Hagemeyer, R.H. "Memorandum to Board of Trustees." *Long Range Planning Report, 1974.* Charlotte, N.C.: Central Piedmont Community College, November 22, 1974.

Hambrick, D., and Mason, P. "Upper Echelons: The Organization as a Reflection of Its Top Management." *Academy of Management Review,* 1984, *9* (2), 193–206.

Hampton, R. *Behavioral Concepts in Management.* 3rd Edition. Belmont, Calif.: Wadsworth Publishing Co., 1978.

Hampton, D.R., Summer, C.E., and Webber, R.A. *Organizational Behavior and the Practice of Management.* 5th Edition. Glenview, Ill.: Scott, Foresman, 1987.

Harrison, M.I. *Diagnosing Organizations: Methods, Models, and Processes.* Newbury Park, Calif.: Sage, 1987.

Havelock, R.G., Guskin, A., Frohman, M., Havelock, M., Hill, M., and Huber, J. *Planning for Innovation Through Dissemination and Utilization of Knowledge.* Ann Arbor: University of Michigan, Center for Research on Utilization of Scientific Knowledge, Institute for Social Research, 1973.

Heller, R. *The Decision Makers: The Men and the Million-Dollar Moves Behind Today's Great Corporate Success Stories.* New York: E.P. Dutton, 1989.

Hellreigel, D., and Slocum, J.W., Jr. "Organizational Climate: Measures, Research, and Contingencies." *Academy of Management Journal,* 1974, *17* (2), 255–280.

Hersey, P., and Blanchard, K. *Management of Organizational Behavior.* Englewood Cliffs, New Jersey: Prentice-Hall, 1982.

Herzberg, F., Mausner, B., and Snyderman, B. *The Motivation to Work.* New York: Wiley, 1959.

Herzberg, F., Mausner, B., and Snyderman, B. *The Motivation to Work.* 2nd Edition. New York: Wiley, 1966.

Hollander, E.P. *Leadership Dynamics.* New York: Free Press, 1978.

Hollander, E.P. "Social Psychological Perspective on Leadership." *Liberal Education,* 1987, *73* (2), 9–15.

House, R. "A Path-Goal Theory of Leader Effectiveness." *Administrative Science Quarterly,* 1971, *16,* 321–338.

House, R., and Mitchell, T. "Path-Goal Theory of Leadership." *Journal of Contemporary Business,* 1974, *3,* 81–97.

Hoy, W.K., and Miskel, C.G. *Educational Administration: Theory, Research, and Practice.* 3rd Edition. New York: Random House, 1987.

Iaffaldano, M.T., and Muchinsky, P.M. "Job Satisfaction and Job Performance: A Meta-Analyses." *Psychological Bulletin,* 1985, *97,* 251–273.

James, L.R., and Jones, A.P. "Organizational Climate: A Review of Theory and Research." *Psychological Bulletin,* 1974, *81,* 1096–1112.

Janis, I.L. *Victims of Groupthink.* 2nd Edition. Boston: Houghton, Mifflin, 1982.

Jelinek, M., Smircich, L., and Hirsch, P. "Introduction: A Code of Many Colors." *Administrative Science Quarterly,* 1983, *28,* 331–338.

Joyce, W.F., and Slocum, J. "Climates in Organizations." In S. Kerr (Ed.), *Organizational Behavior.* San Francisco: Grid Publishing, 1979.

Joyce, W.F., and Slocum, J. "Climate Discrepancy: Refining the Concepts of Psychological and Organizational Climate." *Human Relations,* 1982, *35* (11), 951–972.

Kanter, R.M. *The Change Masters: Innovation and Entrepreneurship in the American Corporation.* New York: Simon & Schuster, 1983.

Kanter, R.M. "Encouraging Innovation and Entrepreneurs in Bureaucratic Companies." In R.L. Kuhn (Ed.), *Handbook for Creative and Innovative Managers.* New York: McGraw-Hill, 1987.

Kanter, R.M. "Change-Master Companies: Environments in Which Innovations Flourish." In R.L. Kuhn (Ed.), *Handbook for Creative and Innovative Managers.* New York: McGraw-Hill, 1988.

Katz, D., and Kahn, R.L. *The Social Psychology of Organizations.* 2nd Edition. New York: Wiley, 1978.

Keller, G. "Shotgun Marriage: The Growing Connection Between Academic Management and Faculty Governance." In J.H. Schuster, L.H. Miller, and associates (Eds.), *Governing Tomorrow's Campuses: Perspectives and Agendas.* New York: American Council on Education/Macmillan, 1989.

Kelly, H.H., Berscheid, E., Christensen, A., Harvey, J.H., Huston, T.L., and Levinger, G. *Close Relationships.* New York: W.H. Freeman, 1983.

Kerr, J., and Slocum, J.W., Jr. "Managing Corporate Culture Through Reward Systems." *Academy of Management Executive,* 1987, *1,* 99–108.

Kets de Vries, M.F. *Prisoners of Leadership.* New York: Wiley, 1989.

Kets de Vries, M.F., and Miller, D. "Group Fantasies and Organizational Functioning." *Human Relations*, 1984, *37* (2), 111–134.

Kimberly, J.R. "Reframing and the Problem of Organizational Change." In R.E. Quinn and K.S. Cameron (Eds.), *Paradox and Transformation: Toward a Theory of Change in Organization and Management*. Cambridge, Mass.: Ballinger, 1988.

Kimberly, J.R., and Quinn, R.E. (Eds.). *New Futures: The Challenge of Managing Corporate Transitions*. Homewood, Ill.: Dow Jones-Irwin, 1984.

Klemp, G.O., Huff, S.M., and Gentile, J.D. *The Guardians of Campus Change: A Study of Leadership in Nontraditional College Programs. Final Report*. Boston: McBer, December 1980.

Kotter, J.P. *The Leadership Factor*. New York: Free Press, 1988.

Kouzes, J.M. "When Leadership Collides with Loyalty." *Forum: The New York Times*, January 24, 1988, section III, p. 3.

Kozmetsky, G. "Creative and Innovative Management." In E.B. Konecci, G. Kozmetsky, R.W. Smilor, and M.D. Gill (Eds.), *Commercializing Technology Resources for Competitive Advantage*. Austin, Texas: IC2 Institute, 1986.

Kozmetsky, G. "The Challenge of Technology Innovation in the Coming Economy." Paper presented at the 13th Annual Symposium on Technology Transfer, Technology Transfer Society, Portland, Oreg., July 1988.

Kuh, G.D. "Organizing in Student Affairs." In U. Delworth, G.R. Hanson, and associates (Eds.), *Student Services: A Handbook for the Profession*. San Francisco: Jossey-Bass, 1989.

Kuh, G.D., and Whitt, E.J. *The Invisible Tapestry: Culture in American Colleges and Universities*. ASHE-ERIC Higher Education Report No. 1. Washington, D.C.: Association for the Study of Higher Education, 1988.

Kuhn, R.L. (Ed.). *Frontiers in Creative and Innovative Management*. Cambridge, Mass.: Ballinger, 1985.

Lacey, R. *Ford: The Men and the Machine*. Boston: Little, Brown, 1986.

Lacoursiere, R.B. *The Life Cycle of Groups: Group Developmental Stage Theory*. New York: Human Service Press, 1980.

LaFollette, W.R., and Sims, H.P. "Is Satisfaction Redundant with Organizational Climate?" *Organizational Behavior and Human Performance*, 1975, *13*, 257–278.

Landsberger, H. "The Horizontal Dimension in Bureaucracy." *Administrative Science Quarterly*, 1961, 6, 299–332.

Lawler, E.E., III. *High-Involvement Management*. San Francisco: Jossey-Bass. 1986.

Lawler, E.E., III, Hall, D.T., and Oldham, G.R. "Organizational Climate: Relationship to Organizational Structure, Process and Performance." *Organizational Behavior and Human Performance*, 1974, *11*, 139–155.

Lawler, E.E., III, and Porter, L.W. "The Effect of Performance on Job Satisfaction." *Industrial Relations*, 1967, *7* (5), 20–28.

Lawless, D.J. *Organizational Behavior: The Psychology of Effective Management*. 2nd Edition. Englewood Cliffs, N.J.: Prentice-Hall, 1979.

Leatherman, C. "Colleges' Failure to Tackle Pressing Academic Problems in 1980s Led to Lack of Collaboration by Professors and Administrators." *The Chronicle of Higher Education*, January 23, 1991, p. A15.

LeCroy, R.J. "Excellence in the Making: The Process of Becoming a Leader." In J.E. Roueche and G.A. Baker (Eds.), *Community College Leadership for the '80s*. Washington, D.C.: Community College Press, 1984.

Levy, A. and Merry, U. *Organizational Transformation: Approaches, Strategies, Theories*. New York: Praeger, 1986.

Lewin, K. "Frontiers in Group Dynamics." *Human Relations*, 1947, *1*, 1–41.

Likert, R. *The Human Organization*. New York: McGraw-Hill, 1967.

Lilly, E. "The American College President: The Changing Role." *Planning and Changing*, 1987, *18* (1), 3–16.

Lincoln, Y.S., and Guba, E.G. *Naturalistic Inquiry*. Beverly Hills, Calif.: Sage, 1985.

Litwin, G.H., and Stringer, R. *The Influence of Organizational Climate*. Boston: Harvard University Press, 1966.

Locke, E.A. "The Nature and Causes of Job Satisfaction." In M.D. Dunnette (Ed.), *Handbook of Industrial and Organizational Psychology*. New York: Wiley, 1983.

Locke, E.A., and Latham, G.P. *Goal Setting: A Motivational Technique That Works*. Englewood Cliffs, N.J.: Prentice-Hall, 1984.

London, M. *Change Agents: New Roles and Innovation Strategies for Human Resource Professionals*. San Francisco: Jossey-Bass, 1988.

Loyd, J.L. "Roles of Administrative Personnel." In B.W. Miller, R.W. Hotes, and J.D. Terry, Jr. (Eds.), *Leadership in Higher Education: A Handbook for Practicing Administrators*. Westport, Conn.: Greenwood Press, 1983.

Lundberg, C.C. "On the Feasibility of Cultural Intervention in Organizations." In P.J. Frost, L.F. Moore, M.R. Louis, C.C. Lundberg, and J. Martin (Eds.), *Organizational Culture*. Beverly Hills, Calif.: Sage, 1985.

Maccoby, M. *The Leader*. New York: Simon & Schuster, 1981.

MacDougall, P.R., and Friedlander, J.H. "The Costs of Innovation." In T. O'Banion (Ed.), *Innovation in the Community College*. New York: American Council on Education/Macmillan/American Association of Community and Junior Colleges, 1989.

Martin, J. "Can Organizational Culture Be Managed?" In P.J. Frost, L.F. Moore, M.R. Louis, C.C. Lundberg, and J. Martin (Eds.), *Organizational Culture*. Beverly Hills, Calif.: Sage, 1985.

Martin, J., Sitkin, S.B., and Boehm, M. "Founders and the Elusiveness of a Cultural Legacy." In P.J. Frost, L.F. Moore, M.R. Louis, C.C. Lundberg, and J. Martin (Eds.), *Organizational Culture*. Beverly Hills, Calif.: Sage, 1985.

Masland, A.T. "Organizational Culture in the Study of Higher Education." *The Review of Higher Education*, 1985, 8, 157–168.

Maslow, A.H. "A Theory of Human Motivation." *Psychological Review*, 1943, *50* (4), 370–396.

Maslow, A.H. "Self Actualizing People: A Study of Psychological Health." In W. Wolff (Ed.), *Personality-Symposium No. 1*. New York: Grune and Stratton, 1950.

McClelland, D.C. "Business Drive and National Achievement." *Harvard Business Review*, 1962, *40* (4), 99–112.

Miles, M.B., and Huberman, A.M. *Qualitative Data Analysis*. Beverly Hills, Calif.: Sage, 1984.

Miner, F.C., Jr. "Group Versus Individual Decision Making: An Investigation of Performance Measures, Decision Strategies, and Process Losses/Gains." *Organizational Behavior and Human Performance*, 1984, *33* (1), 112–124.

Mink, O.G., Mink, B.P., and Owen, K. *Groups at Work*. Englewood Cliffs, N.J.: Educational Technology Publications, 1987.

Miskel, C., and Ogawa, R. "Work Motivation, Job Satisfaction, and Climate." In N.J. Boyan (Ed.), *Handbook of Research on Educational Administration*. New York: Longman, 1988.

Mitroff, I.I., and Kilmann, R.H. *Corporate Tragedies: Product Tampering, Sabotage, and Other Catastrophes*. New York: Praeger, 1984.

Morgan, G. *Creative Organization Theory*. Newbury Park, Calif.: Sage, 1989.

Muchinsky, P.M. "Organizational Communication: Relationships to Organizational Climate and Job Satisfaction." *Academy of Management Journal*, 1977, *20* (4), 592–607.

Nadler, D., and Tushman, M. *Strategic Organization Design: Concepts, Tools, and Processes*. Glenview, Ill.: Scott, Foresman, 1988.

Naisbitt, J. *Megatrends*. New York: Warner Books, 1982.

Naisbitt, J., and Aburdene, P. *Megatrends 2000: Ten New Directions for the 1990s*. New York: William Morrow and Company, 1990.

Nanus, B. *The Leader's Edge: The Seven Keys to Leadership in a Turbulent World*. New York: Contemporary Books, 1989.

Nelson, M.T. "A Case Study of Santa Barbara City College: A Creative and Innovative Community College Organizational Culture." Unpublished doctoral dissertation, Department of Educational Administration, University of Texas at Austin, 1990.

Nystrom, P.C. and Starbuck, W.H. "To Avoid Organizational Crisis, Unlearn." *Organizational Dynamics*, 1984, *12* (4), 53–65.

Offenberg, R.M., and Cernius, V. "Assessment of Idiographic Organizational Climate." *Journal of Applied Behavioral Science*, 1978, *14*, 79–88.

O'Reilly, C.A., III. "The Intentional Distortion of Information in Organizational Communication: A Laboratory and Field Approach." *Human Relations*, 1978, *31*, 173–193.

O'Reilly, C.A., III, and Pondy, L. R. "Organizational Communication." In S. Kerr (Ed.), *Organizational Behavior*. Columbus, Ohio: Grid Publishing, 1979.

Organizational Characteristic: Collaborative Planning and Collegial Relationships. Report No. EA 017 859. St. Paul, Minn.: Minnesota State Department of Education, 1985. (ED 258 361)

Ott, S.J. *The Organizational Culture Perspective*. Pacific Cove, Calif.: Brooks/Cole Publishing, 1989.

Ouchi, W.G. *Theory Z: How American Business Can Meet the Japanese Challenge*. Reading, Mass.: Addison-Wesley, 1981.

Ouchi, W.G., and Wilkins, A.L. "Organizational Culture." *Annual Review of Sociology*, 1985, *11*, 457–483.

Owens, R.G. *Organizational Behavior in Education*. Englewood Cliffs, N.J.: Prentice-Hall, 1987.

Pascale, R.T. "The Paradox of 'Corporate Culture': Reconciling Ourselves to Socialization." *California Management Review*, 1985, *27* (2), 26–41.

Pascale, R.T., and Athos, A.G. *The Art of Japanese Management*. New York: Simon and Schuster, 1981.

Patton, M.Q. *How to Use Qualitative Methods in Evaluation*. Newbury Park, Calif.: Sage, 1987.

Peña, E.E. "Presidential Perceptions of Teaching Excellence of Award-Winning Faculty Members in American and Canadian Community Colleges." Unpublished doctoral dissertation, Department of Educational Administration, University of Texas at Austin, 1990.

Penrose, E. *The Theory of the Growth of the Firm*. Oxford, England: Basil Blackwell, 1968.

Peters, T. *Thriving on Chaos: Handbook for a Management Revolution*. New York: Alfred A. Knopf, 1988.

Peters, T.J., and Austin, N. *A Passion for Excellence: The Leadership Difference*. New York: Random House, 1985.

Peters, T.J., and Waterman, R.H. *In Search of Excellence: Lessons from America's Best Run Companies*. New York: Harper and Row, 1982.

Pettigrew, A.M. "On Studying Organizational Cultures." *Administrative Science Quarterly*, December 1979, *24*, 570–581.

Pfeffer, J. "Management as Symbolic Action: The Creation and Maintenance of Organizational Paradigms." In L.L. Cummings and B.M. Staw (Eds.), *Research in Organizational Behavior*, Vol. 3. Greenwich, Conn.: JAI Press, 1981.

Pierce, J.L., Dunham, R.B., and Cummings, L.L. "Sources of Environmental Structuring and Participant Responses." *Organizational Behavior and Human Performance*, 1984, *33*, 214–242.

Pinder, C. *Work Motivation: Theory, Issues, and Applications.* Glenview, Ill.: Scott, Foresman, 1984.

Pondy, L.R. "Leadership is a Language Game." In M.W. McCall, Jr., and M.M. Lombardo (Eds.), *Leadership: Where Else Can We Go?* Durham, N.C.: Duke University Press, 1978.

Porter, L.W., Lawler, E.E., III, and Hackman, J.R. *Behavior in Organizations.* New York: McGraw-Hill, 1975.

Quinn, J.B. *Strategic Change.* Homewood, Ill.: Dow Jones-Irwin, 1980.

Quinn, R.E., and Kimberly, J.R. "Paradox, Planning, and Perseverence: Guidelines for Managerial Practice." In R.E. Quinn and J.R. Kimberly (Eds.), *New Futures: The Challenge of Managing Corporate Transitions.* Homewood, Ill.: Dow Jones-Irwin, 1984.

Richardson, R. "How Administrators Influence Student Learning." Paper presented to the Illinois Council of Community College Administrators, Champaign, Ill., November 1985.

Roberts, K.H., and O'Reilly, C.A., III. "Failures in Upward Communication in Organization: Three Possible Culprits." *Academy of Management Journal*, 1974, *17*, 204–15.

Roe, M.A. "Identifying Readiness for Leadership: The Behavioral Competencies Associated with Outstanding Community College Presidents and Executive Administrators." Unpublished doctoral dissertation, Department of Educational Administration, University of Texas at Austin, 1989.

Rokeach, M. *Beliefs, Attitudes, and Values: A Theory of Organization and Change.* San Francisco: Jossey-Bass, 1968.

Roueche, J.E., and Baker, G.A., III. *Profiling Excellence in America's Schools.* Arlington, Va.: American Association of School Administrators, 1986.

Roueche, J.E., and Baker, G.A., III. *Access and Excellence: The Open-Door College.* Washington, D.C.: Community College Press, 1987.

Roueche, J.E., Baker, G.A., III, and Rose, R.R. *Shared Vision: Transformational Leaders in American Community Colleges.* Washington, D.C.: Community College Press, 1989.

Roueche, J.E., and Mink, O.G. *Holistic Literacy in College Teaching.* New York: Media Systems, 1980.

Roueche, J.E., and Snow, J.J. *Overcoming Learning Problems: A Guide to Developmental Education in College.* San Francisco: Jossey-Bass, 1977.

Sanford, A.C., Hunt, G.T., and Bracey, H.J. *Communication Behavior in Organizations.* Columbus, Ohio: Charles E. Merrill, 1976.

Santa Barbara City College. *The Community College: A Mission of Excellence.* Santa Barbara, Calif.: Santa Barbara City College, 1989.

Santa Barbara City College Foundation. *The Santa Barbara City College Century Campaign: Toward the Year 2000.* Santa Barbara, Calif.: Santa Barbara City College, 1989.

Santa Barbara City College Office of Planning and Research. *SBCC College Climate Survey.* Santa Barbara, Calif.: Santa Barbara City College, 1989.

Sathe, V. "Implications of Corporate Culture: A Manager's Guide to Action." *Organizational Dynamics,* 1983, *12*, (2), 5–23.

Sayles, L.R. *Managerial Behavior.* New York: McGraw-Hill, 1964.

Schein, E.H. "Organizational Socialization and the Profession of Management." *Sloan Management Review,* 1968, 9 (2), 1–16.

Schein, E.H. *Process Consultation, Its Role in Organization Development.* Reading, Mass.: Addison-Wesley, 1969.

Schein, E.H. *Organizational Psychology.* 3rd Edition. Englewood Cliffs, N.J.: Prentice-Hall, 1980.

Schein, E.H. "The Role of the Founder in Creating Organizational Culture." *Organizational Dynamics,* 1983, *12* (1), 13–28.

Schein, E.H. "Coming to a New Awareness of Organizational Culture." *Sloan Management Review,* 1984, *25* (2), 3–16.

Schein, E.H. *Organizational Culture and Leadership.* San Francisco: Jossey-Bass, 1985a.

Schein, E.H. "How Culture Forms, Develops, and Changes." In R.H. Kilmann, M.J. Saxton, R. Serpa, and associates (Eds.), *Gaining Control of the Corporate Culture.* San Francisco: Jossey-Bass, 1985b.

Schneider, B., and Snyder, R.A. "Some Relationships Between Job Satisfaction and Organizational Climate." *Journal of Applied Psychology,* 1975, *60* (3), 318–328.

Schneider, C., Klemp, G., and Kastendiek, S. *The Balancing Act: Competencies of Effective Teachers and Mentors in Degree Programs for Adults.* Chicago: Center for Continuing Education, University of Chicago, 1981.

Schumpeter, J.A. *Capitalism, Socialism, and Democracy.* New York: Harper and Row, 1950.

Senge, P.M. *The Fifth Discipline: The Art and Practice of the Learning Organization.* New York: Doubleday, 1990.

Sethia, N.K., and Von Glinow, M.A. "Arriving at Four Cultures by Managing the Reward System." In R.H. Kilmann, M.J. Saxton, and R. Serpa. *Gaining Control of the Corporate Culture.* San Francisco: Jossey-Bass, 1985.

Shaw, M.E. *Group Dynamics: The Psychology of Small Group Behavior*. New York: McGraw-Hill, 1981.

Siehl, C. "After the Founder: An Opportunity to Manage Culture." In P.J. Frost, L.F. Moore, M.R. Louis, C.C. Lundberg, and J. Martin (Eds.), *Organizational Culture*. Beverly Hills, Calif.: Sage, 1985.

Simpson, R.L. "Vertical and Horizontal Communication in Formal Organizations." *Administrative Science Quarterly*, 1959, 4, 188–96.

Smilor, R.W., Kozmetsky, G., and Gibson, D.B. *Creating the Technopolis: Linking Technology, Commercialization and Economic Development*. Cambridge, Mass.: Ballinger, 1988.

Smircich, L. "Concepts of Culture and Organizational Analysis." *Administrative Science Quarterly*, 1983, 28, 339–358.

Smith, P.C., Kendall, L.M., and Hulin, C.L. *The Measurement of Satisfaction in Work and Retirement*. Chicago: Rand McNally, 1969.

Stanley, R.R. "The Application of Critical Incident Procedures for an Audit of Organizational Communication." Paper presented at the annual meeting of the International Communication Association, New Orleans, April 1974. (ED 098 624)

Steers, R. *Organizational Effectiveness: A Behavioral View*. Santa Monica, Calif.: Goodyear Publishing, 1977.

Steers, R.M., and Porter, L.W. *Motivation and Work Behavior*. 3rd Edition. New York: McGraw-Hill, 1983.

Stephenson, E.A. "The Impact of Collective Bargaining on Community College Governance and Faculty Welfare." Unpublished doctoral dissertation, Department of Educational Administration, University of Texas at Austin, 1986.

Stodgill, R.M. *Handbook for Leadership: A Survey of Theory and Research*. New York: Free Press, 1974.

Stout, J.K. "The Role of Self-Concept in Interpersonal Communications." *Supervisory Management*, 1984, 29 (2), 12–16.

Tagiuri, R. "The Concept of Organizational Climate." In R. Tagiuri and G.H. Litwin (Eds.), *Organizational Climate: Explorations of a Concept*. Boston: Harvard University Press, 1968.

Tagiuri, R., and Litwin, G.H. *Organizational Climate: Explorations of a Concept*. Boston: Harvard University Press, 1968.

Tagle, T.M. "Leadership Behaviors Perceived to Enable Communication and Relational Strength at Selected Community Colleges." Unpublished doctoral dissertation, Department of Educational Administration, University of Texas at Austin, 1988.

Tannenbaum, R.H., and Schmidt, W.H. "How to Choose a Leadership Pattern." In J.B. Ritchie and P. Thompson (Eds.), *Organization and People: Readings, Cases, and Exercises in Organizational Behavior*. St. Paul, Minn.: West, 1973.

Thayer, L. *Communication and Communication Systems*. Homewood, Ill.: Irwin, 1968.

Tichy, N.M. "Problem Cycles in Organizations and the Management of Change." In J.R. Kimberly, R.H. Miles, and associates (Eds.), *The Organizational Life Cycle: Issues in the Creation, Transformation, and Decline of Organizations*. San Francisco: Jossey-Bass, 1980.

Tichy, N.M. *Managing Strategic Change: Technical, Political, and Cultural Dynamics*. New York: Wiley, 1983.

Tichy, N.M., and Devanna, M.A. *The Transformational Leader*. New York: Wiley, 1986.

Tichy, N.M., and Ulrich, D. "Revitalizing Organizations: The Leadership Role." In J.R. Kimberly and R.E. Quinn (Eds.), *Managing Organizational Transitions*. Homewood, Ill.: Dow Jones-Irwin, 1984.

Tierney, W.G. "Organizational Culture in Higher Education: Defining the Essentials." *Journal of Higher Education*, 1988, 59 (1), 2–21.

Tierney, W.G. "Symbolism and Presidential Perceptions of Leadership." *Review of Higher Education*, 1989, 12, 153–166.

Trice, H.M., and Beyer, J.M. "Studying Organizational Cultures Through Rites and Ceremonials." *Academy of Management Review*, 1984, 9, 653–659.

Trice, H.M., and Beyer, J.M. *Cultural Leadership in Organizations*. Englewood Cliffs, N.J.: Prentice-Hall, 1992.

Tushman, M.L., Newman, W.H., and Nadler, D.A. "Executive Leadership and Organizational Evolution: Managing Incremental and Discontinuous Change." In R.H. Kilmann, T.J. Covin, and associates (Eds.), *Corporate Transformation: Revitalizing Organizations for a Competitive World*. San Francisco: Jossey-Bass, 1988.

Valek, M. "Teaching as Leading in the Community College: An Analysis of Faculty Competencies Developed Through Path-Goal Theory." Unpublished doctoral dissertation, Department of Educational Administration, University of Texas at Austin, 1988.

Vaughan, G.B. *The Community College Presidency*. New York: American Council on Education/Macmillan, 1986.

Vaught, B.C. "An Index of Interpersonal Communicative Competence and Its Relationship to the Selected Supervisory Demographics, Self-Actualization, and Leader Behavior in Organizations." Unpublished doctoral dissertation, North Texas State University, 1979.

Warren, H.F. "Opening Doors and Minds: 25 Years of Touching Lives." *Inside CPCC*, 1988, 2 (7), 12–25.

Waterman, R.H. *The Renewal Factor: How the Best Get and Keep the Competitive Edge*. New York: Bantam, 1987.

Weick, K.E. "Educational Organizations as Loosely Coupled Systems." *Administrative Quarterly*, 1976, 21, 1–19.

Weick, K.E. *The Social Psychology of Organizing*. Reading, Mass.: Addison-Wesley, 1979.

Weick, K.E. "The Management of Eloquence." *The Executive*, 1980, 6 (3), 18–21.

Weish, H.P., and La Van, H. "Inter-Relationships Between Organizational Commitment and Job Characteristics, Job Satisfaction, Professional Behavior, and Organizational Climate." *Human Relations*, 1981, *34* (12), 1079–1089.

Wheetten, D.A., and Cameron, K.S. *Developing Management Skills*. Glenview, Ill.: Scott, Foresman, 1984.

Wiggs, J.L. *The Community College System in North Carolina: A Silver Anniversary History, 1963–1988*. Raleigh, N.C.: North Carolina State Board of Community Colleges, 1989.

Wilkins, A.L., and Ouchi, W.G. "Efficient Cultures: Exploring the Relationship Between Culture and Organizational Performance." *Administrative Science Quarterly*, 1983, *28*, 468–481.

Wrapp, H.E. "Good Managers Don't Make Policy Decisions." *Harvard Business Review*, 1967, *45* (5), 91–99.

Yin, R.K. *Case Study Research: Design and Methods*. Beverly Hills, Calif.: Sage Publications, 1989.

Yukl, G.A. *Leadership in Organizations*. 2nd Edition. Englewood Cliffs, N.J.: Prentice-Hall, 1989.

Zaleznick, A. "Making Managers Creative: The Psychodynamics of Creativity and Innovation." In R.L. Kuhn (Ed.), *Handbook for Creative and Innovative Managers*. New York: McGraw-Hill, 1988.

Zaleznick, A., and Moment, D. *The Dynamics of Interpersonal Behavior*. New York: Wiley, 1964.

Index

AACJC Commission on the Future of Community Colleges, 2, 3, 5, 8, 11, 12, 48

AACJC Presidents Academy, 94

American Association of Community and Junior Colleges (AACJC), 94, 160

Association of Governing Boards of Universities and Colleges, 2

Behavioral events interview, 134

Carnegie Foundation for the Advancement of Teaching, 2

Charismatic leadership. See Transformational leadership

College climate survey, 116

Commitment to Excellence Survey, 37, 39

Communication, 61–62, 63, 75, 76
  assessing effectiveness of, 74–75
  capacity, 74, 75
  direction of, 28, 71, 75, 191, 202
  and organizational climate, 69, 70
  strategies, 66, 68, 70–71, 73, 76
  study of, as used by exceptional leaders, 63–67
  supportive, 29
  and technology, 78

Communication and Relational Strategies Inventory (CRSI), 65, 66

Community College Climate Instrument, 24–25

Community college effectiveness model, 216–226

Community college environment students' assessment of, 224

Community college leadership
  building a teaching-learning environment, 98, 100, 101
  challenges of, 4, 7–8, 9, 10, 11, 12, 21, 45, 46, 48, 79, 97–98, 201
  new paradigm for, 5, 6, 12, 13 (see also Cultural leadership; Organizational culture)
  readiness for, 80, 86, 87–89, 90, 91, 95
  study of teaching beliefs, 100–110
  training and development of, 80, 91–92, 93, 94, 95

Community College Leadership Program, 23, 198

Contingency theories of management, 99

Cooperative system, 62

Creativity and innovation in community colleges, 116–130

Critical incident interview, 134
Cultural elements, 138
Cultural Embedding Mechanisms Framework (CEMF), 14,
  49, 115
Cultural, Environmental,
  Structural, and Technical
  Assessment (CESTA),
  220–221, 222
Cultural leadership
  case study, founder, Central
    Piedmont Community
    College, 133–162
  case study, successor, Central
    Piedmont Community
    College, 163–186
  and creation of climate, 51
  and employee selection, 56–57
  management systems and
    procedures, 58
  modeling appropriate
    behavior, 53–55
  and organizational control,
    57–58
  reaction to crises, 52
  and rewards, 55–56
  and strategic planning, 51,
    54, 58
Cultural network, 20–21

Decision making, 29–30
  in educational systems, 190
  elaboration, 232
  institutionalization of, 232
  interdependence, 232
  reformulation, 232–233
  strategy and policy
    formulation, 231
Delphi technique, 30

Empowerment, 48, 54, 80, 84,
  100, 173

Enabler variables, 191–192
Entrepreneurial spirit, 154, 158,
  162, 184
Exceptional leadership
  behaviors, 50, 55, 66
  beliefs, 54
  and communication, 66, 70,
    72–73, 77
  values, 54
Expectancy theory, 99

Feedback
  effect on organizational
    climate, 76
  to students, 105
  to teachers, 129
Frame-of-reference control, 170
Framebreaking process,
  164–165, 167, 171

Goal formulation, 76
Governance
  assessment of, 222

Hersey-Blanchard model of
  situational leadership. See
  Situational leadership
  styles

Index of Interpersonal
  Communicative Competence
  (IICC), 65, 72
Information flow, 191
Information strategies, 205–206

Job satisfaction
  aspects of, 31
  effect of work environment
    on, 31–32
  and performance, 31
  and rewards, 31
  and turnover, 32

Leadership, 26, 81, 204–205
  maturational stages of, 92
  measure of effectiveness of,
    109
  and organizational culture, 82
  and relationship to followers,
    81, 85, 99, 108, 114
  studies of, 3
Leadership Effectiveness Model
  (LEP), 220
Likert's management systems,
  21–23
  benevolent authoritative, 22,
    39
  consultative, 22, 37, 40
  exploitive authoritative, 21,
    22, 23, 40
  participative group, 21–23,
    37, 40
Likert's Profile of Organizational
  and Performance Characteristics, 23

Motivation
  faculty, 99
  and need for achievement,
    27–28
  and need for affiliation, 27–28
  and need for power, 27–28
  student, 99, 100, 101–110
  theories of, 27
  through participation, 58
  work, 27

Nominal group technique, 30

Organizational climate, 17,
  18–19, 20, 42
  and communication, 28,
    71–72
  community college profiles
    on, 32–42

and decision making, 29
and job satisfaction, 31 (see
  also Job satisfaction)
measurement (assessment) of,
  21, 23
and motivation, 27
and organizational effectiveness, 19
relationship of leadership to,
  24–26
and rewards, 30
Organizational Communication
  Questionnaire (OCQ), 65
Organizational culture, 6–7, 8,
  13, 42, 45, 47, 135, 165
  assessment of, 218–226
  and climate, 15–16, 116 (see
    also Organizational climate)
  creativity and innovation in,
    114–130, 131
  embedding and transmitting,
    48, 50, 110, 111, 113–114,
    115, 185
  hierarchy in, 8–9
  and leader's values, 191
  and leadership, 9–10, 11,
    13–14, 15, 46, 47–48, 50,
    134, 184, 186, 205
  new perspective on education,
    8
  studies of, 49–59, 114–130,
    187–206
  transformation and changes
    in, 80
Organizational development
  dissatisfaction stage, 210, 214
  Lacoursiere's stages, 43, 207,
    209–212, 233–234
  orientation stage, 210, 214
  production stage, 211,
    215–216
  resolution stage, 210, 215

termination stage, 212
Organizational evolution
  contingency viewpoint, 208,
    226, 228–229, 233, 234
  ecological viewpoint, 208,
    226–228, 233, 234
  strategic viewpoint, 208, 226,
    229–231, 233, 234
Organizational growth, 21
Organizational health, 32
Organizational homeostasis,
  160–161, 163
Organizational life cycle, 134,
  208, 230
Organizational power tools,
  150, 158
Organizational structure, 26, 75
Organizational transformation
  commitment and change for,
    171–179
  conditions necessary for, 179
  phases of, 171, 179
  tools for, 179
Organizations
  stages of, 113, 115, 130, 160

Path-goal theory, 99
Personal Assessment of the College Environment (PACE), 218

Reframing process, 163–165,
  171, 177
Reward power, 30
Reward systems, 30

Shared governance, 187, 195,
  198, 202, 203–204
Situational leadership styles
  assessment of, 220
  coaching, 213, 214, 234
  delegating, 213, 214, 215–216,
    234

directing, 213, 214, 234
Hersey-Blanchard model,
  207–208, 212–216, 234
supporting, 213, 214, 215, 234
Socialization process, 142
Span of control, 140
Strategic learning, 232
Strategic planning, 199–200
  staff involvement in, 58
  student involvement in, 59
Strategies for embedding culture
  budgeting, 147–148
  communication and decision
    making, 141–145
  hiring/promotion, 139–140
  planning, 145–147
  systems and procedures,
    140–141
Student Assessment of the College Environment (SACE),
  221, 223–224
Student Follow-up Appraisal
  System (SFAS), 224–225
Student success
  assessment of, by students,
    224

Teaching Effectiveness Program
  (TEP), 221, 222–223
Teaching in community colleges
  assessment of, 223
  behaviors of excellent
    teachers, 101–110
  meeting students' needs,
    101–110
  role of CEOs in, 101,
    110–111
  teachers as leaders, 100
Transactional leadership, 82–83,
  94, 134–135, 160
  contingent reinforcement,
    155–157, 158, 184

management-by-exception,
    155, 156, 184
Transformational leadership, 3,
    12, 32, 82, 83, 84, 94,
    118–119, 134–135, 160, 164,
    204
    and charisma, 155–156, 159,
        181, 182–184
    and communication, 67
    consideration, 155–156, 158,
        181, 183
    and followership, 84–86, 89,
        91, 94, 180

and intellectual stimulation,
    155–156, 159, 181, 182, 183
and self-empowerment, 87, 89
study of, and exceptional
    leaders, 86–91
themes in, 87–88
and time management, 91

Values
    assessment of, 221
Vision
    entrepreneurial, 136, 138, 231
    communication of, 71
    and leadership, 46, 51, 58, 86

About the Authors

George A. Baker, III will assume the Joseph D. Moore Endowed Chair in Community College Leadership at North Carolina State University in the fall of 1992.

Since 1978 Baker has been professor of education at the University of Texas at Austin, where he taught instructional and student development management, organizational behavior, college leadership, and decision making to Ph.D. and M.Ed. students from the College of Education and other colleges in the university. He has chaired the dissertations of more than 60 Ph.D. students in the Department of Educational Administration's nationally ranked higher education, community college, and public school leadership programs. He also serves as director of the National Institute for Leadership and Institutional Effectiveness, a consortium of colleges and universities interested in improving higher education through institutional effectiveness and continuous quality improvement efforts.

Prior to his appointment at the University of Texas, Baker served as visiting professor at Furman University, the University of Rhode Island, Salve Regena College, and the University of Virginia. He was dean of instruction and vice president for general education at Greenville Technical College from 1976 to 1978, and dean of academics at the Marine Corps Educational Center from 1975 to 1976. While at the Naval War College from 1974 to 1976, he served as professor of management and headed the Management Department's organizational behavior group.

A U.S. Marine Corps veteran, he was selected in 1966 to serve on the military staff of President Lyndon B. Johnson, where he worked on the Emergency Task Force in the White House and served as executive officer of the Presidential Retreat at Camp David, Maryland.

Baker earned degrees from Warren Wilson College, at that time a liberal arts community college; Presbyterian College; Shippensburg State University; Duke University; and the Naval War College.

Since 1970, Baker has made keynote speeches at, conducted research for, and provided presentations, workshops, and consultation services to more than 500 universities, colleges, public school districts, and other public and private organizations. He has received numerous awards for

his research, teaching, service, and national leadership in the community college movement, including the 1987–88 and 1990–91 Distinguished
Research Publication awards from the National Council of Universities
and Colleges.

Baker is the author or co-author of more than 75 books, monographs,
chapters, journal articles, and technical reports. In the past five years
Baker has co-written for the Community College Press *Access and Excellence* (1987), *Shared Vision* (1989), and *Teaching as Leading* (1990).

Phyllis Barber is assistant to the president, Central Piedmont Community College, North Carolina.

Charlotte Biggerstaff is director of continuing education, Northeast
Texas Community College, Texas.

G. Allan Clark is assistant to the president, Camosun College, British Columbia.

Rosemary Gillett-Karam is a research associate, College of Education,
the University of Texas at Austin.

Tessa Martinez Tagle is campus president of the Medical Center Campus of Miami-Dade Community College, Florida.

Michele Nelson is acting dean of communications/fine arts, Grossmont College, California.

Eli Peña is chairman of the biology department and director for faculty
development, Texas Southmost College.

Mary Ann Roe is dean of institutional advancement, Texas State Technical College-Waco.